DOING YOUR QUALITATIVE PSYCHOLOGY PROJECT

Edited by

Cath Sullivan,
Stephen Gibson
and Sarah Riley

2nd
Edition

DOING YOUR QUALITATIVE PSYCHOLOGY PROJECT

Sage

1 Oliver's Yard
55 City Road
London EC1Y 1SP

2455 Teller Road
Thousand Oaks
California 91320

Unit No 323-333, Third Floor, F-Block
International Trade Tower
Nehru Place, New Delhi – 110 019

8 Marina View Suite 43-053
Asia Square Tower 1
Singapore 018960

Editor: Charlotte Bush
Editorial assistant: Rhiannon Holt
Production editor: Martin Fox
Copyeditor: Neil Dowden
Proofreader: Bryan Campbell
Indexer: Elske Janssen
Marketing manager: Camille Richmond
Cover design: Shaun Mercier
Typeset by: C&M Digitals (P) Ltd, Chennai, India
Printed and bound by CPI Group (UK) Ltd, Croydon, CR0 4YY

Library of Congress Control Number: 2023934761

British Library Cataloguing in Publication data

A catalogue record for this book is available from the British Library

ISBN 978-1-5297-5441-4
ISBN 978-1-5297-5442-1 (pbk)

At Sage we take sustainability seriously. Most of our products are printed in the UK using responsibly sourced papers and boards. When we print overseas we ensure sustainable papers are used as measured by the Paper Chain Project grading system. We undertake an annual audit to monitor our sustainability.

Contents

About the Contributors

Jo Bryce is a Senior Lecturer in the School of Psychology and Computer Science, University of Central Lancaster. Her research focuses on informing evidence-based approaches to the development and delivery of educational materials and training packages for education and child protection, parents and young people which promote Internet safety and media literacy. She teaches on a variety of topics related to safeguarding online, cybercrime and forensic psychology, as well as qualitative and quantitative research methods.

Michael Forrester is an Honorary Reader in Psychology in the School of Psychology at the University of Kent. His research interests are in early child development, psychoanalysis and qualitative methods. His teaching and research interests are in early child development and qualitative methods. He is co-editor (with H. Gardner) of *Analysing Interaction in Childhood: Insights from Conversation Analysis* (Wiley-Blackwell, 2010) and co-editor (with C. Sullivan) of *Doing Qualitative Research in Psychology* (Sage, 2019).

Nollaig Frost is Professor (Adjunct) of Psychology at University College, Cork and a Visiting Lecturer in Psychology at City, University of London. She teaches qualitative methods and has a particular interest in pluralistic qualitative research approaches. She is author of *Practising Research: Why You Are Always Part of the Research Process Even When You Think You're Not* (Palgrave Macmillan, 2016) and *Qualitative Research Methods in Psychology: Combining Core Approaches* 2e (Open University Press, 2021). She uses qualitative approaches to pursue her research in second-time motherhood, and mental health and well-being.

Stephen Gibson is Bicentennial Chair in Research Methods and Director of Doctoral Programmes in the School of Social Sciences, Heriot Watt University. He is a social psychologist with research interests in obedience and social influence, identity and citizenship, and representations of peace and conflict. His books include *Arguing, Obeying and Defying: A Rhetorical Perspective on Stanley Milgram's Obedience Experiments* (Cambridge University Press, 2019) and *Discourse, Peace and Conflict: Discursive Psychology Perspectives* (Springer, 2018). Between 2020 and 2022 he was joint Editor-in-Chief of the British Journal of Social Psychology.

Siobhan Hugh-Jones is an Associate Professor of Mental Health Psychology in the School of Psychology, University of Leeds. Her work focuses on adolescent mental health, adverse childhood experiences and trauma as well as evidence-based, public mental health approaches to prevention and risk reduction for adolescent mental health in the UK, India and China. She utilises participatory, visual and co-design methods with young people and stakeholders, and typically uses thematic and frame-work analysis. She co-leads the University of Leeds Interdisciplinary Mental Health Network to drive forward interdisciplinary research on national and international mental health challenges.

Nigel King is Emeritus Professor in Applied Psychology at the University of Huddersfield and a freelance qualitative research consultant. He has a long-standing interest in the use of qualitative methods in 'real world' research and is well known for his methodological work on Template Analysis, visual elicitation techniques and interview methods. His substantive interests include how people make meaning from nature/greenspace, experiences of anomalous phenomena in bereavement, and interprofessional collaboration in social and healthcare.

Kathryn Kinmond worked as a senior lecturer at Manchester Metropolitan University teaching social psychology, abuse studies and qualitative research methods, before returning to professional practice as a counsellor and psychotherapist. Her main research and publications have addressed self, identity and experience within a range of topics, including self-harm, spiritual abuse and the use of imagery as intervention following stroke.

Sarah Riley is a Professor in Critical Health Psychology at Massey University, Aotearoa New Zealand. Her award-winning, interdisciplinary research focuses on relationships between discourse, affect, technology and materiality. Recent co-authored books include *Technologies of Sexiness* (OUP, 2014), *Postfeminism and Health* (Routledge, 2019), *Postfeminism and Body Image* (Routledge, 2022); and *Digital Feeling* (Palgrave, 2023); she chaired the British Psychology Society's Qualitative Methods in Psychology section (2017–19), and teaches qualitative research methods.

Cath Sullivan is Senior Lecturer in Psychology in the University of Central Lancashire. Cath has been actively involved in initiatives to support the teaching of qualitative research methods in psychology since 2005 and is a former Chair of the Higher Education Academy 'Teaching Qualitative Psychology' Special Interest Group. In addition to this work supporting and training psychology lecturers who teach qualitative methods, Cath has over ten years' experience of teaching qualitative methods to undergraduate and postgraduate students. Her published articles and book chapters include empirical qualitative papers and pieces about qualitative methodology. She is co-editor of *Doing Qualitative Research in Psychology* (Sage, 2019).

Preface to the Second Edition

Aims of the Book

Welcome to the second edition of *Doing Your Qualitative Psychology Project*. In the chapters that follow, we take you through the process of completing a student qualitative research project. The book is aimed at psychology students, but we also anticipate that it will be useful if you're studying another subject, such as sociology, criminology, geography, education, health and other related disciplines that use qualitative methods. This book will be most useful to those completing an undergraduate final-year project (often called a 'dissertation' or 'thesis'), but it will also be helpful for undergraduate students doing qualitative projects earlier in their degree, and conversely for postgraduate students, especially those doing a qualitative project without a solid foundation in qualitative methods from their earlier studies.

········In a nutshell···

Aims of the book

- To provide a guide to the decisions you need to make at key stages of your project, including:
  - choosing a topic and designing research questions;
  - designing and managing your project;
  - reviewing literature;
  - collecting and analysing data;
  - writing up and evaluating your work.
- To provide useful tips and strategies for your project, including how to deal with challenges and difficulties when they arise.
- To give ideas of ways in which you can build upon and extend your project – for example, as a way of demonstrating your skills when you apply for jobs or courses in the future.

···

Our focus is on helping you to plan and execute the different stages of your project, so we deal extensively with issues such as research questions, planning, supervisory relationships and writing up. Various methods of collecting and analysing qualitative data are considered and we provide overviews and key information to help you to select appropriate methods. Once you've decided on the best methods for data collection and analysis, you will need to read specialist work on those methods and so we also provide suggestions for further reading and information on these. So you understand why this is important, we would like to spend a little time considering what your research project means in the context of your course.

Your Research Project

Your research project allows you to apply and develop the research skills learned earlier in your course and allows your lecturers to assess how well you can apply them to an independent piece of work. It is a complex piece of work that involves many stages. For most students, it is the largest single piece of assessed work that they will do, and it is a time-consuming, challenging and rewarding journey. Many people regard the research project as a key indicator of a student's ability and it often makes a large contribution to the overall mark of a student's degree. Because of this, and because it is a big step towards independence for many students, it can be a daunting prospect. But take heart, the best learning experiences happen when you are just outside your comfort zone, because it is there where you develop new skills and knowledge. Equally, you don't want to be so far out of your comfort zone that you feel overwhelmed. Our motivation for writing this book is to help you stay in that sweet spot, so that you can feel confident for the challenges ahead. After all, part of what is rewarding about doing a research project is its challenging and independent nature.

What's New for the Second Edition?

In this second edition we have made a number of refinements to the book. These are based on our experiences of using the book with our own project students and on feedback that we've received from other lecturers. They are also driven by changes to the qualitative methods landscape that have happened since the first edition was published. These changes include the increased possibilities for using technology, especially the Internet, for conducting and reporting projects, updates to key methods of analysis (e.g. recent changes to thematic analysis), updated ethical guidelines and data protection principles, developments in systematic literature reviewing and the use of quality 'checklists' for qualitative research. Every chapter has had an overhaul, including a rationalisation and streamlining of the pedagogic features (e.g. 'In a nutshell' boxes and activities) and an update to the literature that we draw upon and recommend for you. There has been a slight change to the structure of the book – most significantly we have split the guidance on planning and ethics into two separate chapters so that we can really do these two topics justice. We have also worked to ensure that the chapters are linked together well and that the themes that run through the book are noted frequently to help you keep track of them.

How to Use this Book

We recognise that not all readers will want the same thing from this book. Some will read it from cover to cover before they begin their project; others will come to it at a later stage in their project for guidance on a specific issue; others still may want to supplement their reading around qualitative methods by dipping into particular chapters or sections. We therefore don't want to suggest that there is only one 'right' way to use the book. There is an important conceptual reason for this too – qualitative research tends to be cyclical. This means that rather than beginning with a research question, and then working through the design of the study, data collection, analysis and writing up in a linear fashion, you may find yourself returning to earlier stages to revise your ideas. For example, you might find yourself revising your research question following the initial stages of your analysis, or refining your analysis as you write up your project.

Ultimately, of course, a book is presented in a linear fashion, with different topics presented in a specific order as the contents unfold. In writing and editing this book we have put the chapters in the order in which activities are generally done, making links to other chapters in which specific issues are covered elsewhere in the book so you can see connections between different activities. We have also worked to ensure that each chapter constitutes a useful resource in its own right. Each chapter signposts you to the next steps in developing your project and has suggestions for further reading. This book takes you through the process of doing a qualitative project, but it does not include detailed descriptions of how to do a specific forms of data collection or analysis, which is a book in itself, such as our sister book, Sullivan and Forrester's (2019) *Doing Qualitative Research in Psychology*. We have therefore constructed our chapters on these topics to provide you with an overall guide to that part of the process, and then signposted you to where you can go for further information once you've chosen your direction of travel. The hard work, ultimately, will be yours, but however you decide to traverse the landscape of your qualitative research project, we hope that you will find this book to be a useful source of ideas, inspiration and practical advice.

········· In a nutshell ··· ··· ◆ ···

Useful features of the book

Each chapter contains coverage of the key issues of the topic area being covered, together with some or all of the following features.

- Top tips: useful practical advice for maximising quality.
- Success stories and cautionary tales: examples of triumphs and obstacles in student projects supervised by the authors. These are drawn from our experience as supervisors, but we have changed names and other details to protect people's anonymity.

(Continued)

- 'In a nutshell' boxes: these highlight key points, give summaries of concepts, approaches and overviews of key ideas as well as offering definitions of key terms.
- Flow charts: these are used to represent the key processes you need to go through and guide you in making decisions that are right for your project.
- 'Want to know more ...?' boxes: these provide suggestions for further reading.

Outline of this Book

We start off with a chapter we have written to help you get started with your qualitative project. Chapter 1 covers the foundations of doing a qualitative project. It's important that before we start talking about the specifics, we take a step back and talk you through some of the core principles of good academic work, from which you can build a solid foundation for your project. So, that chapter discusses theoretical principles that underpin qualitative methods (aka 'methodology'), as well as decision making and critical thinking. We also introduce the key idea of the *methodological kite*, which runs through the book and aims to help you develop a coherent project.

In Chapter 2, Kathryn Kinmond and Sarah Riley explain the process for coming up with research question(s). They distinguish between a research topic, aim and research questions. They explain how to write a good research question and start you thinking about research design. The flexible and cyclical nature of qualitative research means that you will need to treat the development of research questions as something you review and refine throughout the project. The importance of consistency between your type of research question and the methods you use is highlighted and tips are given to help you through the process.

In Chapter 3, Sarah Riley and Cath Sullivan take you through the process of planning your project. The chapter discusses planning for methods, for your dataset, for recruitment and for the resources that you'll need. It also considers writing a proposal and planning your timetable. This chapter emphasises the importance of planning to ensure that your data collection and analysis run as smoothly as possible and shows you how to put together a project plan that you will be able to refer to throughout your project.

Cath and Sarah are back in Chapter 4 to take you through the process of doing ethical research. All researchers must gain permission from their institution before doing research. This means you must get ethical approval for your project before you begin. In this chapter we consider how you can ensure that the planning described in Chapter 3 is ethical and apply for ethical approval. We discuss the importance of ethics and highlight some key ethical issues that you will need to consider. We aim to leave you in a position to submit your project for ethical approval.

Chapter 5 turns to the management of your project, and outlines strategies for conducting the various stages as smoothly as possible. In it, Sarah Riley and Nigel King consider four major areas of management in detail, which are: time management; the student–supervisor relationship; the impact of the researcher on the research; and the impact of the research on the researcher, including learning how to negotiate emotional aspects of research.

In Chapter 6, Jo Bryce and Michael Forrester explain how to do your literature review. The chapter provides practical tips on issues such as how to search for literature and review abstracts in order to determine whether the studies they outline are relevant to your research question. It also includes guidance on weaving your review into a coherent narrative when it comes to writing up your project. This will help you make sure that your review doesn't merely describe previous work in your area, but provides an argument for why your particular research question is worth addressing.

Next, we consider the processes and decisions involved in selecting an appropriate method of collecting your data. Siobhan Hugh-Jones and Stephen Gibson do this in Chapter 7 which considers key methods of data collection – including various forms of interviewing, diary methods, Internet data and naturalistic data. They revisit and develop key themes that we introduced in Chapter 1, including methodology and decision making, linking these to what data to collect and how to collect it. The chapter also signposts you to other resources for exploring particular methods in more detail. It finishes by explaining practical issues that you need to consider such as data storage and deciding how much data you will need.

Stephen and Siobhan return in Chapter 8 to help you to select an appropriate and practical method of analysing your data. First, they review the assumptions and technical elements of a number of commonly used analysis methods: thematic analysis; discourse analysis; interpretative phenomenological analysis; grounded theory; narrative analysis; and conversation analysis. There you will find useful hints to help you select a method that fits with other aspects of your project (such as your method of data collection and your philosophical approach). The chapter also considers key issues in transcription, describes some common challenges for qualitative analysis and offers suggestions for how to meet these.

In Chapter 9, Cath Sullivan, Nollaig Frost and Kathryn Kinmond explore the ways in which the quality of research can be evaluated. Essentially, this involves learning how to tell good qualitative from not-so-good qualitative research, and making sure that your project doesn't fall under the latter heading! The chapter considers the nature and importance of criteria for judging the quality of research, such as reflexivity and the use of evidence. Then, you are guided through a process that you can use to put together a set of quality criteria that will help you to be confident that your project is a high-quality piece of research.

In Chapter 10, Sarah Riley returns with the most comprehensive explanation of report writing you will ever need! Beginning with a consideration of the aims of report writing, this chapter introduces the structure of the qualitative project write-up and provides detailed guidance on writing each section and subsection. Particular emphasis is placed on the 'analysis' section, which typically includes substantial quotations from your data together with your analytic commentary and is thus usually the longest part of any qualitative report. The chapter concludes by providing some tips on how to write clearly and concisely.

In Chapter 11, the three of us return to explore a range of ways in which you might extend your research project. These include the possibility of publishing your work and using it as the basis for developing a proposal for further study. This chapter also highlights the transferable skills you will have developed during your project and considers how you can draw on the experience when it comes to applying for jobs or courses. But perhaps most importantly, this chapter celebrates your achievements, and achievements to come, and welcomes you into the community of qualitative researchers.

We hope you will enjoy reading this book as much as we've enjoyed putting it together; or if that's too much to hope for, we hope you at least find it useful!

Cath, Stephen and Sarah

1
GETTING STARTED WITH QUALITATIVE METHODS

Cath Sullivan, Stephen Gibson
and Sarah Riley

There is a picture of a kite on the front cover of this book because, like a kite, we want your project to soar and to survive any gusts that may threaten to bring it down. Equally, when you've got your eyes on the sky, you need to have your feet firmly on the ground, and so in this chapter we explain three foundational elements you need to do a good project. These elements are (1) understanding the underpinning philosophy of methods (aka 'methodology'); (2) skills in decision making; and (3) critical thinking.

Methodology

Considering methodology means dealing with some weighty issues concerning the nature and purpose of research, the nature of knowledge (in contrast to beliefs, for example), and the nature and role of evidence. In this section we introduce you to some of the debates around methodology that are relevant to your project.

Let's start with the difference between methods and methodology. It can be useful to think of a method as a tool you use in research. For example, you could use an interview as a tool to create a person's life history. But methods are tools that need to be accompanied by an underlying philosophy. Good researchers are aware of the philosophical assumptions that underpin their methods. This underlying philosophy or theory is called the 'methodology'. Considering some of the foundations of methodology will help you to get to grips with your research project, which is why we focus on it in this chapter.

········In a nutshell···· ···

Method and methodology

It is useful to think of your method as how you go about collecting data (for example, interviews or focus groups – see Chapter 7). Your methodology, however, can be thought of as the wider approach you adopt in your project which will inform your decision making about your research question, data collection and analysis (for example, discourse analysis or grounded theory – see Chapter 8). Your methodology can be thought of as the philosophy of research, or the underlying assumptions behind knowledge creation, that informs the use of your methods. This means that taking up a particular methodology often determines the kinds of methods you can use.

The chapters in this book cover the full range of issues involved in conducting your qualitative research project, from managing the relationship with your supervisor to writing up your report. At the heart of any research project, however, is methodology, and many of the chapters cover various methodological issues about which you will need to make important decisions. Although most of these are presented in stand-alone chapters (for example, Chapter 2 on research questions and Chapter 7 on data collection), you will notice, as you read the book, that many of the issues involved are interconnected. For example, the decisions you make concerning data collection will be related to the decisions you make regarding your research question, your analytic approach, and so on. This is because the philosophies underpinning methodology include questions around 'what can we know?' and 'what is reality?' These questions are, respectively, questions of epistemological and ontology.

········In a nutshell··· ···

Key methodological decisions

- What is your topic?
- What do you want to find out about your topic? (Research Question)
- What data are you going to collect? (Method)
- How will you analyse your data? (Analysis)
- What assumptions will you make about reality (ontology) and what it is possible to know (epistemology)?

The trick is to make these decisions in advance, while allowing sufficient flexibility to adapt to unforeseen problems or opportunities. We offer some tips for making decisions

later in this chapter. To emphasise the interconnectedness between the key methodological decisions that you need to make, we invite you to think of your project as being
like trying to fly a kite on a blustery day. Thinking about these key methodological
issues as different points of your kite highlights how they all depend on each other (see
Figure 1.1).

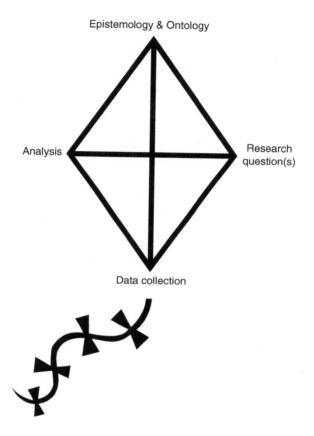

Figure 1.1   The methodological kite

For the kite to fly, all four points need to be connected firmly to one another. If any
of the links are missing or loose then the kite is liable to fall to the ground, or not even
get airborne at all! This also highlights how the decisions you make about each aspect
of your methodology can't simply be made in a straightforward, linear fashion – one
after another, such as research question → data collection → analysis. Instead, try to
plan how each element of the kite fits together at the outset (see Chapter 3 for more on
planning your project). This doesn't mean that things are completely set in stone. You
are likely to develop your ideas and may want to move the project in a different direction. But if you think you're ready to begin collecting data without considering all four

aspects of methodology and the connections between them, then you will almost certainly be storing up trouble for yourself!

Although some authors (for example, Howitt, 2019) suggest that you should start with a problem, and then select an approach that allows you to address that problem, things are not necessarily as straightforward as that. Other researchers (for example, Potter, 1998a) have argued that the way in which we conceive of the problem we want to investigate will already involve a range of (possibly tacit) assumptions about the nature of the world, what it is possible to find out and how we should go about doing that. One of the key points of this book is therefore to encourage you to think about these assumptions at the outset. Rather than thinking of a problem and choosing a methodology to address it, your reading around qualitative research might lead you to conceive of problems in new ways, to think of new problems to address and to recognise that 'problems' themselves might not exist independently in the world, waiting for researchers to address them.

So, by making sure you're clear that each point of the methodological kite is connected with the others, you give your project the best possible chance of success. This book aims to help you do just that. Indeed, three of the points of the kite have whole chapters devoted to them (Chapter 2 on research questions; Chapter 7 on data collection; and Chapter 8 on analysis). The other element of the kite, epistemology and ontology, is something that will crop up repeatedly through this book. To get you started, we want you to take a moment or two to get to grips with these terms (think of them like spiders, they are more scared of you than you're scared of them).

Epistemology and ontology

····In a nutshell···· ·

Epistemology and ontology

Epistemology: A theory of knowledge that specifies certain criteria by which we can answer questions such as 'What counts as valid knowledge?' and 'How do we know what we know?' From the Greek episteme (knowledge) and logos (word, account; and as the suffix -ology, branch of knowledge). At its simplest, then, epistemology deals with questions concerning knowledge about knowledge. For example, is the knowledge that we generate in a research project about reality, or about people's interpretations of reality, or about shared social meanings that shape people's interpretations of reality?

Ontology: A theory of existence that specifies certain criteria by which we can answer questions such as 'What is real?' and 'What exists?' From the Greek on (being) and logos, ontology is therefore quite literally the study of being.

These are big branches of philosophy. As researchers, we are borrowing from these philosophies and applying their thinking to psychological research. It's not a perfect fit because we are using philosophical concepts designed for one thing (asking big questions about the world) to do something else (creating high-quality psychological research to make knowledge about people). So, to continue the spider metaphor, feel free to tread lightly around them, but don't be too anxious about them. All you need is to catch them in a glass so you can see and manage them from afar. And take comfort that by the end of this chapter, you will start to understand them a bit better.

. . . .

There is every chance that you may not really have come across detailed discussion of epistemology and ontology in other parts of your course. However, all research, whether qualitative or quantitative, involves making epistemological and ontological assumptions. The dominant position within many disciplines (including psychology) is one based upon a modified version of a philosophy known as positivism. This suggests that we can uncover the nature of reality through observation, and that which we perceive is that which exists. Ultimately, few researchers of social and behavioural aspects of the world would consider themselves to be straightforward positivists, with its implication of rather naive faith in the reality of what we observe (visual illusions anyone?). However, research that uses experimentation (or quasi-experimentation, as in studies that manipulate variables with questionnaires) can be thought of as occupying a position which has been termed post-positivism. This position (associated with the philosophy of Karl Popper) acknowledges the limitations of pure positivism, and instead suggests a much more cautious approach based around the principles of 'falsification' and 'hypothetico-deductivism' (McGhee, 2001).

· · · · · ·**In a nutshell**· ·

Positivism

Positivism is a philosophy that suggests that all that can be known is that which we observe.

Post-positivism is a philosophy which suggests that to ensure that we can give ourselves the best possible chance of trusting the observations we make, we should test our ideas using the principles of hypothetico-deductivism and falsification.

Hypothetico-deductivism is the idea that we should make formal theories about the world, from which we can then derive testable hypotheses.

Falsification is a principle that means that we should never seek to prove our hypotheses, but that we should always seek to falsify them. When hypotheses derived from a particular theory withstand repeated attempts at falsification, we can be more confident that the theory reflects some feature of how the world really is.

. . . .

Ultimately, post-positivism leads to an approach that views our goal as scientists as deploying a neutral and unbiased approach to observations so that we give ourselves the best chance of uncovering reality, but with some caution about what we may observe directly. Such an approach is therefore realist in both an epistemological and an ontological sense. In short, this means that we can assume that the world objectively exists, and we can have objective knowledge about it. This position is represented in Figure 1.2.

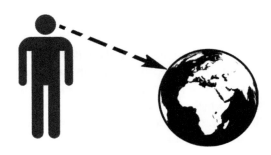

Figure 1.2 The realist approach – we can have direct access to the world, provided we have the right tools.

Realism: a philosophical position which assumes that there is an objective reality out there (ontological realism) and that with the appropriate scientific techniques, we are able to increase our knowledge about it (epistemological realism).

In contrast, many researchers have increasingly been drawn to alternative positions that emphasise the limitations of (post-)positivism and suggest that the goal of achieving objective knowledge about the world is more problematic than might be assumed. Broadly speaking, these alternative positions can be characterised as phenomenology and social constructionism (see Figures 1.3 and 1.4).

In French, the word *'rivière'* means a body of water flowing within the country; in English the word 'river' means a body of water that flows into the sea, a lake, or another river; and in te reo Māori (the language of the Indigenous people of Aotearoa New Zealand) *'wai Māori'* means a flowing body of water that is ordinary with no spiritual significance. Social constructionists can use this example to highlight that a French, English or Māori speaker may look at the same flowing body of water, but their understanding of it (flowing within a country, to the sea, or not spiritual) is shaped by their language (and the culture and geography that shapes that language) and that they cannot 'know' that water outside of these linguistic concepts. These arguments have been drawn upon by qualitative researchers using discourse analysis (see Chapter 8 for more details).

A further contrast which is relevant here is that between realism and *relativism* – a thoroughly constructionist position involves the adoption of a relativist approach. Relativists assert that we can no longer ground our knowledge or action in terms of

Figure 1.3 The phenomenological approach - neither researcher nor participant has direct access to reality, but we can make sense of people's subjective experience of the world, so long as we bear in mind that this will always be mediated through language and embodiment (including our physiology).

Phenomenology: The study of how phenomena (such as events, objects, emotions) appear to us in our conscious experience.
For an example of how phenomenology has been drawn upon by qualitative researchers, see the discussion of interpretative phenomenological analysis in Chapter 7.

what is 'real' or 'true' in the way that this is usually understood. Instead, they suggest that knowledge and reality will always be relative to the historical, cultural and social context.

····· ·In a nutshell· · · ···

Relativism

'A form of more or less systematic doubt about the possibility of objective, socially independent foundations to knowledge' (Hepburn, 2000: 93).

· ·

Figure 1.4 The social constructionist approach – neither researcher nor participant has direct access to reality; rather understandings about what 'reality' is are socially and culturally produced. Researchers look at the meanings people use to make sense of themselves and their social and natural world. The focus is therefore often on how reality is constructed through language and in people's social interactions with each other.

Constructionism: A position which challenges the notion of objectively existing reality – and even of any notion of 'real' experience – and suggests instead that 'reality' depends on one's cultural and interactional context. Often referred to as social constructionism. This is often the hardest one for psychology students to get their heads around at first, so it might be useful to give an example.

Some authors suggest that relativism means that all perspectives must be treated as equally valid. A common objection to such extreme versions of relativism is therefore that it results in a morally problematic view of the world as it appears to suggest that 'anything goes'. However, this position is not typically adopted by relativists themselves. For example, the exasperation is palpable when Jonathan Potter (1998b: 34) argues, 'No! Please! How many times does it have to be repeated that "anything goes" is a realist slur on relativism.' In contrast, Potter and his colleagues have argued forcefully that relativism compels us to confront the absence of timeless hard-and-fast rules underlying our moral positions. We thus must make value judgements on social and political issues without the comfort blanket of 'reality' to keep us safe and warm (see Edwards et al., 1995). As you can perhaps see, what may initially seem to be a somewhat esoteric philosophical debate can lead some researchers to get rather agitated!

Some researchers do, however, accept many of the central claims of social constructionism about the inevitably constructed nature of the world and of our knowledge of the world, but without also adopting a relativist position. This has led to the development of a position known as critical realism.

··· ···In a nutshell··· ··

Critical realism

A position that acknowledges the social construction of reality but suggests that there are nevertheless realities existing independently of human activity (for example, social structure and/or human experience). For more on the relationship between social constructionism and critical realism see Sullivan (2019).

···

Phenomenological approaches (see Chapter 7) can be understood as critically realist in the sense that they assert the reality of experience, while acknowledging the difficulty of achieving objective knowledge of it (Shaw, 2019). Typically, phenomenological research in psychology is critical realist because it seeks to develop methods that will get as close as possible to understanding the reality of another person's experience, while always recognising the limits to that possibility.

Another lens through which to see research is to consider how it theoretically frames issues of power. Post-positivist, social constructionist and critical realist phenomenological research can all be done with a particular political orientation in relation to how cultural ideas of gender, race, ethnicity, class, sexuality, dis/abledness and so forth shape our understandings of people, and thus the psychological research we do about people. This means that psychological research might have, for example, a feminist, anti-racist or Marxist orientation. The role of political orientation has been a source of lively debate (see the 'Want to know more?' box below), and highlights the importance of the politics of research.

Politics and qualitative research

All research decisions are ultimately political in the sense that they have implications for how we might think about and act upon the world. Even the mainstream scientific position of neutral disinterested enquiry is a fundamentally political position insofar as social scientific enquiry has important implications for how people might live their lives. Research is political in the sense that it suggests to us what is possible in the world and, often, what might be the right or wrong course of action. Whatever decisions we make they are likely to involve significant political dimensions; as Billig notes, 'neutrality in the midst of conflict is every bit as much a position – and a controversial one at that – as is partisanship' (1996: 173).

It is also worth noting that there is nothing intrinsic to qualitative methods that makes them a force for good. Many students and researchers (ourselves included) have been drawn to qualitative methods over the years as they see them as providing tools for challenging the more troubling and oppressive aspects of mainstream practice. However, at times this has arguably tipped over into assuming that qualitative methods are politically more promising than quantitative methods – this is not the case (see Parker [2005] for some relevant arguments; and see Martín-Baró [1994], for a quite brilliant – and ultimately tragic – use of quantitative methods in the service of emancipation).

The philosophies underpinning methodology excite some people and frighten others. If you are on the frightened side of the continuum what is important to know is that you don't have to understand it all, you only have to know that these debates exist. As we take you through the process of doing a qualitative research project, you will start to see how these ideas are applied in practice, and through that they will start to make more sense. That you will ultimately have to make decisions about methodology takes us to our next main element of this chapter; that is, how to make good decisions.

Want to know more about methodology?

Howitt, D. (2019) *Introduction to Qualitative Research Methods in Psychology: Putting Theory into Practice* (4th edn). Harlow: Pearson. (Especially Chapters 1 and 2.)

Sullivan, C. (2019) Theory and method in qualitative psychology. In C. Sullivan and M.A. Forrester (eds), *Doing Qualitative Research in Psychology: A Practical Guide* (2nd edn). London: Sage. pp. 17–34.

Riley, S., Brooks, J., Goodman, S., Cahill, S., Branney, P., Treharne, G. and Sullivan, C. (2019) Celebrations amongst challenges: Considering the past, present and future of the Qualitative Methods in Psychology (QMiP) Section of the British Psychological Society. *Qualitative Research in Psychology*, 16 (3), 464–482. DOI: 10.1080/14780887.2019.1605275

Riley, S. and LaMarre, A. (2023) Developments in qualitative inquiry. In M. McCullen (ed.), *APA Handbook of Research Methods in Psychology* (2nd edn). Vol. 2: *Research Designs: Quantitative, Qualitative, Neuropsychological, and Biological*, H. Cooper (Editor-in-Chief).

Tuffin, K. (2005) *Understanding Critical Social Psychology*. London: Sage. (Especially Chapters 2 and 3.)

Wigginton, B. and Lafrance, M. N. (2019) Learning critical feminist research: A brief introduction to feminist epistemologies and methodologies. *Feminism & Psychology*. https://doi. org/10.1177/0959353519866058

And if you want to know even more, then try dipping into some of the debates among discourse analysts in the 1990s (for example, Edwards et al., 1995; Gill, 1995; Hepburn, 2000; Newman and Holzman, 2000; Parker, 1998a, 1998b, 1999a, 1999b, 2000; Potter et al., 1999). Some of these might be heavy going at times if you're new to these issues, but the lively and sometimes even entertaining (no, really) way in which they're conducted makes them a great way to get to grips with the key differences between positions.

Decision Making

As you work on your research project, you will need to make a series of decisions. Throughout this book we help you identify those decisions and provide you with information and ideas that will aid you in making them. Decision making involves a series of steps, skills and processes. To achieve your aims, you have to make practical decisions about what to do, when to do it, how to do it and where. At times when we find making decisions hard, such as when we are stressed or when the outcome is very important to us, it can be useful to break down the decision-making process into smaller components – what psychologists call sub-goaling.

········ In a nutshell ···

What is decision making?

Decision making is about deciding upon a course of action to take in a situation where there is more than one option (Adair, 2022).

· ·

To make a decision we must figure out what our objective is, collect information about it, identify possible options for moving towards it and evaluate those options so that we can make a choice (Adair, 2022). To do this, we need to also think about consequences and risks (Adair, 2022) and we also need to combine decision-making skills with critical evaluation (discussed further below) so that we can evaluate whether our decisions are working out for us.

····**··In a nutshell**··· ·· ·····

Decision making in your research project

Examples of some of the kinds of decisions you will need to make include:

- deciding on a topic area for your project;
- selecting literature to include in your literature review;
- identifying appropriate methods of data collection and analysis;
- deciding on sub-goals and deadlines as you work towards your final deadline;
- selecting material to include in your project write-up.

···

As you will see, doing your project involves you moving from one decision-making situation to another. So, at the start, we want to share with you some advice about how to make these decisions as quickly and confidently as possible.

Decision-making tips

Take ownership

Remember from the outset that your project is an independent piece of work, your chance to show that you can really shine when you work on your own. Your supervisor will help and guide you, but the sooner you begin to own your decisions the better off you will be in the long run. When you decide something (such as what your method of data analysis will be), it is you that will have to write a justification for it in your write-up. So, even if your supervisor can think of ten good reasons for you to use, for example, grounded theory (see Chapter 8), you will be the one who must give a good argument for that choice in your write-up. So, it's important that take responsibility for the decision and make sure you can defend it.

Focus on your goals

When we make decisions, it is usually for a reason – that is, we have some long-term purpose in mind. Imagine that you are trying to choose between several potential methods of recruiting participants. It is easy to slip into a state where the only goal we can see is that we must make the decision. Often, there is no problem with this, but when you are finding it hard to decide it can be useful to think about what your goal is. This will help you to think through what criteria you should use to evaluate the options you have. Your goal, the reason you are making this decision, is that you are trying to identify a method that will allow you to get the kind of data you need, from the people who are likely to have it, and in a way that is practicable and achievable for you. As you can see, thinking about the ultimate aim here gives us a set of criteria that you can use to judge the different options.

Find a reason

Research has shown that when people are choosing between two options, they tend to try and look for reasons to accept one possible course of action and reject the others (for example, Shafir et al., 1993). This means that decisions can be especially hard when a clear reason to do something, or not do it, doesn't really stand out. This can lead to us feeling paralysed and not actually making a choice (Ayton, 2005). Imagine, for example, that you are struggling to see which of two methods of analysis you should use, and obvious reasons for rejecting or selecting options do not immediately appear. In this instance, one thing that you could do to help yourself is to find out as much as you can about these methods and any underlying methodologies associated with them. Try and ask yourself critical questions that can help you find a reason for a decision. Information is key here, so try to:

- Read as many relevant sources of information about these methods as you can.
- Talk to your supervisor about the suitability of different methods.
- If you are working in a group – either informally or formally – speak to your fellow students, who can be good sources of information, as they have to negotiate similar issues to your own.
- Consider the practical consequences and feasibility of each option, such as how much time it would take and whether you have the training and resources you need.
- Write lists to get yourself thinking in concrete ways about the advantages, disadvantages and key features of the various options.

Remember that, in a situation where there don't seem to be any particularly salient or obvious reasons, you can help yourself by gaining more information.

Don't sweat the small stuff

Designing and conducting your project involves many decisions and, inevitably, some of these are more important than others. One way to help you put your energies where they will bring the most reward is to try and distinguish those decisions that are the most important. This can be challenging, especially at the beginning, and this book, along with the other things you read, and discussions with your supervisor, should help you to do this. Some tips that can help with this are:

- Consider the consequences. Some decisions are very important because they have big consequences for other stages of the project. For example, the method of data collection that you choose will have big implications for the kind of analysis that you can do, and how well you can do that analysis (see Chapter 7 for more on this). Try and identify the big decisions that have many consequences.

- Think about the justification. The most important decisions that you make will tend to be those that need to be fully justified in your write-up. Your research questions, for example, will need to be fully and convincingly justified in your write-up.

Efficiency or outcomes?

Many decision-making models rest upon the idea that certain choices have greater 'utility' – that is, will bring a more positive or valued outcome. However, one thing that you need to consider is that you may often be in a situation where there are several possible options that are equally as good. Or, at least, where the differences in how positive the outcomes will be are so small as to make little practical difference.

Often students get bogged down at the early stages of their project because they find it hard to make decisions. Understandably, given the importance of the project, students worry that they will make a wrong choice. This can often happen in relation to the choice of a topic area (see Chapter 2). However, at this stage, you are probably going to be faced with a huge array of potential research areas that are all equally interesting and equally suitable from an academic point of view. It's important to make a relatively informed choice at this stage but remember that making a choice too late and getting behind is probably more of a risk than making the wrong choice when your choices are between three equally suitable and equally interesting topic areas. You may find that it is useful to set yourself firm deadlines for key decisions to keep yourself from getting behind (see Chapters 3 and 5 for more on this).

········· In a nutshell ···· ···

Help yourself to make decisions

- Be aware of when decisions are needed and notice when you have made a decision.
- Gather information and talk your decisions through with your supervisor, other lecturers or fellow students.
- Consider at every stage whether you will be able to justify your decisions and how you will do it – this is crucial for doing a good write-up.
- Record your decisions in a research diary; it can be easy to forget what you did, and why, at an earlier stage (see Chapter 9 for more on diaries).
- Be aware that sometimes your choice is between several equally good options, and at times you will need to just force yourself to choose rather than risk falling behind.
- Ensure that you represent your decisions effectively in the appropriate section of the write-up (see Chapter 10 for more on writing up).

· ·

Decision making involves judgement (about the expected outcomes of options, for example, or their likelihood) and the appraisal and processing of information. It is therefore related to another foundational skill that underpins the research project; critical thinking, and we will consider this in the next section.

Critical Thinking

Critical thinking is a term used a lot in relation to good work done by students. In this book for example, many of the contributors talk about critical thinking, and the institutions that you and they are part of will have critical thinking as part of their marking criteria. Indeed, being able to think critically is a core component of higher education. But despite so many people saying that critical thinking is important, actual definitions of what it is and how to do it are rather thin on the ground.

··· ··· In a nutshell ··· ···

Critical thinking

Critical thinking involves developing the ability to:

1   Evaluate other people's academic work according to appropriate criteria and being able to make links between other people's work, other relevant literatures and your own work.
2   Present your own work in a way that convinces your reader (including the markers) that you are knowledgeable about the topic of your project and the research methods you've used.
3   Demonstrate to your reader that your knowledge has been applied so that your research project meets the quality criteria for an excellent project.

···

The emphasis on the importance of critical thinking, without guidance as to what it involves, can make the idea of critical thinking a daunting one. However, critical thinking is a skill you can learn and it's one that you may be more familiar with than you think. Music reviews, for example, can demonstrate a range of critical thinking techniques. A music review will often describe the music by highlighting important features of it, and discussing how these features distinguish it from previous work by the band or other similar bands. Reviews often locate the music being reviewed within a particular genre, and then give an evaluation of the music in relation to this genre. Such analyses allow reviewers to make evaluative judgements about the pleasures (or not) of listening to the music and how the music develops or represents a genre.

The processes involved in writing a music review are like those you need to go through when critically reading an article or developing your own project so that it will stand up to scrutiny. These processes involve locating the research project within relevant research methods literature or previous research on the subject; and evaluating the study both in terms of the contribution it makes to this literature and the persuasiveness of the argument (in music review terms, the equivalent of whether it develops the genre and how it sounds). To do this kind of academic critical thinking in relation to qualitative research projects you need to understand:

- quality criteria in relation to qualitative methods in general;
- quality criteria in relation to the specific methods you're using (or that the article you're reading is using);
- argumentation, rhetoric and persuasion.

We discuss qualitative research methods in general in Chapters 7 and 8 and refer you to books on specific qualitative methods for the detailed discussion you need for method-specific criteria (for example, Sullivan and Forrester, 2019). You will also find a detailed discussion of quality criteria for qualitative methods in Chapter 9. Here, then, we focus on argumentation, rhetoric and persuasion.

Argumentation, rhetoric and persuasion

Sarah once went to a museum of fashion with a builder friend. Knowing his interests didn't lie in clothes, she was surprised when he seemed happy to spend time there. All was revealed, though, when they left and the first thing he said was, 'Did you see how they'd built that glass staircase?' While Sarah had been looking at the museum's content, he'd been looking at the museum's structure. Together they'd evaluated the whole thing. In the same way, critical thinking requires you to evaluate the content of a research report and the way its arguments are constructed.

We need to consider how arguments are constructed because poor thinking can be dressed up in ways that make it seem plausible. Psychological research shows that people can be persuaded to believe all kinds of things that are not particularly rational. So good-quality thinking involves developing the skills we need to rationally judge the quality of research by evaluating the logic of the arguments it uses.

Applying critical thinking means that we can be persuaded by good-quality arguments and have the skills to reject the claims of poorer-quality ones. To develop this aspect of critical thinking, try asking the following questions about a report you're reading, or if you have already started yours, about your own project:

- Are the arguments given supported by evidence? And has this evidence been accumulated through appropriate methods such as exhaustive literature searches or systematic data collection and analyses?

- Is it a balanced analysis of the evidence? Do the authors examine alternative viewpoints fairly, but when relevant also show when there is strong support for a consensus?

- Given that all research comes from a specific standpoint, does the report recognise its standpoint and how that affected the study, or is the standpoint implicit and not addressed? (See the discussion of 'reflexivity' in Chapter 9 for more on this.)

- Is the ordering of the points logical so that gradually a complete and consistent account is built up?

- Was the study justified and explained in 'watertight' rhetoric (that is, persuasive arguments)? For example, if you follow their arguments to their logical conclusion, do they still stand? What are the implications for their arguments? Are there absences that would allow you to question the logic (such as not reporting studies that take a different approach)? Do they play a 'numbers game', where the authors report a bigger number of participants or hours of analysis from a larger dataset than the dataset that they actually analysed, so making their present study look bigger than it is? Do they use precise terms that can be easily defined and studied, or do they use vague concepts that can't easily be evaluated? Do they make false analogies or unwarranted leaps in the logic, such as arguing that one thing leads to another when it may not?

- Is the document consistent? Does the report draw on the same theoretical or methodological framework throughout? Does information on participants or other procedures remain the same throughout? Have the authors ensured that the connections between the corners of their methodological kite are strong?

- Do the authors demonstrate that their work meets appropriate quality criteria? For example, do they demonstrate a good understanding of the methods and procedures they've used? Does their work make a contribution to the literature they're addressing and demonstrate rigour or transparency?

- Does the outcome of the work generate new ideas or ways of implementing others' ideas in new and potentially useful directions?

- Is it written clearly? Good writing is clear and concise and takes the reader on a journey that is so well articulated and signposted that the reader focuses on the content of the message and not the delivery. Conversely, poor academic writing often 'hides' behind big words and uses overly complicated sentences or obtuse writing that obscures ideas rather than clarifies them (see Billig, 2013, for an excellent, student-friendly critique of academic writing).

With time, asking such questions can become second nature for experienced researchers. However, for a student developing their skills it can be hard to know when or how to ask them. If you thought about each of these questions overtly for every paragraph you read or wrote you'd soon lose focus on the actual study. So take your time to become familiar with them and practise using them gradually. To help you get started, we finish this section with a table that identifies some of the common problems students have with critical thinking, with some suggested solutions.

Want to know more about critical thinking?

Cottrell, S. (2023) *Critical Thinking Skills: Effective Analysis, Argument and Reflection* (4th edn). London: Bloomsbury.

Critical thinking challenges

When you are learning and developing your critical thinking skills, there can be challenges and difficulties. We have outlined some of these in Table 1.1, along with some suggested solutions for you to try.

Table 1.1 Common critical thinking challenges and some suggested solutions

Challenges	Possible solutions
Feeling overwhelmed by what you have to do	• Read though the questions previously listed regularly so that you are familiar with them, and they can be in the 'back of your mind' when you are reading or writing. • Remember it is a skill that takes time to develop so you will not be able to do everything at once. • At the end of a paper or a significant section that you have written, go through the questions given previously and see if you can answer them easily. If you cannot, ask yourself if it is because you have not read closely or consciously enough or if it is because there's a problem with the article. • When you read an article, make brief notes summarising the key points (for example, research question, topic studied, method used, findings, what you liked or disliked about it, how it might relate to your own work or to other literature). This writing should develop your thinking, it will give you a summary of the articles you have read so that you can build up a database you can use for your literature review and it will allow you to develop links across the papers more easily.
Finding it difficult to do a balanced critique of a study, perhaps because all the points made seem good, or you can criticise easily but find it hard to see positives.	• At the end of each main section (for example, introduction or method) write one advantage and one disadvantage about the decisions made there. • Think of different options the researchers could have chosen for each decision they made. Considering the advantages and disadvantages of your suggestions might help you either identify better ways of doing things or better realise the logic behind the decisions made. • Consider what level of knowledge you could develop that may help you. For example, would it help if you knew more about qualitative research methods in general, the specific method used, or the topic being discussed? If you can work out which then you can find the right supplementary reading to help you.

Challenges	Possible solutions
	• If you cannot change your cognitive assessment, consider your emotional response. How do you feel when you read it? Your 'heart' may tell you something your 'head' has missed. For example, you may read something and feel that it is odd, or it makes you feel uncomfortable. Do not ignore these feelings but work out why. For example, you might develop an ethical critique (see Chapter 4) because when you read the method section you felt 'I wouldn't like that to happen to me'.
Having difficulty making useful notes that do not just repeat what the authors are saying.	• Develop your critical thinking by trying to make links across the papers you read; note the author's position as succinctly as possible, how they tried to make their argument sound plausible and any assumptions in the work. • Put the paper to one side and have a short break, such as making a cup of tea. When you come back try to write your notes without referring to the paper itself. The break may allow you to mull over the key points without having to rely on the exact words used by the author.
Finding it difficult to identify what is important	• Read the article through once so you get a sense of the main points, then go back through each section, summarising each subsection and writing one advantage and one disadvantage for the decisions made there. • Compare the abstracts of different articles. Since abstracts summarise the key points of a paper, they can help you identify what is important.
Not feeling motivated to do more than read an article.	• Develop your critical thinking by joining or starting a reading group. Reading groups let you learn techniques for critical thinking from each other and can help motivate you to do the work if you have to discuss it with others.
Being unsure how to develop self-awareness to know what your standpoint is or what implicit standpoints other researchers may take.	• Do the findings resonate with what you believe or don't believe, and could this be affecting your evaluation of the study? • Read more on principles of qualitative research methods to get a better sense of what standpoints are out there, which one resonates with you and the implications for taking that position and not another.

Conclusion

We called this chapter 'getting started with qualitative methods' because we wanted to cover the foundations of doing a qualitative project. We have not shied away from the difficult questions or from encouraging you to think about process as well as content. These are big issues, and you don't have to know it all or be able to do it all before you start a project. Rather, we have shown you some of the issues that will be shaping your experience of doing a project so that you can start your journey that bit better prepared.

References

Adair, J. (2022) *Decision Making and Problem Solving: Break through Barriers and Banish Uncertainly at Work*. London: Kogan Page.

Ayton, P. (2005) Judgement and decision making. In N. Braisby and A. Gellatly (eds), *Cognitive Psychology*. Oxford: Oxford University Press. pp. 382–413.

Billig, M. (1996) *Arguing and Thinking: A Rhetorical Approach to Social Psychology*. Cambridge: Cambridge University Press.

Billig, M (2013) *Learning to Write Badly: How to Succeed In The Social Sciences*. Cambridge: Cambridge University Press.

Edwards, D., Ashmore, M. and Potter, J. (1995) Death and furniture: The rhetoric, politics and theology of bottom line arguments against relativism. *History of the Human Sciences*, 8, 25–49.

Gill, R. (1995) Relativism, reflexivity and politics: Interrogating discourse analysis from a feminist perspective. In S. Wilkinson and C. Kitzinger (eds), *Feminism and Discourse: Psychological Perspectives*. London: Sage. pp. 165–86.

Hepburn, A. (2000) On the alleged incompatibility between relativism and feminist psychology. *Feminism & Psychology*, 10, 91–106.

Howitt, D. (2019) *Introduction to Qualitative Research Methods in Psychology: Putting Theory into Practice* (4th edn). Harlow: Pearson.

Martín-Baró, I. (1994) *Writings for a Liberation Psychology*. Cambridge, MA: Harvard University Press.

McGhee, P. (2001) *Thinking Psychologically*. London: Palgrave.

Newman, F. and Holzman, L. (2000) Against against-ism: Comment on Parker. *Theory & Psychology*, 10, 265–70.

Parker, I. (1998a) Against postmodernism: psychology in cultural context. *Theory & Psychology*, 8, 601–27.

Parker, I. (1998b) *Social Constructionism, Discourse and Realism*. London: Sage.

Parker, I. (1999a) Against relativism in psychology, on balance. *History of the Human Sciences*, 12, 61–78.

Parker, I. (1999b) The quintessentially academic position. *History of the Human Sciences*, 12, 89–91.

Parker, I. (2000) Critical distance: reply to Newman and Holzman. *Theory & Psychology*, 10, 271–6.

Parker, I. (2005) *Qualitative Psychology: Introducing Radical Research*. Buckingham: Open University Press.

Potter, J. (1998a) Discursive social psychology: From attitudes to evaluative practices. *European Review of Social Psychology*, 9, 233–66.

Potter, J. (1998b) Fragments in the realization of relativism. In I. Parker (ed.), *Social Constructionism, Discourse and Realism*. London: Sage. pp. 27–46.

Potter, J., Edwards, D. and Ashmore, M. (1999) Regulating criticism: Some comments on an argumentative complex. *History of the Human Sciences*, 12, 79–88.

Riley, S., Brooks, J., Goodman, S., Cahill, S., Branney, P., Treharne, G. and Sullivan, C. (2019) Celebrations amongst challenges: Considering the past, present and future of the Qualitative Methods in Psychology (QMiP) Section of the British Psychological Society. *Qualitative Research in Psychology*, 16 (3), 464–82. DOI: 10.1080/14780887.2019.1605275

Riley, S. and LaMarre, A. (2023) *Developments in Qualitative Inquiry*. In M. McCullen (ed.), APA Handbook of Research Methods in Psychology (2nd edn). Vol 2: *Research Designs: Quantitative, Qualitative, Neuropsychological, and Biological*, H. Cooper (Editor-in-Chief).

Shafir, E., Simonson, I. and Tversky, A. (1993) Reason-based choice. *Cognition*, 49, 11–36.

Shaw, R. (2019) Interpretative phenomenological analysis. In C. Sullivan and M.A. Forrester (eds), *Doing Qualitative Research in Psychology: A Practical Guide*. London: Sage. pp. 185–208.

Sullivan, C. (2019) Theory and method in qualitative research. In C. Sullivan and M.A. Forrester (eds.), *Doing Qualitative Research in Psychology: A Practical Guide*. London: Sage. pp. 17–34.

Sullivan, C. and Forrester, M. (eds) (2019) *Doing Qualitative Research in Psychology: A Practical Guide*. Sage.

Tuffin, K. (2005) *Understanding Critical Social Psychology*. London: Sage.

Wigginton, B. and Lafrance, M.N. (2019) Learning critical feminist research: A brief introduction to feminist epistemologies and methodologies. *Feminism & Psychology*. https://doi.org/10.1177/0959353519866058

2
COMING UP WITH RESEARCH QUESTIONS

Kathryn Kinmond and Sarah Riley

Qualitative researchers ask questions about people's everyday lives and experiences, considering such issues as communication processes, lived experience, and how shared cultural ideas shape people's understanding of themselves and the world. So as a qualitative researcher, you will have the privilege of exploring what is important to people and why. To do that well you need a good research question and research design, and this chapter will help you do that.

This book takes you through the key stages of doing a successful project, and in this chapter we focus on helping you understand research questions. Before you develop your research question(s) you first have to identify a topic, so we'll start there. Then we talk you through what makes a good research question. Finally, we explain how research questions link with research design. This chapter will look at:

- Deciding the area and topic of your project.
- Identifying a specific issue that you can address.
- Good research questions and how they differ from research aims.
- Writing your research question.
- Research design considerations.

Deciding the Area and Topic of Your Project

In Chapter 1, we noted that some researchers start with a problem, and then select an approach which allows them to address it. Other researchers argue that when we identify a problem, we are already making a range of (possibly tacit) assumptions about the nature of the world, what it is possible to find out and how we should go about doing that. Learning to do a qualitative research project involves starting to recognise those assumptions. To do this, get familiar with the discussion on epistemology in Chapter 1. Then, when you read academic articles during your literature review (see Chapter 6), pay attention to those authors who discuss their approach or epistemology. And consider whether this view of the world resonates with you or offers a viewpoint about your research topic that you would like to take.

Before you get to a literature review though, you need to have an area and topic to review. An area might be a broad theme (such as health, childhood or crime) or a type of psychology (such as social, occupational or developmental); and these might overlap. For example, taking a developmental approach to a childhood issue. A topic is a specific issue you want to look at. Combining an area and topic would give you, for example, a developmental approach to studying children's use of social media. This might produce quite a different project to, for example, a social psychology approach to studying children's use of social media. This is because different approaches in psychology draw on different theories of how people work. You don't have to know about all these differences before you decide an area and a topic, but you can get a good-enough feel for them by thinking about how the different modules you've studied have framed their area and which ones resonated with you enough that you would like to know more. Students often need help choosing an area and topic, so below we discuss four ways to find a research focus that interests you.

Top tip

Identifying a project topic

- Consider the classes, courses or modules you enjoyed the most.
- Reflect on what readings you found most interesting.
- Look up staff homepages for their research interests and what they like to supervise.
- Get inspiration from you own life experience, work experience or the communities you're connected with.

You can decide which area to focus on by considering what lectures, tutorials, seminars, modules, courses, readings, YouTube videos or podcasts you have enjoyed while studying psychology. There may be a particular topic you really enjoyed in your studies, or which sounded interesting, but you didn't have the opportunity to cover fully. Your project is likely to be the biggest piece of work you do in your degree, it will take up a lot of your time, and require intensive periods of focus. So, you want it to be something you are interested in. That way, you've got a fighting chance of sitting yourself down and doing it. Most students are really proud of their project, not just because it is a big piece of work but because they feel ownership of it. So, when picking a topic, ask yourself, can you imagine working on this topic for a significant amount of time and being that proud student on handing-in day?

If you have not yet studied any topics that really interest you, then think about the topics and issues that distract you when you are supposed to be reading for an assignment, or that engage you in conversations with friends, family, co-workers or perhaps your lecturers. Is there someone in your department who might supervise the project on this topic? Or if you already have a supervisor, discuss with them whether it's possible to develop a project in this area.

Deciding on an area or topic to study involves matching an area you find sufficiently interesting, and that is suitable for a project, to one that a member of staff in your institution is able to supervise. Choosing an area that's already taught means that you're likely to find a supervisor with an interest in this area. It also means you might have an idea of the field, which can help you in narrowing down your research question and knowing what literature to read. Another way to match your interests to a supervisor is to use your departmental webpages to explore staff research interests in your department. Include looking at people who haven't taught you or who you don't know well – they might be doing super-interesting research that you don't know about. It is often to your advantage if your project fits in with the interests of your supervisor because they will be enthusiastic about the topic and can guide you with expert understanding of the field, and in some departments you may be expected to undertake a project closely allied to the interests of a member of academic staff. If you want to do a qualitative project, also check that your supervisor is able to supervise this.

Your own life or work experiences or knowledge of the communities you're connected to might also be inspiration for identifying a research area. You may have encountered a specific problem or situation you feel is worthy of further investigation, although note that some topics of personal relevance may be difficult to research. Work or voluntary experience may also be a useful source of ideas if you have noticed something worth studying; alternatively, ask the staff there if they have any research needs. There are important distinctions between research and service evaluation, so make sure you run any ideas past your supervisor.

Connecting with an organisation in an area where you want to develop a career can be especially useful. Alternatively, consider your career aspirations and if you can develop any skills or understanding through your thesis that would make you an attractive candidate for future jobs in that field. Jane, for example, wanted to work in advertising, so in her thesis she explored a theory related to people's responses to advertisements. Similarly, if you want to work in human resources, look at organisational psychology textbooks and see what issues stick out for you as interesting.

Getting familiar with a general research area can help you identify a specific topic within that area. But if you need direction, one top tip is to return to articles you found interesting or enjoyable to read and go to the conclusion because usually there is a subsection where the researcher suggests directions for future research. See if any of these sound like the beginning of a research project for you. Also notice how they phrase their research questions, as it could give you ideas for your own.

Another way of finding a topic to study is to look at academic conference programmes. At these conferences, academics present research they are currently working on. If you have a look at the titles of their presentations, you might get inspiration that you could translate into a qualitative student project. With so many conferences now being hybrid delivery or virtual, it's never been easier to look at conference programmes. Try searching for 'British Psychology Society events' or specifically search for the BPS section conferences, especially 'Qualitative Methods in Psychology'. If you hit a paywall, try their social media including Facebook and Twitter. The UK National Centre for Research Methods calls their conference a research methods 'festival', and you can look up past programmes here www.ncrm.ac.uk. Or try SQIP, the American Psychology Association's Society for Qualitative Inquiry in Psychology (http://sqip.org); there are a range of other areas of psychology that have conferences see, for example the International Society of Critical Health Psychology (https://ischp.net). Ask your supervisor for recommendations.

Students can also develop a research project around a theory. In qualitative research, you might not have a theory that you test with a hypothesis, but you can have a theoretical framework that tries to account for, or explain, a particular psychological issue or through which you can explore your participants' experiences. And you can use that theoretical framework to identify a focus for your study. For example, if you were interested in body image, you might find research on the mediating effects of self-compassion for body image. Then, taking self-compassion as a starting point, you might organise your research around the theory, such as understanding the literature theorising why self-compassion works as an intervention and then exploring how aspects of self-compassion resonate (or not) with the lived experience of people who identify as having a positive body image.

Qualitative research is iterative, which means we cycle through the same process, but each time getting more clarity or focus. So it might be that you cycle through a few ideas about area, topic of interest or even a specific research question as your ideas about what to focus on develop. But there is a point where you have to decide on an area, topic and research question, and you do not need to do it alone. Supervisors are often happy to think-through ideas with their students to collaboratively develop a project that will work. The box below gives an example of how a research topic developed during a project.

Success story

Refining and refocusing the research question

Sampat was interested in doing her undergraduate project on how British men in their 70s experienced and coped with the loneliness resulting from their sons leaving home for the first time. Sampat went to the library to search for relevant literature and was surprised to find there was virtually no published academic research on this topic. Coming from India, Sampat's personal experience indicated that this was a major psychological issue within society. However, in the UK most young men leave their parental home when their parents are younger than 70. Indeed, the changing demographics of family life in the UK mean that many sons do not live with their fathers at all. So, an issue that is pertinent to life in India did not appear to be so relevant for people in the UK. It is possible that social change in the UK means that this might become an issue, and it could therefore be a topic that is ripe for study. But, given the time constraints of undergraduate research, Sampat's supervisor helped her to explore the possibilities of developing a research study in a related area such as 'empty nest' syndrome, loneliness and the ageing process.

The aim of research is to generate knowledge that is useful. This could be in relation to creating new insights into an issue or supporting existing research findings and so strengthening their conclusions. Normally researchers are required to say how their research develops knowledge or addresses a knowledge gap. But you are using your project as a training exercise for learning to be a researcher. At undergraduate level, this means that expectations for creating original research may not apply to you. Doing research on a topic already investigated can help support, challenge or develop existing understanding of that topic. If your topic has been researched extensively, try to think (as in Yvette's success story on p. 32) of a slight twist on what has already been done that you can focus on. You can make a case for looking at a specific population that hasn't been studied before, for example, and explain why that population is important. And because qualitative research tends to understand knowledge as produced within a specific context, if contexts change then new research is needed. For example, you could make a case that the Black Lives Matter movement created a new context for understanding racism (it might, for example, frame how victims of racism interpret these experiences). Similarly, technological developments also create new contexts to study. For example, there is a long history of feminist research on make-up, but YouTube make-up tutorials are a relatively new cultural phenomenon that can be studied in a variety of novel ways. We might, for example, do a thematic analysis of the talk; a multimodal discourse analysis of the interconnected talk, visual and moving elements (e.g. holding product up to camera); or interview people who like to watch these videos. None of these projects were possible before the advent of the YouTube make-up tutorial.

Students can also make a case for a qualitative study on a well-researched topic if most prior research has been quantitative. For example, a lot of research about students shared living was done using quantitative methods, such as correlations between proximity and friendship. But what it's like to share a living space with a peer group is relatively under-explored qualitatively, and a prime topic for qualitative research, given its interest in lived experience, and how shared taken-for-granted ideas structure people's sense-making.

Final considerations when identifying a topic or area is if it can be researched qualitatively and with the resources and timeframe you have to do your project. A topic needs to be feasible in terms of your resources and timeframe; it also needs to be ethical. We guide you with these issues in Chapters 3 and 4, but you also need speak to your supervisor. For now, note that often less is more – in that it's easier to get good marks if you do a small, focused, feasible project really well than an over-ambitious, complex, hard-to-organise or under-resourced project. It is great to be ambitious but find ways to convert that ambition into something that is doable. So, for example, if you are interested in mental health, it's unlikely that you will have the skills or the time to negotiate access to mental health service users so trying to do that is both unfeasible and unethical. However, it is likely that you could interview staff working in the field to explore their understanding of the issue.

Activity 2.1

Can the topic be researched qualitatively?

Ask yourself, which of these topics and issues can be researched qualitatively?

1   The link between playing violent computer games and violent behaviour in children aged 10-15 years.
2   The link between living near to someone and being friends with them.
3   The experience of living with an autistic child.
4   The success of a healthy eating programme in schools.

Answers are at the end of the chapter.

What Makes a Good Research Question?

Qualitative researchers do lots of different kinds of research projects using different kinds of methods. But what we share in common is an interest in analysing talk, text, image or movement without converting it into numbers and doing statistical analysis on those numbers. The data we use – talk, text, image or movement – usually helps us gain insight or understanding into how people communicate or make sense of their world. So qualitative researchers are usually interested in:

• examining processes of interaction and communication;
• understanding how people experience an issue and interpret those experiences;
• analysing language to explore how ideas about the world underpin what we can say, think, feel or do;
• analysing images or movement to understand how or what people are communicating.

Our research questions usually map onto one of those interests. For example, if we are interested in interaction we might ask: 'How do people refuse an invite to something they cannot or do not want to go to?' Or, if we are interested in experiences, we might ask instead: 'What are the kind of feelings people have and how do they interpret those feelings when they say no to an invitation?' Or, if we want to look at our underlying sense-making, we might ask: 'What are the broader forms of common sense (or "discourses") which underpin people's talk of refusing invitations?' Or, if we want to understand the impact of a person's movements, we might ask: 'What does the way that person moves tell us about their experience of that event?' Or if we want to explore images, we might look at Internet memes of refusals and ask: 'How is emotion represented in these memes?' These are all relevant questions to ask, and all can offer interesting findings – including, respectively, that people pause and then give an excuse; in Britain people often feel guilty; people tend to construct refusals as dilemmatic activities related to managing their own and other people's feelings; eye contact is important; there is a shared understanding that social relationships can be awkward.

Given the topic of this chapter, the smart reader (that's you by the way) might already have guessed that the above questions are examples of research questions.

········In a nutshell········· ·

What is a research question?

A research question is a question posed by the researcher that can be answered by the project's proposed methods of data collection and analysis.

· ·

Research projects differ in terms of how many research questions they aim to answer. You might have one research question, two or more distinct research questions, or one main research question with some subsidiary research questions. But the nature of these questions, how we create them and how they link to design remain the same. A good research question also tells you something about the participants involved or for whom the study is most relevant. So, research questions often refer to a particular group that we are interested in; overseas students, for example, might experience particular tensions in working out how to say 'no' in a new country where they are unsure of cultural norms in communication. Context-specific questions are important, because most qualitative researchers understand knowledge to be produced in context, rather than representing universal psychological processes (see Chapter 1 for more discussion on this issue).

A good research question may give you a hint about the underpinning epistemology or approach of the research, although not all questions do, and different epistemologies might share some terminology. See Table 2.1 below, Chapter 1 for discussion of epistemology and Chapter 8 for more information on methods of analysis.

Table 2.1 How research questions can hint at epistemology or approach

	Focus of study	Epistemology 'hint' words in the research question	Example research question	Want to read more?
Phenomenology	People's lived experience and how people interpret that experience	'experience'	How do women experience voluntary childlessness?	Shaw, R. L. (2011). Women's experiential journey toward voluntary childlessness: An interpretative phenomenological analysis. *Journal of Community & Applied Social Psychology, 21*(2), 151-163.
Discursive approaches related to discursive psychology or conversation analysis	The interactional functions of people's talk	'doing' 'account' 'functions' 'talk'	What are the interactional functions of making 'mmm' sounds while eating?	Wiggins, S. (2002). Talking with your mouth full: Gustatory mmms and the embodiment of pleasure. *Research on Language and Social Interaction, 35*(3), 311-336.
Discursive approaches informed by poststructuralism (including Foucauldian-informed discourse analysis)	How particular understandings of reality are created in language	'taken for granted' 'common sense' 'discourse' 'talk'	What discourses structure couples' talk of engaging with health-related lifestyle advice after one of them has a diagnosis of CHD?	Robson, M., Riley, S., Gagen, E. & McKeogh, D. (2022). Love and lifestyle: how 'relational healthism' structures couples' talk of engagement with lifestyle advice associated with a new diagnosis of coronary heart disease., *Psychology & Health.* doi 10.1080/08870446.2022.2033240

When you first start working with qualitative methods you may not know your epistemology or approach because you are still learning. If this is you, start with a broad research question (e.g. how do people who do 'extreme sports' explain why they do this?) or even just a topic to think about ('extreme sports'). But as you develop an understanding of research methods – by reading research methods literature and published research studies on your topic – you will be able to develop your research question so that it maps onto the approach to knowledge that underpins your project.

Top tip

Ground your research question in the literature

Some of the first psychologists sat in their armchair and introspected. But there's been a lot of developments in our discipline over the last hundred years or so, and that luxury is not open to you. As you can see from the directions we've given you above, we offered ways in which you can connect with existing research, such as through what you've learnt in class, or when reading academic literature. It's important to derive research questions from existing work so that:

- there is a good reason for asking them;
- they are not naïve or otherwise problematic;
- they are useful to ask because they haven't been done to death.

Good research questions in qualitative research are relatively short, clear and focused on a particular issue. But qualitative research projects often start off with relatively broad questions because qualitative research tends to be exploratory – in the sense that we rarely have hypotheses or predictions. Indeed, going to look for something that you expect to find is the hallmark of a limited qualitative project. You might start off with a broad research question that you refine as you get a better understanding of the literature or, later in the project, you might revisit your research question based on the patterns in your data. When refining initial research questions in these ways, you would consider whether to keep them broad or make them more specific and focused. You might add more questions or rewrite them to shift the focus. When you are reviewing your research question, speak with your supervisor, as they can help you think this through for your specific study. They can also help you to consider how many research questions will work for your methods and aims and why this is appropriate.

─Success story─

Developing a research question

Yvette was interested in talk during family mealtimes. She started off with a broad research question: 'How do families talk about food during family mealtimes?' Once she had read more literature on this topic, she became interested in research by discursive psychologists whose research concerns were around how people account for their food preferences. Given these researchers had done a lot of work in this area already Yvette tried to think of a specific context that was less researched and realised that previous studies hadn't focused much on special occasion meals. So, Yvette tightened the focus and direction of her research question to ask: 'How do people account for their food preferences during special family mealtimes?' This was a good research question because it had information about the population being studied (families), the topic (explaining food preferences during family mealtimes), it gave a hint at the kind of approach being taken since discursive psychologists often ask about how people 'account' for an issue and it was contextually focused on specific, special mealtimes. It met the criteria we outline above – it could be answered, it told us the population, it gave us a hint at epistemology (the word 'talk' points to some kind of discourse analysis), it was short and was clearly focused on a topic.

When thinking about research questions, it's useful to know the difference between research questions, aims and objectives. As we said above, a research question is a question posed by the researcher and which is answered by their proposed method of data collection and analysis. Answering that question should enable you to meet the bigger aim of the project. A project aim is the wider goal. So, for example, Yvette's aim is to better understand interactions during special family mealtimes. To meet that aim, she may have several objectives, which are the goals of a project. Yvette's objectives might be to i) identify patterns in special family mealtime talk and ii) analyse that talk with reference to how food-choices are managed. She can meet her aim and objectives by answering her research question ('How do families talk about food during special family mealtimes?').

In this example, Yvette already had an idea of the area and topic of her project and reading in this area then allowed her to develop her specific research question. Many students though do not start with a very clear idea about the project they want to do. If that's you, don't worry! Use the advice above to find an area of interest and then narrow down to a topic, which will take you to that currently elusive research question.

Writing Your Research Question

Once you have a good idea of your topic, issue and the kind of question you want to answer with your research project, you are ready to write a brilliant research question. Earlier on we highlighted key aspects of a good research question; these include:

- a question that can be answered by your proposed qualitative method of data collection and analysis;
- tells you something about the kind of participants involved;
- hints at (or at least is consistent with) the underpinning epistemology or approach of the research;
- is focused, contained and doable with the resources you have.

Any research question you write should actually be phrased as a question (this sounds obvious, but you might be surprised by the number of students who don't do this). Start with words like 'what' or 'how'. Note that research questions that start with the word 'do' are closed questions, inviting a 'yes' or 'no' answer, rather than a deep engagement with the complexity of the issue. So, avoid starting with 'do' if you can help it.

You also need to decide if you are going to have a broad question (that you may or may not narrow later), such as: 'What are the concerns of parents of primary school aged children about their children's health?' Or if you will be more focused, either because you have a clear idea of what you want to look at or because you are writing a set of more specific research questions. An example of a more focused version of the question above is: 'How do parents account for the content of their children's packed lunch in the context of wider discourses around healthy choices?' In either case, make sure you include in your question the group of participants involved and a clear topic (whether it's something broad like 'health' or something more specific like 'discourses of health when discussing packed lunch'). Avoid being so narrowly focused as to be unidirectional or leading since we want to explore the issue from our participants' perspective not our own. The latter works because pack lunches require parents to make decisions and there already exists research showing that parents have to negotiate a discursive world that connects good parenting to healthy eating in their children.

Activity 2.2

Broad or narrow?

Consider the following questions. Are they too broad, too narrow, or about right?

1   How far do male nurses embody a male hegemonic identity?
2   What is the experience of living with diabetes?
3   Do children sent to day-care have problems?
4   How do football fans' online message boards account for their team's poor performance?

Answers are at the end of the chapter.

Remember that a project aim is the wider goal. So, for example, the broad question of 'why do people self-harm?' is likely to be a general aim since a study is likely to contribute to understanding this issue, rather than to answer it in full. If your research question is this broad, start to focus it down on a specific element. For example, something like: 'How do counsellors understand the reasons for self-harming behaviour in adolescents?' This is more focused, is easier to research (in part because of ethical issues – see Chapter 4) and can be addressed more fully and in more depth by a specific project.

Qualitative research enables exploration of dimensions of the social world, including features of everyday life such as the understandings, experiences and imaginings of research participants, the ways in which social processes, institutions, discourses and relationships work, and the significance of the meanings they create. It is good for exploring complex, interconnected issues, processes, experiences, or other forms of meaning making associated with them, which is why these words tend to appear in the research questions of qualitative projects. This is in contrast to quantitative research which tends to look at differences between groups or between two time periods in the same group or asks cause-and-effect questions. Questions, about influences, for example 'Does the media influence body image?', tend to hint at a quantitative, cause and effect project.

Qualitative and quantitative methods do share some features; for example, methods in both traditions involve systematic and detailed analysis of data with the aim of addressing a specific aim or research question. But they tend to be suited to different things. This means that while many topics can be addressed by either qualitative or quantitative research, it is the research question, rather than the topic, that tells us which methodological approach is being used. For example, the topic of interventions for stroke patients can be investigated using a quantitative approach seeking to measure the efficacy of specific interventions (e.g. Chatterton et al., 2008) or by exploring the qualitative experience of a how an intervention made patients feel and how far they felt it aided recovery (e.g. Ewan et al., 2010).

Activity 2.3

Writing research questions

List three psychology questions that you'd like answered. The list may consist of a number of inter-related questions, or a set of very different questions. For each question:

1   Describe the area: e.g. is it social psychology or developmental psychology? This will help you locate your study in a particular literature and give you direction for reviewing the literature (see Chapter 6).

2   Describe the topic: e.g. is it social media, healthy eating? This gets your mind focused as to exactly what you are going to be looking at.

3 Write the question: starting with a question word such as 'how', 'why' or 'what' and then making sure you include a group of people (e.g. students, adolescents, parents), a word that hints at your approach (e.g. experience, discourse) and your topic.

4 Write a couple of sentences as to why it is important to answer this question. For example, does it address a gap in the literature, inform future practice or help us understand an important issue better? This helps you justify your research question since a strong research question should pass the 'so what?' test. It will also help you frame your research proposal and provide a clear and strong rationale for why you asked that question (see Chapter 3).

Review what you have written for Activity 2.3. Consider which questions seem most interesting to answer or most possible to answer given your resources. Take this to your supervisor who can help you think through the advantages and disadvantages and make your final decision. For a summary of this process, see Figure 2.1.

From Research Question to Research Design

Your research design is how the overall components of your study come together. A key feature of an excellent project is coherence in your design, which is when there is coherence between your research question, underpinning approach to knowledge (epistemology and ontology), and methods for collecting and analysing data (the four corners of the methodological kite, introduced in Chapter 1). This is because it shows that you understand the principles underlying these separate components and that they can be combined in ways that align with these principles. An example design statement might be, 'a phenomenological thematic analysis of five interviews with people who experienced long Covid'. This is a qualitative research design where the components 'fit', since phenomenological research requires in-depth descriptions by participants of their experiences, often focusing on a small number of participants because understanding individual experience is valued, and thematic analysis can be applied to the in-depth discussions produced in interview data.

As Figure 2.1 suggests, developing a coherent design might require you to cycle between developing research questions and familiarising yourself with the sorts of approaches available to you. If you set your research question before you know which approach or method you're going to use, you may be storing up trouble for yourself further down the line! See Chapters 7 and 8 for more on data collection and methods of analysis. We also give guidelines for thinking about methods in Chapter 3. Reading these will also help you here.

Previously we noted that qualitative and quantitative projects tend to have different kinds of research questions, because their approach to knowledge is often different. So, when considering your design, ask yourself, are you interested in making a claim about

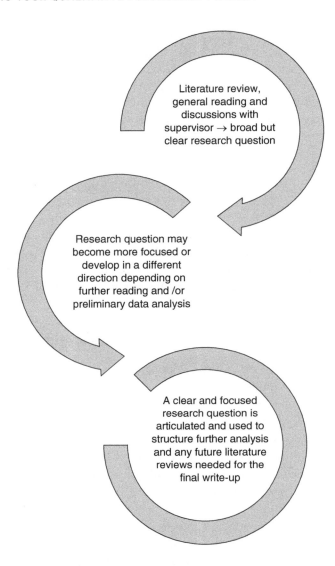

Figure 2.1 Developing your research question

the nature of reality or how people interpret their reality? For example, do you want to know how people really talk, and want to study patterns in communication – as in our earlier example of how people do refusals? Or if you are interested in interpretation, is how people describe and understand their experiences what you want to know more about? Or perhaps you are interested in how people use shared forms of sense making (discourses) to make sense of themselves and others? We have two caveats here. First, you are unlikely to be able to answer this well unless you read more literature on your topic and get a feel for the kinds of questions and approaches to knowledge available – doing a qualitative research project is an opportunity to enter a new world for thinking about people, let yourself get lost a little in it before you make your decision. Second, some qualitative work is underpinned by the same approach to knowledge as quantitative work, but many qualitative researchers would question any simplistic assumptions about language mirroring reality. So, if you are interested in understanding experience or meanings it is likely that your study will be an interpretive one (see Chapter 1 and below).

Philosophical issues, like whether knowledge gives us access to reality or interpretations, are not easy topics to understand but having a general familiarity with the ideas will help you understand what you read and the assumptions underpinning your project. Below, we use the example of carrying out research on healthy eating to help you see how epistemology, aims, research questions and research methods might be brought together to form coherent designs. Take heart! Over time this will become more familiar and the ideas easier to work with.

··· ··In a nutshell··· ···

Forming coherent designs

Nurses sometimes find it hard to eat healthily at work. Below are different ways of researching this issue:

Realist/positivist/post-positivist approaches understand that a real world exists independently of human perception and interpretation and is available to be discovered. Applying this to our topic:

- Aim: to understand what limits nurses' access to healthy food.
- Research question might use language relating to influence, cause and effect, or understanding.
- Example research question: what factors do nurses describe as influencing their eating at work?
- Kinds of methods: realist-informed thematic analysis of interviews or food diaries; discursive psychological analysis of nurses' naturally occurring talk (e.g. in their kitchen) - recorded with permission of course!

Phenomenological approaches in psychology are interpretative, focusing on understanding what is experienced and the way it is experienced, treating experience as a thing people encounter but also a process in which they are active.

- Aim: to understand the lived experience of the nurses and how they interpret this.
- Research question might include words like experience, meaning or understanding.
- Example research question: what is the lived experience of eating at work for nurses?
- Kinds of methods: interpretive phenomenological analysis of interviews with nurses, phenomenologically informed thematic analysis of nurses' eating diaries.

(Continued)

Social constructionist and poststructuralist approaches are interpretative, focusing on how the specific socio-historical discursive context shapes how people can make sense of themselves and their world.

- Aim: to identify how participants construct their reality, the common sense and discursive resources they use to do this and wider discourses (broad understandings about the world) that support this sense making.
- Research question terminology might include words like talk, experience, discourse, construct, account.
- Example research question: what discourses structure nurses talk of eating at work?
- Kinds of methods: discourse analysis of interviews with nurses, social constructionist informed thematic analysis of nurses' eating diaries.

. . . .

Want to know more about philosophy and research?

For useful explanations of the philosophical assumptions relevant to different research approaches see:

Riley, S. and Chamberlain, K. and (2021) Designing qualitative research in psychology. In U. Flick (ed.), *SAGE Handbook of Qualitative Research Design*. London: Sage.

Sullivan, C. (2019) Theory and method in qualitative psychology. In C. Sullivan and M. A Forrester (eds), *Doing Qualitative Research in Psychology: A Practical Guide* (pp. 17-34). London: Sage.

As mentioned above, qualitative designs are often iterative. When you have a prediction design, which is more likely with quantitative studies, then the design should be linear. This means that if a hypothesis is not supported, researchers should not try to find other statistically significant connections in the data because this increases the chance of a Type II error (that they are finding patterns in the data that are meaningless). In contrast, qualitative researchers do research to gain understanding and insight, and this means you can cycle back and forth through the stages of research process. For example, if your analysis brings up an issue that was unexpected, you might go back to your literature to see where this issue is discussed, and bring that new knowledge into your analysis, and in some cases you might develop your research question in response to what is in your data.

Earlier we gave a story about Yvette whose research question was: 'How do families talk about food during special family mealtimes?' It was a great research question that could have taken her the whole way through her project. But even with a great question, sometimes there may be further iterations. If, for example, she found an unexpected pattern in her data that she wanted to explore in more detail, Yvette could tighten her research question further to explore it. In our own research on family meal-times we were surprised, for example, to find a lot of talk about money and economic power in food discussions, such as when a daughter in her 20s said to her parents: 'When I contribute, I'll make decisions in this family' (www.youtube.com/watch?v= iYKuTHdFMPw). If this happened to Yvette, she could shift her research question to focus on this issue, such as: 'How does finance talk structure people's accounts of food preferences during special family meals?' Equally she could have kept her broader ques-tion, and instead included talk around money as one of the patterns in her analysis. We give you the story so that, should you come to your analysis and want to change your research question in response to your data, you know that it is possible to do so within exploratory, interpretative qualitative designs. But you should not make this decision on your own – always speak with your supervisor to evaluate the pros and cons of mak-ing a change like this. We return to this issue when considering planning in Chapter 3 and in managing your project in Chapter 5.

Conclusion

Research questions can and might change, but in the short time that students usually have to complete a project, it's preferable to have a clear, answerable and well-justified research question relatively early on in your project so that you can dedicate time to addressing that question well. Here, to sum up, are our final top tips for great research questions.

—Top tips—

Make your research question excellent

- Take time to decide upon your research area.
- Consider your research topic carefully.
- Make sure the question can be researched qualitatively.
- Check that the question is grounded in relevant research.
- Make sure that your research question is focused.
- Ask yourself whether the research question asks precisely what you want to ask.
- Check that your question passes the 'so what?' test.

Your final step before you can start formally planning your study is to explicitly write down your research question(s) (see Activity 2.3 above if you need some pointers). To complete your design statement, you also need to consider the implications of this question for what kind of data you need to collect and what kind of method of analysis you plan to use. In the next chapter we discuss this and other steps in planning what you are actually going to do to address this question, which means it is time to turn to Chapter 3.

Answers to Activity 2.1

1   As currently phrased, this would be more suitable to a quantitative project measuring the correlation between hours of playing violent games and subsequent violent behaviour. A qualitative project might explore the experience of playing violent computer games, or the way in which the link between violent computer games and violent behaviour is socially constructed by the media.

2   The use of the term 'link' hints at a correlational and thus quantitative study. Instead, a qualitative project could ask questions about the quality of relationships occurring between people living in close proximity to each other, or how physical or geographical distance shaped their experience of their friendships.

3   This maps well onto qualitative research that is interested in experience; see, for example, research using a phenomenological approach (Chapter 8).

4   If your measure of success was a change in eating choices/practices, then this topic would probably be well suited to a quantitative study. However, you might use a mixed quantitative and qualitative method study, measuring eating choices (e.g. how much fruit was eaten) and also exploring how the pupils talked about those choices. Or you could do a fully qualitative project exploring what healthy eating means to children (which might yield important findings about reasons for – and barriers to – the success of the programme). Alternatively, you might evaluate the programme by looking at the discourses of healthy eating used by those delivering the programme – do they, for example, perpetuate stigmatising fatphobic discourses?

Answers to Activity 2.2

1   This question offers some room for development. Definition of terms will give it better focus.

2   This question is too broad. It is unclear whether the study will look at people with insulin-dependent diabetes or non-insulin-dependent diabetes and what exactly it is aiming to investigate. The question needs focus.

3   This question also needs focus because it is unclear what type of 'day-care' or what 'problems' are included.

4   This question is specific enough to make for a manageable project. It is clear what type of data is needed and where it can be found. The focus on 'accounts' also points to the appropriateness of a qualitative (most likely a discourse analytic) approach.

References

Chatterton, H., Ewan, L., Kinmond, K., Haire, A., Smith, N. and Holmes, P. (2008) Observation of meaningful activities: A case study of a personalized intervention on post-stroke functional state. *Journal of Neurologic Physical Therapy*, 32, 52–9.

Ewan, L.M., Kinmond, K. and Holmes, P.S. (2010) An observation-based intervention for stroke rehabilitation: Experiences of eight individuals affected by stroke. *Disability & Rehabilitation*, 32, 2097–106.

3
PLANNING YOUR PROJECT

Sarah Riley and Cath Sullivan

This chapter focuses on planning your project. Our aim is to help you identify the key stages of doing a successful project, starting from the point of having research questions (see Chapter 2). We leave you at the point of having completed a comprehensive plan for your project.

Planning your project is vital. This is likely to be the biggest independent piece of work that you do for your degree. The way you tackle a large project is to break it down into smaller, manageable chunks, but it can be a challenge to identify the many small steps that lead to success. In this chapter, we help you do this by showing you what you need to consider when planning for your project. Good preparation is the key to a good outcome – whether it's planning for a big night out, taking part in a sports tournament or doing a research project.

····In a nutshell····

Why planning is important

If you have a plan, you have a well-thought-out study. Well-thought-out studies are likely to:

- have phases (e.g. data collection and analysis) that fit together better (remember the lesson of Chapter 1 – you need your kite to stay airborne!);
- be high quality (through knowledge and application of best practice);
- involve fewer unpleasant surprises (for example, finding out later that the data you collected won't allow you to answer your research questions);
- give you a sense of achievement by creating sub-goals and meeting them;
- be completed on time;
- be more enjoyable, and therefore be less stressful.

To plan your project, you need to turn your research questions into a project plan that outlines what you are going to do. To do this, you will work through several phases, which are summarised in the box below and form the structure of this chapter. As you plan your project you will need to think about the ethical issues that it raises (see Chapter 4) and to draw upon material about ethics and various other aspects of research methodology. The other chapters in this book will help you to do this.

···· ···In a nutshell···· ···

Planning phases

Planning a successful and ethical project should include the following phases:

- Plan your methods: data collection and analysis.
- Plan your data: sampling and recruitment.
- Plan for the resources you need: information, support, materials and equipment.
- Plan for ethical approval.

Having done the above, you'll be able to:

- create a plan that outlines the key steps to complete your project;
- write a proposal;
- successfully apply for ethical approval.

··

In the rest of the chapter, we outline the key tasks for writing a comprehensive project plan. Assessing situations and making decisions that allow you to move your project forward requires a set of skills that develop over time. Your student research is part of a process that allows these skills to develop, so don't expect to know everything; remember that you're learning on the job. Try to find a balance between being as prepared as possible and recognising that you will learn through doing along the way. Planning your project is about being in a position to make the best possible decision you can at the time you make it. Below we give you some tried and tested tips for this.

─Top tip─────────────────────────────────

Know your stuff!

- Give yourself a good understanding of the relevant literature. Read reports of similar research projects and qualitative methods books.
- Weigh up decisions by writing down the pros and cons.

- Imagine carrying out your plans. Are they feasible? Have you forgotten to factor in something important? For example, if you're working with school children, have you scheduled your data collection during term time?
- Consider your interests and experiences. In which areas do you need to get more experience to help things go well?
- Be realistic in what you can do in your time frame.
- Look up the marking criteria for your project and think about how you can meet them.
- If you feel unsure of how to proceed, return to your research question and consider how your plan can best help you answer your question.
- Always run key decisions past your supervisor and get their help when you need it.

From Research Questions to Project Plan
Planning your methods

Your first objective in planning your project is to work out the best methods to address your research question(s) (see Chapter 2). You'll need to identify methods for collecting and analysing data that are practical within the timescale and with the resources you have. In Chapters 7 and 8, we discuss methods for collecting and analysing qualitative data in more detail, so you can use those chapters to help you with this. When identifying potential methods to use, it's useful to ask yourself the following questions:

- What methods have been used in previous similar studies?
- Did these previous methods prove useful?
- What other methods do I know about and what are their potential uses?
- What resources do these different methods require (including time) and do I have access to them?

Considering your research questions will usually give an indication of which methods will be suitable. For example, if you want to see how people make sense of an issue together, focus groups or recordings of naturally occurring talk between several people will be useful. This is because they are methods where you can see people making sense of an issue together, whereas individual interviews would only allow you to see personal reflections of these processes. Similarly, particular methodologies (the wider approach to research methods that you are using) are often closely linked to the use of specific methods, so your decisions about what methods to use may be already structured by your methodology. For example, if you want to use the methodology of discursive psychology, then you might think of using methods that record 'naturally occurring' talk (which is talk that would have occurred if your research project didn't exist). If you're struggling with these questions or think that you don't know enough about what methods might appropriate for your study, try the following:

- Look up previous work in your topic area.
- Read through some qualitative research methods books.
- Speak to your supervisor.
- Join or start a conversation in a relevant online space (e.g. one for psychology students or qualitative researchers – ask your supervisor for recommendations).

If you want to use a method you haven't already been trained in, first consider the implications. For example, will it make things unnecessarily difficult for you and jeopardise your mark? Or, conversely, will it help you demonstrate initiative and originality? Also check whether you can access training (for example, could you sit in on a relevant class) and whether there is appropriate supervision available for using this method. Discuss these issues with your supervisor.

The decisions you make about your research questions and methods will be informed by a range of issues, including your personal perspective. It's useful to reflect on how your perspectives inform your choices about your project, so that you can explore what shapes it. This kind of self-reflection allows you to make more self-aware decisions and is an important aspect of 'reflexivity'. Chapter 9 considers reflexivity in more detail and gives ideas on how to build self-reflection into your project.

Top tips

Planning for methods

There are many useful resources for qualitative researchers that will help you with project design. These include:

- Looking at contemporary research including conference presentations to get ideas for methods (see links in Chapter 2).
- University libraries have qualitative research methods books, either in hard copy or as e-books, and you should also be able to borrow from other libraries through inter-library loans. Read these books to learn about issues, methods and debates in qualitative research.
- Some libraries have electronic resources, like https://methods.sagepub.com/, which can be useful for particular methods in qualitative psychology.
- Dig out your research methods lecture notes from courses you've taken - you may be surprised by how much in there is useful now!
- Browse academically credible web resources, such as the online journal *Forum: Qualitative Social Research* (www.qualitative-research.net/index.php/fqs).
- In Google Scholar or another academic database, type in the name of your topic and then a particular qualitative method or epistemology. For example, if you were interested in alcohol drinking, search for 'drinking and phenomenology' and 'drinking and discourse analysis' (see Chapter 6 for more on finding literature).
- Have a look at an example plan - see Chapter 5.

Planning your data

Your project aim should have already got you thinking about your dataset. Because qualitative research projects are usually in-depth, small-scale projects, it is often clear at the outset what particular group of people, or type of material, you will need to gather your data from. For example, your research aim could be to investigate the experiences of university students who are also parents, or to examine how trans issues are represented in mainstream news media. As these examples illustrate, sometimes the data for qualitative projects involves recruiting people and other times it might mean gathering a dataset from pre-existing materials. In order to plan for collecting your data, you need to decide what kind of data will allow you to answer your research questions and then plan for how you will get this data. If you are unsure about what data you need, then a useful strategy might be to return to your research questions and consider what information will help to answer them or perhaps to revisit your research questions because they might not be specific enough (see Chapter 2).

Identifying the data you will need

A first step in planning is to identify who your participants will be or what will be the dataset for your project. This is sometimes called sampling, although this word borrows from quantitative research designs and has a different meaning there (we discuss this further below). In qualitative research we aim to create datasets that help address our research questions. There are a number of different methods of gathering data, and the one that is right for your project will depend on your research questions and what you want to be able to claim from your data analysis. It will also depend on the time and resources that you have.

Qualitative projects normally seek to develop deep understanding or insight into the subjective interpretations of experiences, communication processes or wider forms of sense making that happen in a specific context. To develop this kind of insight using a small-scale study, which is what a student project often is, you usually need a homogeneous sample (i.e. similar people with shared characteristics related to your study). Recruiting a homogeneous sample is so that you can say something meaningful about the shared experience or sense making of an issue experienced by a particular group of people. For example, one of our students, Lana, was interested in experiences of what she called 'ambivalent racism', the phrase she used to describe experiences that feel racist but may not seem so to other people. Her reading of the literature suggested that this form of racism was linked to ways of talking that were especially prevalent at a particular time in the UK. To explore this, she recruited people who identified as Black British and whose age meant they had experience of the period of time that was relevant to Lana's study. This allowed her to create an in-depth and context-sensitive analysis, which revealed something meaningful about experiences of this form of racism for this group of people. And while she did not seek to generalise to all experiences of racism, her findings addressed her research questions and were transferable. By transferable, we mean that the study added understanding to our knowledge about a subject in ways that may be relevant for other researchers studying this topic, such as helping them develop their design or think about patterns in their data.

Qualitative research projects rarely aim to generalise to a population in the same way that quantitative projects might do. Therefore, they don't tend to use methods of sampling that aim to create a statistically representative sample (which means a sample that is representative of the population from which it is drawn). Students who learn first about statistically representative samples, and then start to learn about qualitative methods, can get the mistaken idea that the only issue in good sampling is statistical representativeness and therefore feel that methods used to create qualitative datasets are less valid. But the key point is that qualitative studies, rather than simply failing to achieve a representative sample, often deliberately use methods that do not aim to create a representative sample. There are a number of methods that have as their goal something other than the creation of a sample that is statistically representative of a population. Two such methods that are often used in qualitative research are 'opportunity' or 'purposive' sampling.

'Opportunity' (sometimes called 'convenience' sampling) involves a researcher recruiting people who they have relatively easy access to. This can include recruiting people you already know. For most student projects this is appropriate, but there are several things you need to consider if planning to do this. You should discuss this approach with your supervisor and devise strategies to address the implications it may have.

Top tips

Recruiting participants that you know

It is not unusual for students to recruit participants from amongst the people with whom they already have some relationship. Key issues to consider are:

- You should reflect on the possibility that things could be revealed during the research that affect your relationship. What if you interview your friends and they tell you something that changes how you feel about them? How much of an issue this is will, as ever, depend on the topic of the research. For example, this would be highly relevant if interviewing them about their experiences of friendship. See Chapter 5 for more discussion of relationships with participants.
- Be careful about what conclusions you can draw from your findings. For example, one of our students, Beth, wanted to look at how older women negotiated contemporary beauty ideals and recruited from her mother's friends. Beth got a good mark for this study, partly because she explored how researching people she knew might have affected her findings and the conclusions she could draw

(for more on the impact of the researcher on the research, see the discussion of reflexivity in Chapter 9).
- Recruiting people you know will also present ethical challenges in relation to consent (see Chapter 4 for more on this).

'Purposive sampling' is a more focused form of opportunity sampling. Researchers recruit participants, or select material, whose characteristics mean they will provide 'information-rich cases' in relation to the research questions (Patton, 2015). For example, Chalkley et al. (2019) wanted to explore in detail children's experiences of being involved in a specific school-based running programme. They used purposive sampling to recruit children from schools where the programme was operating, so that they could specifically explore their experiences of this context using qualitative methods. In purposive sampling researchers make decisions before collecting the data about the people or material that will best allow the research questions to be met. It is therefore also distinct from 'theoretical sampling', which is done during analysis and is focused specifically on recruiting new participants to better understand issues that have come out of that analysis so far (see Chapter 8 for more details or Gordon-Finlayson, 2019).

···· ···In a nutshell··· ···

Purposive sampling

This method of sampling:

- Does not have as its main goal the creation of a statistically representative sample.
- Is aimed at creating a dataset that will be useful for answering the research questions of the project.
- Is usually done at the start of the project, before you begin to collect and analyse data.

···

Occasionally qualitative researchers may have the goal of trying to generalise their findings to a population. This might be likely when qualitative methods are used alongside quantitative methods in a large-scale project. When qualitative researchers want to use sampling methods that aim to produce statistically representative samples, they use methods that are similar to those used in quantitative research. The small-scale nature of student research projects means that they often work best as a detailed exploration of a specific context. So, information about purposive sampling is likely to be of more use to you at this point.

—Top tips—

Successful sampling

The method of sampling you choose should be the one that will:

- best help you address your research questions;
- work within the time and resources that you have.

—Want to know more about choosing the data you need?—

There are many good sources, including the following for general discussion on sampling:

Robson, C. and McCartan, K. (2015) *Real World Research* (4th edn). Chichester: Wiley.
Schreier, M. (2018) Sampling and generalization. In U. Flick (ed.), *The SAGE Handbook of Qualitative Data Collection* (pp. 84–98). London: Sage.

Discussion of dataset size can be found in Chapter 7.

Recruiting people

Once you know what kind of dataset you need, the next step is to work out how to collect it. In many cases, this will lead you to planning the recruitment of people who will volunteer to take part in your study. Your first step here is to plan how you will access people who meet your criteria. For example, you might approach people on campus until you get enough participants, or recruit a small number of people and then ask these people to recommend you to other people in their social networks (what's known as 'snowballing' as the participant numbers increase as the project gains momentum). Will you use advertisements, perhaps placing them on notice boards or on social media sites? Are you able to recruit your participants directly or do you need to go through other people who can advertise your study to people for you?

People who control your access to potential participants are called 'gatekeepers'. They can be extremely helpful, but sometimes they can feel like a barrier to your research. Plan time to work with gatekeepers, and in some instances the participants and their community. This will allow you to build relationships and trust and identify their needs and concerns so that you can make sure that your project addresses them. You will also need to plan how to make participating in your project attractive to potential participants, so that it is easier to recruit people. For example, plan a project on a topic that people want to talk about or plan to give your participants a more tangible benefit, such as feeding their responses back into a relevant institutional policy. If you do pursue this latter option, it is advisable to discuss it with your supervisor (and also see the discussion about offering incentives to participants in Chapter 4) as you do not want to find yourself promising more than you can deliver. As with all your planning activities, work out what is feasible with the resources and time that you have.

You should also plan for how you will communicate with prospective participants, with any gatekeepers, and also with actual participants. In some cases, you may communicate with people face to face, but it is increasingly common to use digital communication such as email or messaging. In Chapter 7 we discuss the use of technology to collect data but before you can get to that stage, you must work out how to communicate effectively with people to invite them to participate in your project. The obvious bonus of using email and instant messaging is that it allows you to reach many more people as you will be less restricted by geographical location. But you should also reflect upon how this might affect things like your ability to build rapport with people and make a personal connection. Crucially, you also need to remember than any information you collect in these communications will need to be stored and handled in ethical ways (see Chapter 4 for more on this).

Top tips

Recruitment

Recruitment tends to go well when:

- People find your study interesting and relevant and can see benefit in participating (or in helping you recruit participants).
- You recruit through an appropriate medium or use several recruitment methods. For example, recruiting people on Instagram for a project on people who use Instagram would give access to appropriate participants, but a project on experiences of healthy eating that recruits only through Instagram might give a particular kind of perspective.
- You approach the participants in a positive and pleasant manner.
- Your method is convenient for participants (for example, people might be keener to take part online because they won't have to travel).
- You identify and address any concerns that participants may have (as the public are often aware that psychologists sometimes design studies involving deception or that reveal people's negative characteristics).
- You build in time to reflect on your relationships with potential and actual participants, which will improve your project by increasing your self-awareness about the decisions you've made.

───Success story and cautionary tale───

Recruitment

Amir wanted to recruit people involved in 'free party' events for his study on social identities in youth cultures. A friend who was involved in a range of music scenes gave him the phone number of Louise. Louise agreed to meet Amir at a party, but when Amir arrived, Louise had already left. On the phone, Louise told Amir to look for a guy called Steve driving a blue car. Seeing a group of people standing around some parked cars, Amir asked for Steve and soon found himself explaining the situation to him. Steve walked Amir around the party, introducing him to everyone he knew. Steve also told Amir of subsequent parties and introduced him to people there. Amir ended up joking that Steve wasn't a gatekeeper, but a 'gate opener'.

A very different experience happened to Jess when doing research in schools on body image. Jess emailed the head of a local school, who said the school would support the project and to contact the relevant year leader. This year leader appeared very interested and arranged to meet with Jess and three student representatives to discuss the project. At the meeting all parties were enthusiastic about the project and the students agreed to help with recruitment and to participate themselves. When Jess tried to arrange another meeting with the school, all emails and phone messages were ignored. Jess then changed the project, interviewing university students instead to retrospectively explore key moments that shaped their body image during their school years.

What do these stories tell us? That you never quite know how a project will go, so:

- sometimes you're un/lucky;
- be flexible;
- respond to opportunities (safely);
- use the resources you have to hand (such as friendship groups);
- have a plan B, in case participants withdraw; and,
- reflect on how your relationships with your participants and potential participants might affect your project or interactions with others.

Creating datasets of existing material

Using existing material as data can be a good option for qualitative research. Students often wish to explore psychology topics that are highly sensitive and involve groups of people who are at risk and who students are unlikely to have the skills to work with safely. Using existing data doesn't remove the need to deal with such topics sensitively and ethically (seen Chapter 4), but it can sometimes be the only feasible way of carrying out student research in these areas. Potentially suitable existing material includes archived data, news media content, social media content (e.g. Twitter, Instagram), blogs and online news articles, advertisements, company documentation and policies. This makes for a lot of opportunities to study sensitive issues without working directly with people at risk.

····In a nutshell····

Archival data

There are a number of data archives, for example the UK Data Service, where researchers have deposited sets of qualitative data that can be reused by other researchers in the future. These can sometimes be used for secondary analysis in student projects. Figshare.com is another repository for researchers who upload their anonymised datasets released under a creative commons licence. These repositories are related to the 'Open Science' initiative, which is a drive for greater transparency in research (Riley et al., 2019). Similarly, many academic journals require a statement from authors as to where interested readers might access the data on which their article was based. When reading articles for your literature review, pay attention to these data access statements – they might give you access to a large database on which you could base your research project.

These different kinds of pre-existing data sources are discussed in more detail in Chapter 7. The key thing at this stage is to consider how you might plan to get a sample of this kind of data. Although a representative sample may not be the goal, researchers still need a systematic sampling procedure that is appropriate for the research questions and the proposed data analysis method. For example, a student wanting to perform a discourse analysis of how obesity is represented in the media might focus on gathering relevant news articles published around a particular 'news hook' such as when a politician was reported as having an eating disorder; or you might look at a particular time of year, such as January, when diet talk is fashionable in the press. To do this, you would need to have clear decisions made about what would count as 'news media'. There are databases that allow you to search for news articles with certain inclusion criteria, such as topic, dates and type of media. Then, you would need to use a transparent and meaningful set of criteria to help determine which of these news articles are relevant to the topic of obesity. For example, you might decide that the word 'obesity', rather than other words with a similar meaning, has to be used. These relevant articles would then be selected into your dataset, and you would discard the irrelevant articles. As you can see, sampling of material tends to be done in stages and, at each stage, you need clear and appropriate criteria so that you can justify why some material was included for analysis while other material was not. Otherwise, you might find yourself applying different rules for inclusion and exclusion at different times, which is a hallmark of a poorly designed project.

---Top tips---

Planning for a dataset of existing material

If you want to use existing data for your study, here are some key things to consider in planning for this:

- What material is right for my research question and planned methods of analysis?
- Is it legitimate to access and use it?
    - What permissions or consent do I need from the people that created the material?
    - Are there any copyright or intellectual property issues?
    - How do I approach ethical approval (see Chapter 4)?
- How will I access it and how can I get help with that?
    - Experienced researchers know about appropriate, systematic and meaningful sampling procedures for existing texts, so ask your supervisor.
    - Check what access your institution has to sources of archive data or existing material (e.g. databases of news media such as Nexis).
    - Your librarian may also help you identify ways of searching for available materials.
- How will I develop a systematic and transparent method for selecting the material (inclusion and exclusion criteria)?
- Will I need to download and store online material and how do I do that?
    - Think about whether the source, especially for online material, is likely to change. Will your data potentially disappear if you haven't downloaded a copy?

Planning resources: Information, support and equipment

Your qualitative research project will need a range of resources, including information, support and equipment. At this planning stage your goal is to have a sense of what these resources are and how you'll use them.

Planning your information needs

All qualitative researchers need to develop their knowledge of the topic they're study-ing and the methods they're using. While these forms of knowledge should develop throughout your project, there is usually a bigger focus on them at the planning stages of the project when you're working out what to do. There may also be a focus towards the end of the project, when you will want to check for newly published research or for literature that has come to take on more relevance as your project developed.

Reviewing relevant literature is a significant activity for any qualitative research project, and Chapter 6 is dedicated to talking you through this.

Planning for support

Students who do well in their research projects tend to be proactive, independently using the various information resources they have to plan their project. However, great projects also involve students consulting with their supervisor and drawing on their experience to improve decision making. So, talk to your supervisor about the frequency and timing of meetings, agree a plan on how often to meet, but also review it and ask for changes if it isn't working for you. See Chapter 5 for more on the student–supervisor relationship.

Top tip

Being independent

Don't confuse independence with never asking for help. You must take ownership of your project, but this includes recognising when you need help and working out how to get it. Your supervisor can discuss your ideas and strategies with you and help you to do the problem solving that is needed to get your project done. They will not be able to do it for you, but they will be a great sounding board for helping you to work out how to do it for yourself. You'll need this kind of support to do your best work, so plan for how you'll get it.

Other staff who can offer you support include technicians and librarians (university libraries often have a dedicated member of staff to support students and staff in a faculty, school or department). Other students can also be a source of support. Try setting up regular study group meetings with other students working on similar topics or with similar methods. At these meetings you could discuss a reading (for example, on a method), talk about the decisions you've made regarding your projects, or look at each other's data or analysis (although be mindful of your institution's rules on collusion here). Many qualitative researchers do this kind of small-group work because other people's perspectives can be invaluable in the development of one's thinking, especially when it comes to interpreting data. Study group meetings tend to work best when everyone involved contributes and there is a theme for each meeting (for example, to read a paper). They do not work if participants compete or create anxiety through comparisons; walk away from groups that do this! Look for individuals who you think might work well with you or ask your supervisor to pass your contact details to others they are supervising who are doing similar work.

Planning equipment needs

Qualitative researchers often use specialist recording and transcribing equipment. While some students get by using the technology that they have to hand, such as mobile phones, specialist recording and transcription equipment often makes things easier, more pleasant and potentially more ethical depending on your data security. If you are doing online interviewing, you also need to check you have the right equipment and skills.

Traditionally, qualitative researchers listened to audio recordings of their interviews and manually typed in the talk. This process is called transcription (see Chapter 7) and it takes a long time – researchers typically plan for four hours of transcription time for one hour of talk. Recently, voice recognition software has transformed this process making it far less time consuming, and now many people run their audio files through such software, and then listen carefully to the recording to manually correct any errors and add the required formatting.

Top tips

Equipment for transcription

Below are links to transcription software that have at least some features that are free to use. See what will work best for your computer's operating system:

- https://otter.ai/login
- www.inqscribe.com/
- www.nch.com.au/scribe/index.html
- https://sourceforge.net/projects/audacity/
- https://dirtdirectory.org/resources/inqscribe-0

If you are doing online interviews (e.g. using Zoom or MS Teams), you may find that these have recording and transcription functions, depending on what version you have.

Check if your university has paid for qualitative analysis computer software such as NVivo - these also have voice to text functions.

Whatever software you use there will be errors, so you need to listen to your own audio files and manually finish your transcription. Also, bear in mind data security when using online transcription tools (see Chapter 4).

If you do not use dedicated voice recognition software:

- Try to borrow a transcription machine from your department or library with a foot pedal as this allows you to keep your fingers on the keyboard for faster transcription.
- The free software Audacity will allow you to play an audio file and transcribe it manually: https://www.audacityteam.org/.
- Use the voice recognition function on Word by listening to your interview and speaking it out loud into Word; this will give you a first rough draft relatively quickly, and then you can listen again to create a polished transcription.

When you use equipment to record people during your project, you will always need to fully consider issues of data security and you will need to be clear when recruiting participants about how you will keep their data secure. You may also want to advise them about the implications of any technology being used (e.g. applications for online interviewing) for data security. Your supervisor will help you with this and it is also discussed further below.

Top tips

Planning for equipment needs

- Talk to your supervisor about which equipment would be best and how to gain access to it.
- Find out as much as you can about what is available and how the system works for borrowing equipment so that you can build this into your planning.
- Find out how you can reserve equipment and what demand is like.
- Work out how long you might need it for and check that you can borrow it for this amount of time, as sometimes there are time limits on equipment loans.
- Explore online resources that may be helpful (e.g. for transcription).
- Try to plan for equipment failure. For example, have spare batteries or extra recording equipment.

Planning the development of materials

As well as the recruitment materials discussed above, depending on your project you may also need to develop materials to facilitate rich and detailed talk, such as interview or focus group schedules (see Chapter 7), which list questions and prompts to ask during interviews. Other materials that can be used to facilitate rich talk include vignettes (hypothetical stories about other people), 'memory work' (where participants share a previously prepared story of a memory), television clips and photographs (which depending on your project you might provide, or you might ask your participants to provide). Consider if these materials already exist (e.g. a news story used to prompt discussion in an interview) or whether you will need to write them (e.g. a vignette). Have a look at qualitative methods research to get ideas for the kind of materials you might use. Try making a list of the materials you might need and discuss your ideas with your supervisor. For further advice on equipment, materials, data collection and transcription see Chapter 7. You'll also need materials related to ethical practices such as consent forms and participant information sheets, which we discuss in Chapter 4.

What now?

As you get to the final stages of designing and planning your project, you will be able to write a proposal. If you are required to produce a proposal, then you will be given specific instructions about what you should include by your lecturers. Always follow your institutional guidelines.

···· ···In a nutshell··· ···

Project proposals

A project proposal is an outline of the project that gives an overview of the basic rationale of the project, states the aims and describes the methods for the collection and analysis of data.

· ·

Even if you are not required to write a formal proposal, we recommend you still develop a short project proposal on one side of A4 paper. This will let you see the structure of your project in a single glance. You can do this as a piece of text, or in some schematic form, such as a flow chart or mind map (see, for example, www.ayoa.com). Remember to include information on the background to the study and the reasons why it is important, your research questions, and your methods for collecting and analysing data. In this way, you can articulate why your study is important; what you're going to do; when, how and with whom you're going to do it; and what equipment you'll need. Put dates against when you need to do these actions and you have a well-justified and structured plan that can form your timetable (see Chapter 5 for timetabling once the project has started). Put your timetable somewhere you can see regularly, and you will have a plan you are likely to follow and all the cognitive load of trying to remember what you should be doing, and when, is gone. This is why we said at the beginning of the chapter that having a good plan increases the chance of you enjoying your project and finding it less stressful.

─Top tips─

What makes a good proposal

Good proposals:

- specify clear aims, objectives or questions to investigate;
- argue for and justify the topic to be investigated and the research questions;
- propose a method which will allow answers to the questions to be found or the aims of the research to be met;
- clearly identify the nature of data that will be collected;
- document the method in sufficient detail to allow replication;

- provide a clear account of the data analysis that will be undertaken, describing the steps involved and how they will enable the research questions to be answered;
- give a thorough treatment of the ethical issues relevant to the research;
- are well organised, easy to follow, and compel the reader to accept that the research needs carrying out and will be conducted competently and ethically;
- follow the guidelines/criteria given by your institution.

Chapter 5 contains an example of a project plan, which you can use to help you do yours, and also discusses timetables in more detail. Having a plan is important, but be flexible, plans will need to be reviewed and sometimes revised as you go along. Students can also sometimes get stuck at the planning stage, so knowing when you have done sufficient planning and can move on to writing your ethics submission is key.

Top tips

Evaluating your plan

To work out whether you've done enough planning to move onto the next stages, you need to be able to answer the following questions:

- Why is my study important?
- What has been done before?
- What are my research questions?
- What research method will best let me answer my research questions?
- What is my data collection strategy and rationale?
- What equipment, materials and skills do I need? And how will I gain access to or develop them?
- Where will I go for support in doing my project and how can I plan for this?
- Will my data need recording and transcribing or other forms of work before I can analyse it?
- How am I going to analyse the data in a way that lets me answer my research questions?

If you can't answer these questions, then you need to go through another cycle of planning. Qualitative research is often cyclical (see Chapter 5 for discussion of cyclical designs), so don't think of this as a waste of time, but part of the sharpening up processes that go into making an excellent research project. Speak to your supervisor as necessary to help you answer these questions.

Conclusion

In this chapter we have discussed the process of planning your project, and this is sum-marised in Figure 3.1. This brings us to the topic of the next chapter: your ethics application. Submitting a successful ethics application is a significant part of conduct-ing a research project because all research, including that done by students, must be subject to ethical review and approval. At the start of this chapter, we suggested that you use Chapter 4 to help you think ethically while planning your project. It's also common for your project plan to be adapted as part of the process of applying for and gaining ethical approval.

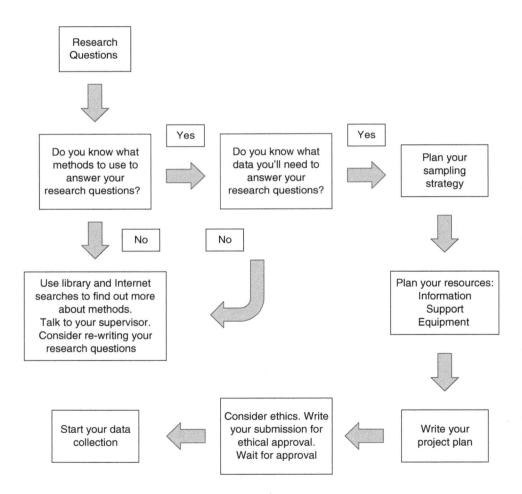

Figure 3.1 The planning process

References

Chalkley, A.E., Routen, A.C., Harris, J.P., Cale, L.A., Gorely, T. and Sherar, L.B. (2019) 'I just like the feeling of it, outside being active': Pupils' experiences of a school-based running program, a qualitative study. *Journal of Sport and Exercise Psychology*, 42(1), 48–58.

Gordon-Finlayson, A. (2019) Grounded theory. In C. Sullivan and M.A. Forrester (eds), *Doing Qualitative Research in Psychology: A Practical Guide*. London: Sage. pp. 284–312.

Patton, M.Q. (2015) *Qualitative Research and Evaluation Methods* (4th edn). London: Sage.

Riley, S., Brooks, J., Goodman, S., Cahill, S., Branney, P., Treharne, G.J. and Sullivan, C. (2019) Celebrations amongst challenges: Considering the past, present and future of the Qualitative Methods in Psychology (QMiP) section of the British Psychological Society. *Qualitative Research in Psychology*, 16(3), 464–82.

Robson, C. and McCartan, K. (2015) *Real World Research* (4th edn). Chichester: Wiley.

Schreier, M. (2018) Sampling and generalization. In U. Flick (ed.), *The SAGE Handbook of Qualitative Data Collection*. London: Sage. pp. 84–98.

4

DOING ETHICAL RESEARCH

Cath Sullivan and Sarah Riley

All researchers must gain permission from their institution to conduct their planned research. This means you must get ethical approval for your project before you begin. In this chapter we consider how you can ensure that the planning described in Chapter 3 is ethical and apply for ethical approval. We discuss the importance of ethics and highlight some key ethical issues that you will need to consider. We aim to leave you in a position to submit your project for ethical approval.

Find out about your university's approval procedure as you start to plan your project. If you plan to work with another organisation, you must fulfil any ethical requirements of that organisation too. The UK National Health Service (NHS), for example, has its own ethics approval process that often requires specialist knowledge and a significant amount of time. See your supervisor for advice on NHS ethical approval if this is relevant to you.

Getting permission to conduct your research involves you assessing the ethical issues that are involved in your research and outlining how you will address these issues. Your objectives for planning ethical research should be as follows:

- Understand research ethics and how these apply to your project.
- Know your institution's ethics procedure, including deadlines and timescales for applications.
- Find out whether you need ethical approval from anybody other than your institution and, if so, know that process too.
- Ensure that your project will be conducted ethically, meeting any relevant ethical guidelines (e.g. in the UK, British Psychological Society guidelines).
- Write and submit an ethics application in good time for you to do your study and gain approval.

········· **In a nutshell** ··· ···

The importance of ethics

Fully considering your project's ethical issues is essential for:

- avoiding harm to your participants;
- protecting the reputation of your discipline and institution;
- fulfilling your responsibility to do ethical research;
- passing your assessment!

···

Understanding Research Ethics

Research ethics is about designing morally acceptable research. Deciding what is morally acceptable is a subjective process and ethical standards are therefore derived through agreement by groups of people. This means that ethical standards change over time and are subject to some discussion and debate. Ethics applications are often evaluated by a committee, which may pass an application, reject it, or ask for changes to the study. Ethics is also an ongoing concern as issues may arise throughout the project and researchers should remain alert to the ethical implications of their work as it progresses. We advise you to review your ethics application as you carry out your project, keeping alert for ongoing ethical issues that arise and discussing these with your supervisor.

——Cautionary tale——

Unexpected revelations

Sameeha, who was interested in the relationships between identity and consumption, interviewed five people about their music collections. Two of the participants described traumatic life experiences, such as having an eating disorder and a miscarriage, which they associated with particular songs. Sameeha hadn't expected to hear such personal and painful accounts and didn't know how to respond.

What can we learn? Plan for the unexpected. Have some set phrases ready for difficult situations, however unlikely you think they'll be. For example, if a participant is upset, offer them the chance to stop the interview or take a break. When we ask people to share aspects of their lives with us, it is our duty to make this experience a safe one. It's also important to have relevant sources of help to hand (such as contact details for organisations that offer support and advice in those areas, or resources for counselling or medical advice) so that you can provide these for your participants in case they need help or support afterwards.

Some qualitative researchers argue that qualitative research tends to be more ethical than other forms of research. This is based on the idea that participants in qualitative research are less likely to be deceived and more likely to be empowered and given voice. However, not all researchers agree with this (see Willig, 2012, for further discussion) and qualitative research will only be ethical if we focus carefully on the ethical implications of our work. The way we tend to collect data means that we often ask participants to disclose personal information and to do this we form a relationship, or at least a rapport, with our participants. This combination of creating a relationship and asking for personal information may make participants vulnerable to disclosing more than they had wanted to, feeling exposed or even used. So, even projects that seem to have few ethical issues need to be carefully considered.

········**In a nutshell**········ ···

Ethics

Ethics is about:

- 'making ... decisions about what would be morally right and wrong to do' (Chamberlain, 2004: 129);
- making sure your project follows any relevant guidelines for good ethical conduct - such as those written by your institution or by a relevant professional body (for example, British Psychological Society ethical guidelines which can be downloaded from their website: www.bps.org.uk/).

··

The specific ethical issues that arise will be different for each project. But there are several key ethical issues that occur in almost all projects, which we will consider in the rest of this chapter. These are:

- doing genuine and competent research;
- valid consent;
- confidentiality;
- anonymity;
- harm and distress;
- deception and debriefing;
- right to withdraw;
- effects beyond the participants.

Genuine and competent research

Research needs to be conducted honestly. This means being truthful about how you conducted your research and what you found. Practices such as inventing data, deliberately reporting data in a way that is knowingly misleading or lying about what you found are clearly unethical and are also breaches of student discipline.

Research also needs to be conducted competently. Without the necessary skills to do research properly, researchers may make crucial mistakes that lead to untrustworthy findings, waste the time of their participants or even cause them harm. When judgements are made about this, the level of training a researcher has had is considered. This is one reason why you have a supervisor and why, in many cases, you will be steered towards methods that are appropriate for somebody with your degree of training. But don't worry if things don't go quite according to plan all the time. For example, all qualitative researchers will have experienced interviews that didn't go as well as they hoped (see Roulston, 2014). Reflecting on such experiences, in discussions with your supervisor and in your project write-up, will help you to develop your skills and do a good project.

Valid consent

Consent in research is valid when participants make a free choice to participate before the research starts. This choice must be based on full information about what participation will involve and the opportunity to reflect on what the implications would be for them.

This is complex because not all projects require consent (e.g. media analysis of news articles). In most studies consent is needed, and it's usually given by the participant themselves. But sometimes (e.g. research with children) you must get consent from the participant themselves and somebody else (e.g. parents or guardians). You should discuss the type of consent needed with your supervisor, and it will also be a major part of the ethical approval process. Ethics policies and guidelines (e.g. those of your institution or the relevant professional body) will help you too. Figure 4.1 illustrates the kinds of consent that may be needed for different types of qualitative projects.

Psychologists have a long and controversial history of conducting studies where observations are made without consent (covert observation). For example, Festinger and colleagues' work on cognitive dissonance was influenced by early covert observations (Roulet et al., 2017). Internet research and the increased use of data archiving that is linked to Open Science have recently highlighted the issue of gathering data without obtaining consent. Data from archives can often be re-analysed (see Chapter 3), but it is important to check what the original participants consented to. If doing Internet-based research, you need to be aware of how online environments blur the boundaries between public and private spaces and create opportunities for data collection that may make consent difficult or impossible to obtain.

Projects where consent is needed include:
Studies where you recruit people specifically to take part, such as interviews.

Observational studies of public settings in which people would not normally expect to be observed.

Online environments (e.g. social media, discussion forums) where content is only visible to people who are registered and logged into a site.

When might participants not be able to consent for themselves?
When they are under 16 years of age.

If they have an intellectual impairment that limits their capacity to consent.

Projects where consent may not be needed include:
Observational studies of behaviours in a public place, where being observed is expected.
Analysis of existing data from an archive, providing original consent includes future analysis.
Collection of internet data that is publicly available.
Analysis of publicly available media data (e.g. news articles, TV).
Analysis of freely available documentation (e.g. government policy documents).

Figure 4.1 Consent for different types of qualitative projects

Many researchers draw upon existing guidance about observational research as a guide for Internet research. The latest version of the British Psychological Society's guidelines for ethical research (BPS, 2021a: 23), for example, says that covert observation without consent 'is only acceptable in public situations where those observed would expect to be observed by strangers'. Guidance of this type has been around for a long time but applying it to online environments isn't straightforward because it requires us to consider which online places count as public spaces. Researchers have tended to consider things like whether the online material can be viewed without registering or logging into a site, how likely people are to use what appear to be real names when posting and whether people posting the information are warned that they are posting in public. In recent years, additional guidance has been provided about ethical issues in Internet research (e.g. BPS, 2021b) and you should consult this for more specific advice if needed. Also remember that, even if consent is not required for your data, you will still need ethical approval and to fully consider the ethical issues that arise from your project.

Want to know more about the ethics of online research?

Guidance from the Association of Internet Researchers:

Association of Internet Researchers (2019). Internet Research: Ethical Guidelines 3.0. Available from https://aoir.org/ethics/

(Continued)

The British Psychological Society's Guidelines for Internet-Mediated Research (2021) can be downloaded here: www.bps.org.uk/news-and-policy/ethics-guidelines-internet-mediated-research

Detailed discussion of the ethics of online research can be found here:

Woodfield, K. (Ed.) (2018). *The Ethics of Online Research*. Bingley: Emerald Publishing.

In research where consent is gained, participants must be competent to give their own consent. If your research involves working with anyone who has an intellectual impairment that inhibits their ability to consent, or anyone under the age of 16, you will normally be expected to gain consent from somebody else on their behalf. In the case of children, this means gaining parental consent, or equivalent consent from somebody who is legally responsible for that child in place of their parents (in loco parentis). In the UK, it is not always entirely clear when research is being done with children because although the point at which adulthood is legally reached is 18, there is also legislation that defines those aged 16 and over as having the capacity to consent to things such as medical procedures (BPS, 2021a). Decisions about age and consent therefore need to be considered carefully for each individual project. If you are dealing with populations who are incarcerated, permission may be required for you to approach people to invite them to participate in your study, but they should ordinarily give their own consent. The fact that they are incarcerated does not in itself mean that anybody else can consent on their behalf. It is also important to be sensitive to the potential coercive effects of requests for participation coming through third parties with a high level of power over potential participants (for example, teachers, prison staff, clinicians, doctors).

When consent has been obtained from some other individual, this doesn't mean that the participant is obliged to take part. In the case of children, for example, parental consent does not mean that the child shouldn't also be participating voluntarily. Gaining the permission of a participant who has had somebody else consent for them is known as gaining their 'assent'.

· · · · · · ··**In a nutshell**· · · ·· ·

Participant assent

If doing research with somebody who is unable to consent for themselves:

- You must get consent from somebody who is legally able to consent for your participants.
- The person giving consent must be well placed to consider whether it is in the participant's interests to participate and to consider any risks and benefits for them.

- You must also get permission (assent) from the participant, and this must be monitored on an ongoing basis.
- If your participants are not able to communicate their assent verbally (e.g. infants) you must monitor their behaviour and responses for any sign that they are uncomfortable or unwilling to continue (e.g. looking away).

. . . .

Your participants can only give their informed consent if you have been clear with them about who is doing the research, what participating in it will mean for them and what will be done with the information they give. And this needs to be communicated to them in language that they can understand. At the heart of consent in research is a paradox. We are asking participants to be fully informed about doing something that they haven't done yet. So, participants might change their minds once they start, making consent an ongoing process. Monitor consent by frequently checking that participants are still happy to proceed. You can do this by asking verbally and reading body language. See also information about participants' rights to withdraw from research, discussed below.

---Top tips---

Communicating with potential participants

You can help make sure people fully understand your research by:

- Avoiding unnecessary jargon. Trying to work out when a technical term is unnecessary (and therefore counts as 'jargon') can be hard, because sometimes we need to use the technical terms to ensure accuracy. But we must use everyday language whenever it's possible to do so. For example, instead of saying this study is about 'the role of body art in self-identity', you could say 'this study is about what your body art means to you'.
- Thinking carefully about who your audience will be. What type of people are you writing for and how likely are they to understand the concepts and words you're using to describe the study? Will they have English as a first language? What level of literacy are they likely to have?
- Focus on what is needed to make a choice about consent. In your proposal, you may well have written about what previous studies found in a way that uses technical language (e.g. 'studies have found that professional identity is integral to decision making'). But will this really help somebody who is trying to decide whether to take part? Probably not. A focus on what participation will involve (e.g. 'if you decide to take part, you will be invited to an interview with the student researcher, where you will be asked about ...') is likely to be more effective.

During the informed consent process, you are likely to communicate in various ways with your participants. This might be through email, phone or talking face-to-face, and also through formal documents such as participant information sheets and consent forms. You need to tailor this communication so that it is clear and understandable for your participants. Copies of forms, and templates for things like emails, will usually need to be included in your ethics application, so all communication must be planned in advance. To do this, write templates of the emails you will send to participants or gatekeepers as well as notes about what you plan to say when you speak to them. It's common to write a participant information sheet that can be given to potential participants so that they can read about the study and make an informed decision. Exactly how this is worded will depend upon your study but below is an example from a study on mindfulness that shows the kinds of things that are often included.

Once a participant has informally agreed to participate, the next step is usually to gain a written record of consent. Typically, this is recorded on a consent form, which each participant signs to indicate their agreement and confirm that they've been fully informed about the study. Many research methods books, including Robson and McCartan (2015), offer templates to develop materials such as consent forms. Below, we offer you one example from the study of mindfulness mentioned above.

One way of increasing the chances of gaining consent from potential participants is to use rewards or incentives. This has ethical dimensions that must be considered carefully in the context of the specific project in which their use is planned. We must balance the size of any incentive against any potential risks involved in participating. Obviously, it is vital to prevent harm wherever possible and minimise risk (this is discussed in more detail below) but there may be occasions where participation in research involves a small risk for participants (risk of becoming distressed if discussing sensitive topics, for example). In these situations, any incentives to participate must not be so great that people might give consent even when they have decided that doing so might be distressing, harmful or unpleasant for them. In essence, it's appropriate to give a small incentive but we must be careful that this is not so great that it overrides a participant's urge to say no for some non-trivial reason.

········· **In a nutshell** ···

Rewards and incentives for participants

Examples of rewards that are sometimes given in return for participation in research include:

- paying participants for their time;
- reimbursing travel expenses;
- providing gifts or vouchers;
- entering participants into a prize draw;
- offering students course credit or similar rewards.

···

Experiences of a Brief Mindfulness Intervention:
Invitation to Participate in Research

My name is Phil Jones and I am studying for a degree in psychology at Central University. As part of my course I am doing a research project under the supervision of Dr Chris Neville that explores experiences of mindfulness. As you have recently done a mindfulness course, I would like to invite you to also take part in my research project. This sheet gives details of what participating in my research would involve, to help you decide whether you would like to volunteer.

What would participating involve?

If you volunteer to take part you would be invited to join me for an online interview in an MS Teams meeting lasting approximately an hour. This would cover topics such as your reasons for being interested in mindfulness, your experiences of practicing mindfulness & any impact of mindfulness on your thoughts, feelings or other aspects of your life. You would be free to tell me what you want about your experiences & avoid any topics that you prefer not to discuss.

What happens to the information provided?

The interview will be audio recorded. You can choose whether to also allow a video recording to be made by opting to switch your camera on or off. The recordings will only be viewed by me and by staff at Central University who have a legitimate need to see them (e.g., staff supervising or marking my work). The recordings will be used to create a written version of the interview (a transcript). When I create these I will not use your real name and will also remove any information that could potentially reveal your identity (such as names, places, job titles). I will use a system of numerical codes to keep track of which anonymised transcript belongs to which participant, but anything with your name on will be kept separately from this list of codes and from the interview transcripts and recordings. I will use these transcripts to write a report that will be in the public domain and will contain direct quotations from the interviews. However, I will make every effort to ensure that you are not identifiable from the quotations used.

What if !volunteer &then change my mind?

Also, if you agree to take part in an interview, the interview can be stopped immediately at any time. If you want to withdraw from the study after attending an interview, you will be able to do so up until two weeks after your data has been collected (so two weeks after your interview) & you will not need to give any reason for doing this. Once I have had your data for two weeks, it will no longer be possible for you to withdraw. If you want to withdraw, please email me using the address below.

Want to know more?

If you would like to ask further questions about this study, or would like to volunteer to take part, please contact me using the contact details below. You can also contact my supervisor if you wish.

Phil Jones, psychology student, Central University pi1123@central.ac.uk

Dr Chris Neville, Lecturer, School of Psychology, Central University CN1187@central.ac.uk

If you experience any distress in connection with the issues raised in this study, support can be obtained from Mind (www.mind.org.uk,), a national charity providing information & support for psychological well-being.

Figure 4.2   Sample information sheet

Experiences of a Brief Mindfulness Intervention:
Interview Consent Form

I wish to volunteer to participate in a semi-structured interview as part of the above-named research project. I agree to the following (please initial):

I have read a participant information sheet that explains what the interview involves and how my data will be stored and used.

I am aware that the interview will be audio recorded.

I consent to anonymised quotes being used from my interview transcript in the public domain (for example in reports or presentations that describe the research and its findings).

I am aware that I can leave the interview at any time I wish but that once the interview is finished I have got 2 weeks in which to withdraw any information I have given from the study.

I am aware that confidentiality will only be breached if I reveal information that suggests that myself or somebody else is in danger of being harmed.

I have had the opportunity to ask questions about the interview.

Any questions that I have asked about the interview have been answered satisfactorily.

Student researcher name: ----------------- Signature: ----------------   Date: -----------------

Participant name: ----------------- Signature: ----------------   Date: -----------------

Want to know more?

If you would like to ask further questions about this study, or would like to volunteer to take part, please contact one of the research team using the contact details below:

Student Researcher, Phil Jones, School of Psychology, Central University, PJ1123@central.ac.uk
Supervisor, Dr Chris Neville, School of Psychology, Central University, CN4578@eecentral.ac.uk

To raise concerns about this research with somebody independent of the research team, please contact the University Ethics Officer for Ethics (EthicsOtfice@centralac.uk).

Figure 4.3 Sample consent form

If you are considering using any kind of incentive, talk this over with your supervisor, provide details of it in your ethics submission and show that you have considered any ethical ramifications. You should also bear in mind that some universities may have specific rules that ban or limit the use of incentives and rewards in student research projects (in order to prevent wealthy students from gaining unfair advantage, for example).

Another thing that might help increase your chances of getting participants is to recruit people that you already know. In Chapter 3 we noted several things you should consider if planning to do this. One of the most important considerations is the possible impact of recruiting people we know on the consent process. It's likely that the people with whom you already have a connection, especially a close one, will be motivated to help you complete your project. They will know how important it is to you. This could inadvertently put pressure on them to agree to, or continue with, something that they might otherwise prefer not to do. In that sense, it can act in a similar way to providing incentives, as discussed above. You should discuss with your supervisor what strategies you can take here – for example, taking extra steps to emphasise voluntariness and being particularly vigilant for any signs that consent might be being given reluctantly or might be wavering part way through. You could also discuss this explicitly with potential participants that you already know, so that they are prompted to reflect on it. Tell them clearly that you don't want them to do something they are unsure of simply as a favour to you – and make it convincing! You should also be clear in your ethics application what issues arise here and what steps you plan to take.

Confidentiality

The issue of confidentiality in research is not as straightforward as it may at first seem. In everyday talk 'confidential' is often understood as meaning 'I tell you and you tell nobody else'. Since our aim as researchers is to communicate our findings, we will usually want to tell others about what our participants have told us. This means that if we just say to our participants 'this is all confidential' they could misunderstand this and think that we will not pass on any of their information. To avoid this, we need tell potential participants what we mean by 'confidentiality' and explain clearly what will be done with the information we plan to collect, who it might be shared with (and who it won't, in some cases) and in what format it might be shared or presented. Often what we plan to do is to share the things our participants have told us, but in a form that makes it impossible for people to work out who they are (we discuss this 'anonymity' more later). Confidentiality also links to data storage, because the information on participants that we collect must be stored securely in order to protect confidentiality. More of that later when we talk about data protection.

There are also limits to confidentiality. In some exceptional circumstances researchers will pass on information from a research participant to a third party, such as when there is a significant likelihood of serious harm to an identifiable individual, whether that is the participant themselves or somebody else. For example, when Lucy did body image research in a school, she had to be clear with her school-aged participants, before they consented, that if they disclosed information that suggested that they were at risk of harm (from themselves or someone else) she would need to share this information with their school.

This allowed Lucy to manage her responsibilities to treat the participant's account as confidential and her wider responsibility to protect people from serious harm. This practice is often standard for research in schools. It's not always possible to identify all limits to confidentiality before the research commences, although clearly all reasonable attempts should be made to do this. If a situation like this arose that was unanticipated, it would be important to talk the dilemma over with your supervisor, possibly in conjunction with your department or university's ethics committee, to identify the best course of action. This issue is also interesting because it highlights that ethics is not just a static thing that is established before your research begins but is a dynamic process that is ongoing throughout the project.

Top tips

Confidentiality

Data where confidentiality issues are particularly important includes:

- Contact details and any communication with participants that could identify them, e.g. emails, consent forms.
- Data files that contain the real names of participants and their pseudonyms or transcript numbers.
- Raw data including audio files of participants talk, or other data that could identify them, e.g. Facebook posts, transcripts if you have not anonymised them.

When considering issues of confidentiality, make sure you can answer the following questions about your study:

- How will I store the data so that confidentiality is protected?
- How will I use the data, to whom will I reveal it and in what format?
- How do I make it clear to my participants how I will store their data and what I will do with it?

Confusion sometimes arises about the distinction between confidentiality (which is about what we will do with information we collect) and anonymity (which is about whether that information reveals a participant's identity). Next, we consider anonymity in detail, and we suggest that you pay careful attention to the distinction between this and confidentiality.

Anonymity

Participants' anonymity must be protected so that they can't be identified from any data or documents associated with the project that enter the public domain. It's good practice to plan for how you will anonymise your data before you start your project.

Occasionally we may ask participants to consent to research where they will not be anonymous, but this is not common. To do this, you must have a compelling reason and be sure your participants fully understand the implications. For example, in a study on identity and social networking, participants might be currently happy to have screenshots of their Facebook page, complete with photos of drunken nights out, included in your project write-up. But they may be less keen in years to come when they discover that your write-up is available online and prospective employers might see it.

Qualitative raw data (e.g. audio files, downloaded forum posts) are often not anonymous and so it is important that this is stored securely and not shared beyond those you have told participants could see it, for example you and your supervisors or staff who will be marking your work.

········ **·In a nutshell·** ·· ···

Protecting anonymity

Qualitative researchers protect anonymity by:

- giving participants pseudonyms (false names), and we prefer these to participant numbers to avoid dehumanising participants and improve readability of your work;
- changing or removing identifying information (for example, place names, job titles);
- checking that all these procedures have been carefully done for all data that might be shared, published or otherwise introduced into the public domain (for example, interview transcripts included as appendices in a report);
- anonymising transcripts of audio recordings as the transcription is done, which removes the chance that transcripts with identifying information in them might be accidentally shared.

In interview studies, it is usual to protect anonymity by altering details when interviews are transcribed (that is, when a written version of the recorded interview is created). To illustrate, in an interview a participant might describe themselves in a way that could enable someone else to identify them, for example, by saying: 'Well … it all started when I was headteacher of Middlewood Primary School in Birmingham …'

If you transcribed this talk and included it in your write-up, you would need to change the identifying markers, which in this case is the name of the school and the city. You could do this by using pseudonyms or cutting out this information: 'Well, it all started when I was headteacher of [name of primary school] in [name of City] …'

Sometimes even this might provide enough information for people to guess who your participants are; for example, if you recruited in an area where there were few primary schools. In such cases you would reduce the information further, for example changing 'headteacher' to 'senior teacher'.

Data from which people can be identified (e.g. where you saved their names, email or phone numbers to organise meeting with them, audio files of interviews, un-anonymised transcripts) are considered 'personal data', which means that relevant data protection legislation will apply. Data protection legislation, often based upon the EU General Data Protection Regulation (GDPR), exists in most countries (Information Commissioner's Office, no date). In the UK, the relevant national legislation is the Data Protection Act (2018). This legislation sets out rights and responsibilities for how personal data should be collected, stored and used. Your institution will have policies and procedures for dealing with personal data under GDPR, which will help you plan a study that's compliant with the legislation. Because data needs to be stored within the legal jurisdiction where you carried out your study, saving it in a cloud service whose servers are in another country might mean that you are breaking data protection laws. So, save your data in password-protected online storage that is recommended by your university.

Top tips

Data protection

Speak to your supervisor about whether GDPR applies to your project and, if necessary, how you should deal with this. It is likely that GDPR will apply if your project involves the following:

- You are collecting data relating to a specific individual.
- That individual can be identified from the data you are collecting, either:

  o   directly, for example, through their name being included, or
  o   indirectly, through something like an Internet IP address.

Remember that this is not just about your research data but about any information that is being collected. You must also consider things like names and email addresses that are collected as part of the research process. If you are using online methods for data collection, you must think about where the recordings will be saved and whether this is GDPR compliant. Some basic things you can do:

- Identify two password-protected, safe storage places for your transcribed data, e.g. a university server and a password-protected external hard drive. This means you have a back-up of your data. Make sure that your university's rules allow the use of these storage places.
- Identify 'personal data', where GDPR applies (e.g. participant contact details, names, lists that link real names to pseudonyms, audio files). Store and use this in a GDPR-compliant way. Also, identify data that are not 'personal data' (e.g. anonymised transcriptions of participants' talk) and where GDPR doesn't apply. Make sure that

these two kinds of data are stored separately and that access to one type doesn't inadvertently give access to the other. For example, make sure that if you have a list of participants' real names and contact details that also includes their pseudonym, you store this securely away from the anonymised transcripts with pseudonyms.
• Know your university regulations for when and how different types of data need to be destroyed.

If you are using images, note that there are various debates about how to manage anonymity with visual data – for example, using photographs that do not include people's faces or using software (for example, Photoshop) to blur faces. If this is relevant to you, read visual research methods texts for ideas and discuss your options with your supervisor.

Want to know more about the ethics of visual research?

The ESRC (Economic and Social Research Council) is the biggest funder of social science research in the UK. It offers various documents about research methods produced by its National Centre for Research Methods. A useful document, entitled 'Visual Ethics: Ethical Issues in Visual Research', can be found at: http://eprints.ncrm.ac.uk/421/

Harm and distress

Potential for harm must be considered and areas where harm could occur must be identified. You should also talk this through with your supervisor and any other people who might help you to identify sources of harm (sometimes non-psychologists can give us a better idea of how participants might respond to certain materials or issues). You also need to consider whether your participants are particularly vulnerable, for example if you are working with people who have experienced some kind of trauma that relates to the research question.

Activity 4.1

Where's the harm?

Below are two examples of research proposals that were submitted for approval. Measures were put in place to deal with the potential sources of harm before approval was granted and these studies were conducted. For each example, see how many potential sources of harm to

(Continued)

the participants you can list, and ways to deal with these issues so that participants either do not experience harm or have the harm minimised and are able to give fully informed consent.

> Example 1: A student wanted to find out about people's attitudes towards illegal downloading of music and piracy. He planned to run focus groups asking people about their experiences and attitudes.
>
> Example 2: A student on a Psychology and Counselling course wants to explore how counsellors deal with clients who come to them with specific issues relating to their experience of rape and sexual assault. She plans to advertise on a forum used by counsellors to recruit people for individual interviews.

See the end of this chapter for our thoughts on this.

As these examples illustrate, 'harm' is conceptualised quite broadly, and you need to think hard about any possible sources of harm while you design your research. It can help to imagine doing the project as a participant, what would you think and feel during each step of the process?

· · · · · ·**·In a nutshell**· ·

Potential sources of harm

Harm can include many things such as:

- physical harm;
- embarrassment or personal offence;
- trauma;
- the reduction or erosion of one's rights;
- loss of property or reputation;
- psychological distress;
- feeling unsafe.

· ·

Once potential sources of harm have been identified, steps must be taken to prevent them from causing harm. Sometimes people want to talk about difficult topics, and they might get upset doing it. This doesn't necessarily mean they shouldn't take part, but we must exercise great care and be confident in such situations that they have genuinely chosen to do something they find slightly upsetting. Researchers must finely balance avoiding harm and not being afraid of people's emotions. We also don't wish to communicate to people that their emotions are inappropriate or should be hidden. However, as trainee researchers, you should err on the side of caution in terms of harm until you have more experience of doing sensitive research.

Your focus should be on the prevention of harm. But it might also be appropriate to have some measures in place in case the prevention doesn't work. It is appropriate for participants to direct questions about the research itself to the student researcher and their supervisor. And many universities also ask that people affected by research are given details of somebody independent of the research project to whom they can address queries or concerns. But participants may also need extra information or support because participation has created some difficulty for them or raised issues (e.g. discussing their experiences might have created unanticipated distress, or they might be worried about their physical health after discussing this in an interview). Any additional information or support should be provided by somebody who is not involved in the research and has appropriate skills, qualifications or knowledge. Participants might be guided towards their doctor, a professional counselling service, or organisations such as Childline or Victim Support (in the UK). In psychological research, participants may be especially likely to mistakenly assume that the researcher can also take on a therapeutic role. Even in cases where research is being carried out, or supervised by, somebody who is qualified to provide relevant information, support or therapy we must direct participants elsewhere for support. This ensures that the support comes from people who are appropriately qualified, and that a clear distinction is kept between the researchers and anybody providing support. For further discussion on managing the relationship with your participants, see Chapter 5. While it is important to identify external sources of support for your participants, this should never be a substitute for making all reasonable attempts to prevent harm from occurring.

Want to know more about harm to participants?

For an example of a reflection on the potential harm to participants of a study on illegal drug use see:

Measham, F., Aldridge, J. and Parker, H. (2001). *Dancing on Drugs: Risk, Health and Hedonism in the British Club Scene*. London: Free Association Books.

Deception and debriefing

Deception (either by deliberately misleading or by omission of important information) has often taken place in psychological research. We can probably all describe Milgram's (1974) famous obedience experiments where he convinced participants that they were giving real electric shocks to other participants. Deception conflicts with the principle of obtaining informed consent and studies employing significant deception are unlikely to gain ethical approval. There are no set rules about when deception is allowed, but if you answer 'yes' to the following questions then your research is likely to involve unacceptable levels of deception:

- Does the deception hide something about the procedure that is particularly likely to be crucial for consent (for example, does the researcher plan not to tell people that the interview is likely to take four hours? Or does the researcher plan to interact with people online without saying they're going to use these interactions as data for a research project)?
- Is the thing that is not revealed to them particularly likely to lead to harm or distress (for example, are they not told that they are going to be asked about their experiences of exam stress and how they cope)?

At the end of the data collection, researchers often 'debrief' participants about the study. It is common in experimental studies for participants to not be told the key aim of the study, and so this often needs explaining to them at the end, and often such studies have a written debrief. In qualitative studies, we usually provide all the information that is needed at the start of the study and so a debrief may be verbal rather than written. You also want to be mindful about not overloading participants with lots of official-looking paperwork, as that can be stressful. Unless you are keeping an element of your project hidden from your participants until you have completed the data collection, try to put all the information they need to understand the study on the participant information sheet, including where they might go for further support. And when you finish data collection with them, give a verbal debrief, for example reminding them what the study was about and asking them if they have any questions or comments. At that stage, you can also check that they still have access to the full information you gave them earlier and, if needed, give this again. If, however, you have hidden some aspect of your research from them earlier, in a way that is still considered ethical, give them a verbal and written debrief with information.

Whatever your project involves, take steps to help your participants leave you in a good psychological state. If, for example, they have talked about a difficult issue make sure you've chatted in a relaxed way at the end to lighten the mood, so that they can leave you feeling secure and not emotional. In interviews, for example, we often finish with an upbeat question (e.g. what's the best aspect of being a parent?); these questions help set a positive frame before participants leave us.

Top tips

Debriefing

Debrief sessions should involve:

- explaining the study in more detail, if needed, and answering questions;
- fully explaining any deception if it has been used;

- thanking the participant for their time;
- reiteration of contact details for researchers if they have questions afterwards;
- providing sources of help and support in case the measures taken to prevent distress don't work;
- checking that participants still have access to the full information they were given earlier.

In addition, your debrief session might involve:

- providing a written debrief for participants to take away;
- offers to send their transcript, a summary of findings or the report (although your final project report that you hand into your institution is not always the best thing to send to participants as it is written for an academic audience);
- an opportunity for participants to talk without being recorded about the topic or their experience of participating in the research (although do not use this as data without their permission).

Right to withdraw

Participants should always have the right to withdraw from any data collection sessions or research procedures (such as an interview). This right should be communicated to them before they give their consent. You also need to consider the issue of withdrawal after data collection. Usually, there will logically be a point when participants can no longer withdraw. For example, a participant can no longer withdraw their data if you have quoted them in a write-up that has been submitted and may be in the public domain. At the consent stage, therefore, explain to your participants their right to withdraw, what this means and the limits to this withdrawal. For example, you should tell participants in an interview study that they can stop at any time during the interview. You might also tell them that they can withdraw their data immediately at the point the interview ends. People who complete the interview might be told that if they decide afterwards to withdraw their data, they can do so but only up until a certain date (such as two weeks after the interview) after which their data may have already been included in the analysis.

If you are collecting data that are anonymous at the point of collection, which is rare in qualitative research, you should be careful to tell your participants that this will mean that they can't withdraw their data once you've collected it. More often in qualitative research, data starts out in a form that is not anonymous (e.g., an audio file created by recording an interview) from which an anonymised version is created (e.g., a transcript with identifying information removed, as discussed above). We suggest that you only anonymise data after any deadlines for withdrawal have passed, as you don't want to spend time transcribing and anonymising data only to find that the participant wants to withdraw. Even after deadlines, it is a common strategy to keep some kind of key that links anonymised data (e.g. an interview transcript) with the other pieces of information you are holding in relation to that individual (e.g. their signed consent form, name, email address). This can be done by keeping a list of pseudonyms or codes that identifies each participant. You can then use this pseudonym or code on other pieces of information so that you can link them. Strategies like this can be used to make sure that, if somebody wants to withdraw, you can be confident that you can find and delete all of the necessary information. Obviously, it is vital that this list is kept securely and that it is not stored with the data.

Effects beyond the participants

Ethics is not just about the effect on the participants, but the potential impact the study has on other people. For example, research materials that might inadvertently reinforce racist stereotypes will be problematic not just because they might cause offence to individuals who read them, but because they reinforce harmful stereotypes in society more widely. Thinking through these broader consequences often involves considering what the media, policymakers or political groups – including those you agree with and those with whom you might disagree – might do with your research findings.

Considering any possible impact of what you write is especially important if you are writing about topics that have potential significance for people or groups who may already be at risk, marginalised or disadvantaged in some way. This is true for projects where you collect your own data and for those where you use existing data sources. For example, John carried out a project on how personality disorders are described in news reports of crime. Although John didn't recruit any participants, he needed to be careful about how he carried out and presented his analysis on this sensitive subject. John's interest in the area was partly coming from a desire to do work that would challenge harmful stereotypes about criminality and mental health and so it was important for him to keep reflecting upon this and write authentically but sensitively on the topic. It was also something that he wrote about in the reflexive account (see Chapter 9) in his project, which showed the markers how he had considered ethics carefully.

Want to know more about the wider impact of research?

For discussion of the wider ethical implications of research that goes beyond the participants:

Summers, K. (2020). For the greater good? Ethical reflections on interviewing the 'rich' and 'poor' in qualitative research. *International Journal of Social Research Methodology*, 23(5), 593-602.

When planning studies, we should also consider any possible risks to researchers. Students are often attracted to doing projects in areas that have personal relevance for them, but this can also raise issues about possible harm. If you are considering doing your project on a topic that is sensitive, difficult or has personal relevance you should discuss this with your supervisor and other people who can support you. Try to consider safeguarding yourself in the same ways you would potential participants. Think through what the effect would be on you of spending a significant time reading about an issue that you might find distressing. For example, if you have a history of distress related to eating, how would you feel when immersing yourself over a long period of time in other people's stories about their struggles with food? If there's any part of you that thinks this might be triggering, find another topic you can do safely. And in terms of planning, if you go ahead, make sure that you have planned for how you can get the support you may need for yourself and how you would check in with yourself to review this process.

Another way in which carrying out research can affect you is that participants might say or do things that you find offensive. In some projects, it will be possible to antici-pate this and try to plan for it as described above. For example, if you have decided to interview people about why they belong to an organisation, this is likely to be an issue. When collecting data about people's perspectives and experiences, we would usually adopt a non-judgemental perspective and try to make participants feel safe to express themselves. But this will also need to be balanced against judgements about what is acceptable to you personally or in a wider sense. In situations like this you might tact-fully challenge or counter things your participants say, or at least signal that you don't share their view. Managing things like this is difficult even for researchers who have much training and experience. This is partly why your supervisor is likely to guide you towards situations where this is less likely to happen. You will also find suggestions for managing your relationship with your participants in Chapter 5.

However, as we noted earlier in this chapter, sometimes things can happen during data collection that are not anticipated. As we suggested above, get your supervisor to help you develop general strategies for what you will do if something unexpected hap-pens. This could include participants unexpectedly saying things that are offensive or research affecting you emotionally when you didn't anticipate it. It is not uncommon for researchers to feel distressed after a participant shares a story of a traumatic experi-ence. One thing that you should never be expected to tolerate is any kind of threat to your safety, including the possibility that a participant might behave in a way that is threatening or aggressive towards you. Your supervisor must help you to identify any implications for your safety as you plan your research, and a risk assessment might need to be completed. Talk to your supervisor about any potential safety issues (for example, collecting data in potentially risky situations, contact with strangers or certain kinds of equipment or substances, conducting research in a private home) and remember that your project should not put you in harm's way without protection. You should always retain the right to stop and withdraw from any situation that you feel is unsafe.

Want to know more about ethics?

For general coverage of ethical issues in qualitative research:

King, N. (2019) Research ethics in qualitative research. In C. Sullivan & M. Forrester (eds),
    Doing Qualitative Research in Psychology: A Practical Guide. London: Sage. pp. 35–59.
The British Psychological Society's Code of Human Research Ethics and the Ethics Guidelines
    for Internet-Mediated Research can be downloaded from their website (www.bps.org.uk/).
For the guidance provided by the Australian Psychological Society, see this website: www.
    psychology.org.au/About-Us/What-we-do/ethics-and-practice-standards
And, for New Zealand, guidance can be found here: www.psychology.org.nz/members/
    professional-resources/code-ethics
Guidance for the US (www.apa.org/ethics/code) and Canada (https://cpa.ca/aboutcpa/
    committees/ethics/codeofethics/) are also available online.

Conclusion

You should now be in a position to apply for ethical approval for your project. As you have thought through the ethics and prepared your documentation, you may have amended your original plan. In the next chapter, we move on to consider how you can manage your project once ethical approval has been granted and your study is under way.

Answers to Activity 4.1

Below are the two example research proposals that we met earlier. Here are our thoughts about some of the potential sources of harm that these might involve. These are not the 'correct' answers, and are not necessarily exhaustive, but will help you think the issues through some more. Compare these notes with your own and discuss with your supervisor if you wish.

Example 1: A student wanted to find out about people's attitudes towards illegal downloading of music and piracy. He planned to run focus groups asking people about their perspectives and attitudes:

- The student researcher can give assurances about how they will handle anonymity and confidentiality in relation to what is said in the focus groups, but what if a participant fails to treat what other participants say as confidential? It would be useful to warn participants explicitly about this before consent. Also, the focus group could start by making an agreement between those present about sharing things outside of that discussion.

- Participants might put themselves in harm's way by revealing information about their involvement in criminal activities. At recruitment, we must stress that the focus is on people's views and perspectives, rather than details of their activities. And we can warn them against revealing anything incriminating. Researchers do, of course, carry out studies where details of crimes are revealed, but this complex ethical and legal area is not something to be tackled in a student project.

Example 2: A student on a Psychology and Counselling course wants to explore how counsellors deal with clients who come to them with specific issues relating to their experience of rape and sexual assault. She plans to advertise on a forum used by counsellors to recruit people for individual interviews:

- Simply advertising a study on this topic could cause distress to people who have been affected by rape or sexual assault. Although focusing on professional experiences, we can't assume that counsellors have not been negatively affected by sexual assault. This topic demands careful thought about recruiting and approaching people. Counsellors are trained in dealing with difficult psychological experiences and belong to networks that can provide support with their own psychological well-being. So, that is helpful here. The student could recruit through word of mouth, in conjunction with a counselling psychologist that she knows, who could help identify people who it is safe to approach. A practitioner could also suggest sites for counsellors that might be appropriate for advertising the study, or those best avoided. This would help the student take steps to make sure adverts are only seen by counsellors who are currently well enough to practise. Signposting to support services could go on the adverts and information sheets so that anyone who is distressed but doesn't decide to take part can still access support. Potential participants must be encouraged to consider how participating might affect them and they will need to time to reflect on this.
- Participants might experience distress and difficulty during an interview on this topic. Planning for this should include steps that can be taken during the interview if a participant becomes emotional or distressed. This is very delicate, as we must avoid giving people the impression that their distress should be hidden or is shameful or inappropriate (which can happen inadvertently if an emotional participant is hastily bundled out of an interview). We must plan ways to support people, acknowledge their emotions and empower them to make decisions about participation that are in their interests.
- Participants might experience difficulty after taking part. It's essential to ensure that signposting takes place for people so that they can access support. Remind them in a verbal debrief at the end of the interview that sometimes talking about sensitive issues can have a delayed impact, and make sure they still have the information sheet.
- Remember that you can answer questions about the study and signpost participants to support services but you as the student researcher cannot offer psychological support.

References

Association of Internet Researchers (2019) *Internet Research: Ethical Guidelines 3.0.* [downloaded from https://aoir.org/ethics/]

British Psychological Society (2021a) BPS Code of Human Research Ethics. [downloaded from www.bps.org.uk/guideline/bps-code-human-research-ethics]

British Psychological Society (2021b) Ethics Guidelines for Internet Mediated Research. [downloaded from www.bps.org.uk/guideline/ethics-guidelines-internet-mediated-research]

Chamberlain, K. (2004) Qualitative research, reflexivity and context. In M. Murray (ed.), *Critical Health Psychology*. Basingstoke: Palgrave Macmillan. pp. 121–36.

Data Protection Act (2018) Available at: https://www.legislation.gov.uk/ukpga/2018/12/contents/enacted (Accessed 14 February 2022).

Information Commissioner's Office (no date) Guide to the UK General Data Protection Regulation (UK GDPR). [Downloaded from https://ico.org.uk/for-organisations/guide-to-data-protection/guide-to-the-general-data-protection-regulation-gdpr/ on 25.5.21].

King, N. (2019) 'Research ethics in qualitative research', in C. Sullivan and M. Forrester (eds), *Doing Qualitative Research in Psychology: A Practical Guide*. London: Sage. pp. 35–59.

Measham, F., Aldridge, J. and Parker, H. (2001) *Dancing on Drugs: Risk, Health and Hedonism in the British Club Scene*. London: Free Association Books.

Milgram, S. (1974) *Obedience to Authority: An Experimental View*. New York: Harper & Row.

Robson, C. and McCartan, K. (2015) *Real World Research* (4th edn). Chichester: Wiley.

Roulet, T.J., Gill, M.J., Stenger, S. and Gill, D.J. (2017) Reconsidering the value of covert research: The role of ambiguous consent in participant observation. *Organizational Research Methods*, 20(3), 487–517.

Roulston, K. (2014) Interactional problems in research interviews. *Qualitative Research*, 14(3), 277–93.

Summers, K. (2020) For the greater good? Ethical reflections on interviewing the 'rich' and 'poor' in qualitative research. *International Journal of Social Research Methodology*, 23(5), 593–602.

Willig, C. (2012) *Qualitative Interpretation and Analysis in Psychology*. Maidenhead: Open University Press.

Woodfield, K. (ed.) (2018) *The Ethics of Online Research*. Bingley: Emerald Publishing.

5
MANAGING THE PROJECT

Sarah Riley and Nigel King

Having developed a clear plan for your research and got it ethically approved, you're ready to start doing your research. This can be an exciting time – you can feel like you're finally doing research and being a 'proper' psychologist. But, it can also be a very stressful period.

Stress can occur when you're not clear on what you're doing, when you're doing it or why you're doing it. Another source of stress can be your supervisor – if they seem unavailable for example, or conversely, that feeling of impending doom when they want to see you and you haven't done any work. And because qualitative projects often involve in-depth interactions with other people, a third potential stressor is the emotional work that comes with such interactions.

A little bit of stress might be good for focusing your mind on your project, but too much stress is never helpful. So in this chapter we outline some of the ways that you can manage your qualitative research project to maximise pleasure and minimise pain. Since the aim of this book is to help you identify key stages of doing a successful project, we start at the point where you've got ethical approval (see Chapter 4) and we leave you at the point of being ready to do a focused literature review (see Chapter 6). In this chapter, we help you with time management; the student–supervisor relationship; and the dynamics between you and your research participants.

· · · · · · In a nutshell ·

Managing the project

Managing your project involves the following key issues:

1   **Time management:**
    creating a feasible project;
    using sub-goals;
    planning for the cyclical nature of qualitative analysis.

(Continued)

2   **The student-supervisor relationship:**
    a unique relationship that develops over time;
    the need to harmonise your working styles;
    how to be proactive.

3   **The impact of the researcher on the research:**
    considering the power dynamics between you and your participants;
    how class, gender, ethnicity, and embodiment may impact on your research.

4   **The impact of the research on the researcher:**
    learning to negotiate the emotional aspects of research, including upset and frustration;
    how research can change our perspectives and relationships.

. . . .

In order to illustrate some of the key issues in this chapter, we will use an example of Suzy's final-year project, described in the box below. As in all successful projects, Suzy faced some challenges along the way. It's how she dealt with these – in discussion with her supervisor – that ultimately make her project a success.

—Success story—

Strangers in a strange land?

Suzy Lee came to Britain from Singapore to study psychology at Goldborough University. Having been attracted to qualitative methods in her second year, she chose to carry out a qualitative project, examining overseas students' experiences of coming to study in the UK. She wanted to use a phenomenological approach to explore this topic, because her interest was in what 'being an overseas student' is like for her participants, and she planned to use semi-structured interviews to collect her data. She completed an ethics application, which was passed following some minor amendments.

Following her first meeting with her supervisor, Dr Hilton, Suzy agreed to carry out and transcribe one preliminary interview, so she and her supervisor could look at it together. She interviewed a close friend and was quite pleased with the data she obtained, though she felt she rushed through some topics and didn't probe enough beyond a fairly superficial level. Discussing her concerns with her supervisor, they looked at the transcript together and concluded that perhaps part of the problem was that the topic was too broad. Suzy therefore changed her aims to narrow the focus down from the experience of being an overseas student as a whole to that of the initial arrival, course induction and the first few weeks of study. They also thought this focus might help participants talk about concrete experiences rather than general ideas about overseas student experience, which would help generate data that would fit better with a phenomenological study.

Suzy then recruited three more participants, through snowball sampling (see Chapter 3); she was happy with the depth and focus of the ensuing interviews, as was Dr Hilton. She carried out some preliminary analysis on all four interviews to present to her supervisor. Through doing this, she noted that the final participant described some very different experiences from the first three. Reflecting on this with her supervisor, she suspected that the national/cultural background of the students was important to these differences: the last participant came from Ghana, while the three previous ones all came from South East Asia (Singapore, Hong Kong and Indonesia). She therefore recruited two more participants from different parts of the world – one from Libya and one from Greece. In between carrying out interviews, Suzy also started on drafts of her literature review and methodology sections.

After transcribing all the interviews, Suzy started analysing the data. Worried that she was several weeks behind her original timetable, she reviewed her plans with Dr Hilton and decided to exclude the first interview from the full analysis; the fact that it was wider in scope than the following ones reassured her that she can present this as a methodologically based decision. She then completed the analysis, and was happy to be able to highlight interesting details in the lived experience of her participants. Having already made a good start on the first sections of her project, and with ongoing advice from her supervisor, Suzy was able to submit the finished work two days before the deadline.

Time Management and Planning

Part of Suzy's story involves focusing on time management and planning at different stages in her project. In Chapter 3 we discussed planning a timetable at the beginning of your project. It's also good practice to revisit your timetable once your project has been granted ethical approval.

Timetables are useful because they help you identify the stages that you need to go through to do an excellent project. Often we think that we know these stages, but it's only when we write them down that we realise there were gaps in our knowledge or problems with what we planned to do (for example, forgetting to factor in school holidays in a school-based project; or planning to recruit students during exam time). Timetables are also useful in helping you keep track of your project, so you can spot if you are beginning to slip behind your schedule, and can do something about it before it gets worryingly late. Having sub-goals in a timetable also means you get the pleasurable experience of ticking actions off your list, and a motivating sense of achievement and progress that comes with doing that. Finally, a good timetable helps you focus on doing the work in hand, rather than using important brain power just remembering all the things you need to do!

· · · · · · · In a nutshell ·

Writing timetables

To write a timetable that will help you to actually manage your project, rather than sit on a pinboard being studiously ignored or making you feel guilty, we recommend that you do the following:

(Continued)

- Outline the activities you need to do ('sub-goaling'; see Chapter 3 for what these are for a qualitative project). The more specific you make these the better. SMART goals are specific, measurable, attainable, relevant, time bound.
- Consider how these activities will flow from one to the other.
- Consider the resources you need for each of these activities.
- Ask yourself if these activities are feasible, especially in the time you've allocated to them.

Don't just take our word for it – these principles follow from Locke's goal-setting theory (see, for example, Locke and Latham, 2002), which is 'probably the most consistently supported theory in work and organisational psychology' (Arnold et al., 2005: 327):

- Add to the above the recognition that qualitative projects often have cyclical not linear designs; that is, you will go back to different phases of the project (literature, analysis, even research questions, while writing up might also lead to a further cycle).

. . . .

Step 1: Outlining your activities

Think through all the steps you need to go through to complete your project. These steps are likely to include the range of activities we list below, which we will discuss in more detail in the following section:

- Identifying a research question, conducting a literature review and developing a conceptual framework for your study.
- Considering the ethical implications of your study and submitting an ethics application.
- Deciding appropriate participants (numbers, sampling and recruitment strategy).
- Identifying equipment needed and where to source this (such as interview guides/schedules, recording equipment, transcription technology).
- Creating a data storage plan including how you will be compliant with data protection laws.
- Recruiting participants (if relevant).
- Collecting data (for example, interviewing participants).
- Transcribing and anonymising data.
- Cycles of data analysis, which may also involve reviewing your research questions.
- Reviewing the literature (for new work and in the light of your analysis).
- Writing up (which in itself is likely to create another cycle of analysis).

For more details on planning for these activities see Chapter 3.

Step 2: Considering the resources, feasibility and flow of activities

Your activities will either flow from one to another or run in parallel. For example, you could recruit all your participants first, or aim to be recruiting and collecting data simultaneously by interviewing participants as you recruit them. If you need to transcribe your data, plan to do that in parallel with your data collection. Doing this also means that you could do a practice analysis on an early transcript while you are still recruiting and data collecting, so that you already have the skills to do your analysis when you finish your data collection. It is useful to imagine yourself doing each activity and seeing how these activities fit together. Write down these activities and against each activity write down the dates when you plan to do them. Ask yourself if what you plan is feasible. For example, can you recruit five participants in a week? And if so, what exactly do you need to do to achieve that? Remember also to plan your activities around other activities that either you or your participants have to do (for example, when you need to focus on exams or other assignments or when participants will be away on school or university holidays).

Step 3: Outline a cyclical design

Traditional scientific research takes a linear design, in the sense that researchers aim to follow a set of processes in this order: identify a theory → create a hypothesis to test the theory → collect data → analyse data → conclude if hypothesis is supported. This model is called 'linear' because one thing follows another in a set order and these activities do not cross over. It is often considered a hallmark of quality in quantitative research. However, for qualitative researchers, data collection, analysis and theory development can all fold into each other and do not need to be kept separate. This produces a cyclical research design, as can be seen in the example of Suzy's project (Figure 5.1).

It may be that your project is much simpler than that shown in Figure 5.1, but even the most straightforward qualitative projects require you to undertake several cycles of analysis (see Chapter 8 for more on analysing your data). During data analysis qualitative researchers often revise their research questions. For example, in talking about her work with chronically ill people, Kathy Charmaz (1995) explains that a project might start with a broad question, such as: 'How do chronically ill people experience their illness?' However, as the data are analysed, key themes that are identified might suggest a more focused question. For example, a prominent theme in participants' talk might be 'disclosure', where chronically ill people describe having to decide whether to disclose their illness when they meet people. The researcher might then reframe the research question to something that more specifically addresses this theme, such as: 'How do

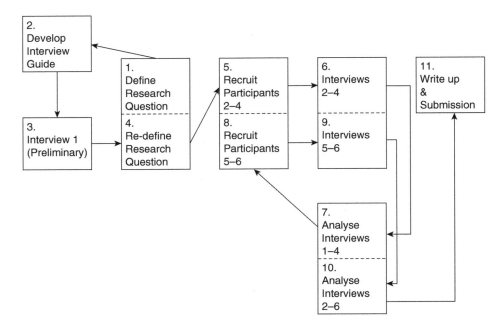

Figure 5.1 Example of a cyclical design, from Suzy's project

chronically ill people manage disclosure?' The researcher would then have to decide if this question can be answered using the current dataset or if the collection of new and more focused data is required. If you feel you need to redefine your research questions in the·light of preliminary data analysis, make sure you discuss this with your supervisor first (see Chapter 2 for more on research questions). All this is perfectly acceptable (indeed, it is positively encouraged) in qualitative research, provided that you ensure the coherence of your project. Remember the methodological kite from Chapter 1: your research question(s), method of data collection, analytic approach and philosophical perspective should all fit together nicely.

Cyclical designs mean that you must leave a significant amount of time to do the analysis – we recommend planning to leave between one-third and one-quarter of your project time for analysis and write-up. Even experienced researchers tend to underestimate how long particular stages of a research project will take, so it is not a bad rule of thumb to work out how long you need for each activity on your timetable – and then double it. The box below shows the timetable produced by Suzy for her project on overseas students' experiences, which was based on the suggestions we outlined in Chapter 3. As we noted in our summary of Suzy's project above, in reality there was some slippage at the data collection and analysis stage, but she was able to retrieve this because she and her supervisor monitored her progress against the timetable regularly. It's also worth noting that your timetable will of course vary depending on the way in which the project is organised at your institution.

Suzy's original project timetable

OCTOBER

Define research question; start literature review/background reading (topic and method); develop interview schedule and other materials; complete ethics application; organise equipment.

NOVEMBER

First wave of participant recruitment; complete equipment booking; carry out and transcribe preliminary interview; revise interview schedule as necessary; work on literature review.

DECEMBER/JANUARY

Recruit rest of participants; interview participants; transcribe interviews; complete drafts of literature review and methodology sections.

FEBRUARY/MARCH/APRIL

Complete transcription of interviews; analysis; review literature for recent work, or work that is now relevant to the analysis.

APRIL/MAY

Write-up and submission.

Planning template

Below is an example of milestones and sub-goals to help you write your timetable. Remember that each project is different, so use it along with your ethics application

Table 5.1 Project planning template

Milestone	Sub-goals	Completion date
Proposal [add date for completion for each milestone]	• Identify a supervisor and topic area (see Chapter 2). And meet with your group if you are doing a group project • Meet with your supervisor. • First round of literature review to develop/confirm research question (see Chapter 6). • Plan project (see Chapter 3 and Chapters 7 and 8 so you know what possibilities are available). • Consider what makes a high-quality project (see Chapter 9). • Write proposal. • Receive feedback on the proposal. • If relevant, complete and submit your proposal.	
Ethics	• Read about ethics (see Chapter 4) and about your institution's ethics approval process. • Complete draft of ethics application and associated paperwork (interview guide, information forms, etc.). • Receive feedback on the ethics application and submit it to review body.	

(Continued)

Table 5.1 (Continued)

Milestone	Sub-goals	Completion date
	• Second round of literature review while you are waiting for assessment – this can be on your topic (see Chapter 6) and/or developing your understanding of the research methods you plan to use (see Chapter 8, then read work on your specific methods of planned data collection/analysis; see Sullivan & Forrester, 2019). • Use this reading as an opportunity to practice your writing by either drafting some of your literature review or your method chapter (see Chapter 10). • Send to your supervisor for feedback. • You may need to amend your ethics form before your ethics application is passed.	
Data collection	• Once you have ethical approval, follow the planned procedure for recruitment. • Do the following activities in parallel but prioritise in this order: 1 Recruit participants (if this is relevant for your study) 2 Data collection 3 Transcription 4 Carry on with literature review 5 Preliminary analysis (see below). Review recruitment throughout this period, and if there are any problems or concerns run them past your supervisor or team members.	
Data analysis	• Preliminary analysis: Take an element of your data and do a practice analysis on it. For example, take one interview, complete a full analysis on it as if it was your whole data set, and write some of this process up (e.g. 1-2 pages with a description of the superordinate themes/main discourses, an introduction to one main theme/discourse, an extract to represent this theme/discourse, and your analysis of that extract in line with your chair is a method of analysis). If you are in a group, you could do this together. Share it with your supervisor for feedback. • Take this learning and apply it to the analysis of your whole data set. This is an efficient way for both you and your supervisor to develop your skills in analysis, and thus develop your overall project. Do not do this activity as a group. • Complete analysis of whole dataset and write it up (see Chapters 9 and 10) (ask your supervisor for feedback). • During this time, you may review your research question (see Chapter 2).	
Write up your project	Consider what should go in each part of your write-up and why (see Chapter 10). Consider how to demonstrate the quality of your project (see Chapter 9). Send your full draft to your supervisor for feedback. Use the time that they are reading your thesis to do references if you haven't already done them. Write the final draft of your thesis, integrating the feedback. Submit. Bask in the glory of a job well done!	

and proposal to help you identify actions relevant for your study and put a date against each one of these actions. Add a fourth column 'completed' for you to enjoy ticking them off.

Timetables: The last word

You can use your timetable to facilitate good communication with your supervisor. Bring your timetable with you to meetings and discuss your plans. Once your project is up and running, keep your timetable somewhere you can see it and refer to it. If you find yourself getting behind you may need to revise it – in which case it's always advisable to consult your supervisor.

Top tip

Keeping track

If you are going to leave your project for any length of time, write yourself a note that outlines what you were doing or thinking at the time. Include, for example, any decisions you had recently made, the rationale behind these decisions and any plans you had to action these decisions. This note will act as an aide-mémoire - bringing you back into the moment when you left your project. If you don't write such a note, you may find that when you come back to your project you've forgotten much of what you'd been thinking and you'll have to spend precious time trying to make sense of your own paperwork!

The Student-Supervisor Relationship

Relationships between students and their supervisors are unique and develop over time as both parties learn about each other's preferred styles of working and approach to qualitative research projects. It might be the first time that you've worked with your supervisor and this can make it intimidating or leave you unsure of what's expected. Here we will start by examining the key issue of communication between student and supervisor, and then look at some of the main causes of problems in this relationship and what you might do about them. We will then pay particular attention to how you can make the supervisory relationship work at its best at the crucial stage of data analysis. These issues are relevant, whether you are having one-to-one supervision, or if your project is with other students. But we recognise that group projects come with their own issues, so we finish this section by discussing some of the issues that can arise when students do projects in groups.

Good communication between you and your supervisor means that you are likely to develop a sense of shared ownership of your project. This will let you feel positive about

and interested in your work and thus more likely to work harder on it and enjoy working on it. And in turn, it means that your supervisor is more likely to give you the focus
and in-depth advice you need to develop the project into an excellent qualitative study.
If that wasn't motivation enough, remember that learning to manage your supervisor
at university will help you develop a set of skills you can transfer into your future (or
current) employment. But perhaps most importantly, it is useful to know that supervising students is often a really rewarding part of an academic's job. For students, this is
often your closest working relationship with an academic whose job it is to support you
to do a large piece of work on something that matters to you. Similarly, supervisors find
the opportunity to support students and watch them grow and create a project of their
own that they couldn't have done without you really rewarding. These kinds of relationships take time to build and they grow over time of the project, but when it comes
to graduation it's their project students that the lecturers look for and cheer on. So, in
this relationship, be authentic, give it your best shot and be honest if you are struggling,
and most of the time you will find your supervisor has your back. Below we outline
some of the ways to facilitate good student–supervisor relationships.

Top tips

How to have a positive student-supervisor relationship

- Develop mutual respect and shared interest in the subject (for example, by reading up on the subject before your first supervision meeting).
- Have regular and meaningful contact (for some people this may be fixed, regular meetings, for others you may want more contact towards the beginning and end of the project - discuss this with your supervisor as your institution may have particular guidelines on the timing and number of meetings).
- Use your timetable to set clear goals and deadlines.
- Have early in-depth discussions to enable clear and shared understanding of the project, and to find out what your supervisor's expectations are for you (such as when you should meet or who initiates meetings).
- Try to recognise your own and your supervisor's preferred communication styles and reflect on how to harmonise these.
- Make notes during your meeting so that you can follow up what you've agreed.
- Keep your supervisor informed if you are having difficulties or if you want to significantly change your plan.
- Use other relevant resources (for example, if you're having literature review problems make an appointment to see your librarian in the first instance).
- If your supervisor has published in the area of your study - read their work.

Troubleshooting: if the relationship sours

The supervisory relationship is often enjoyable and valuable for all parties. But, as with any kind of relationship, things sometimes go wrong. In this section we will consider some of the main causes of problems in this relationship, and how you might try to prevent or alleviate them.

Lack of work by the student(s)

Supervisors know when you haven't done any work and get frustrated if they're having meetings that they think are a waste of time. So, if you haven't done any work and have a meeting set up, then do one of the following:

- Postpone the meeting, but only for a few days so that you can do some work and get on top of the project. If you leave it for longer, you're likely to be avoiding a problem that will only get worse with delay.
- Quickly review what you've done so far on the project before your meeting, so at least you can start from where you left off last time you saw them.
- Be open about your lack of work and explain why. Often students haven't done work because there's a problem, such as time management, not really understanding what to do, not having the confidence to do what's been agreed, personal problems interfering with work or recruitment problems. Your supervisor is there to help make your project run as smoothly as possible, so bring these issues to their attention. Most times they'll have solutions for you; after all, they've probably had to deal with similar problems before with other students or in their own work.

Lack of engagement by the supervisor

You should feel a sense of ownership of your project, and there will be times when your supervisor will encourage this by taking a more 'hands off' approach. Indeed, some students can expect too much input from the supervisor – it is not the supervisor's job to tell you how to conduct your research, or to analyse your data for you. Most supervisors will be good at managing this process, knowing when to give more direction, and when to stand back a little. Occasionally, however, you might encounter a supervisor who perhaps isn't as engaged with your project as they might be.

Managing a supervisor who doesn't seem engaged is a difficult task, particularly because of the power imbalance in the relationship. If you think you have this problem it's probably useful to deal with it in stages. First, reframe your thinking and consider that your supervisor has your best interests at heart, but for some reason is not able to apparently act in that way. This might help you identify ways of improving your supervisor's engagement with you. For example, is it a time-management problem? In general, academics have more emails a day than they can answer, so sometimes they overlook one. So, if you've sent an important email and haven't had a reply after a couple of days, it's ok to send a polite reminder. Similarly, if you think your supervisor only skim reads emails, then make your emails short and clear, and schedule meetings to discuss issues in depth.

If, after trying to see the problem from the supervisor's point of view you are still left with the conclusion that they are not interested in your project, then you need to develop a different strategy. We would always suggest you try to discuss your concerns with your supervisor first, as politely and calmly as possible. Avoid accusations, as these may tend to provoke a hostile response by backing the supervisor into a corner. Focus instead on how you have experienced the supervision process and what you feel about it. It may be helpful to acknowledge that you might have misread the situation, allowing the supervisor to take your feelings seriously without having to become defensive to save face. If such an approach still fails to resolve the situation, you will probably have to involve an outside party (or parties). You may approach another member of staff who you have a relationship with (for example, a personal tutor) to see if they can liaise with your supervisor on your behalf or help you with a strategy for dealing with your supervisor. Alternatively, there may be a lecturer who has overall responsibility for running the project module who is in the best position to help you. Should all such efforts prove unsuccessful, you may decide that the only option is to change supervisors. It is important to find out your institution's criteria for considering such requests. For example, claiming a clash of personalities will probably not get you very far, but if you feel that your study has now developed into an area more appropriate for another member of staff (and perhaps you might strategically find that it does) then you may be able to argue more successfully for a change.

Sometimes these problems are easily resolved and it's a transferable skill to learn to behave in a professional and diplomatic way in the face of difficulties. However, if you are upset or feel you need support, then use the resources you have at your institution to get this support – such as personal tutors, year leaders, programme directors, student representatives or the student union.

The over-controlling supervisor

Occasionally, students may feel that far from being disengaged, their supervisor is assuming too much control over their project. They are telling the student exactly what to do and when to do it and may seem dismissive of your suggestions. If you feel this is happening to you, again we suggest you try to think about how the situation may appear to your supervisor. If you have fallen behind your original schedule, and/or have failed to complete work agreed in the previous meeting, they may feel that they need to impose more direction on you to recover your situation. Once you are back on course, your supervisor will probably allow you to assume more control. Another possibility is that what you perceive as excessive control is just a sign of your supervisor's enthusiasm for your project – this is particularly likely where you are working in an area that is closely aligned to their own interests. In most respects such enthusiasm is greatly to your advantage: you will certainly get your supervisor's full attention, they will be able to direct you to cutting-edge literature, and you will be able to learn directly from their own research experience. So long as you also show excitement about the topic, negotiating for more control over the direction of your project should not be difficult.

The most serious problems relating to supervisor control occur in the very rare instances where a student feels that the supervisor is attempting to use their project purely for the supervisor's own ends, such as to collect additional data for their own research. There is actually nothing wrong in principle with a student's project being incorporated into the supervisor's programme of research, so long as this is done openly and the focus on the project as a major piece of assessed academic work is not lost. Indeed, you may have a lot to gain from such an arrangement, in terms of support, access to resources and perhaps the possibility of publishing your work (see Chapter 11 for more on this). However, if the supervisor appears to be only interested in what your project can do for them, you need to address this just as you would for the case of the disengaged supervisor discussed above. The bottom line here is that your project is your work – in all likelihood the single most important piece of work you produce in your degree. It is never right for your supervisor to take over ownership of it.

Supervisor's lack of qualitative research experience

While most institutions try to match student projects to supervisor expertise, sometimes this is just not possible – perhaps your department only has a few members of staff with qualitative expertise, or your supervisor has been allocated on the basis of topic area rather than methodology. You may then find yourself in the position of knowing more about the methods you want to use than your supervisor does, and feel anxious that they are unable to advise you as to whether you are going about your research in the right way.

Top tips

When your supervisor is not a qualitative researcher

Some strategies for dealing with this situation include the following:

- Share with your supervisor some of the methodological literature you have found most useful.
- Ask whether it is possible to see examples of qualitative projects from previous years.

(Continued)

- Talk about your research with friends from your course who are also doing qualitative projects (though be very careful not to plagiarise their work).
- Ask your supervisor whether you could approach another member of staff for specific expert advice. They may prefer to do this for you on your behalf.

Remember that good supervision is about helping you manage the process of your research rather than the fine detail; methodological expertise on the part of your supervisor is an advantage, but not the most critical aspect of project supervision. A great supervisor is one that guides you skilfully through the process of carrying out your project. They may or may not be an expert in the topic you are researching and the methods you are using, but they will be an expert in how to carry out a project and this is the most important aspect of their role.

Supervision and feedback

At various points during the project, you will receive feedback on your work. Depending on your institution's formal requirements and how you and your supervisor plan your project, this feedback can be on proposals, ethics submissions, practice analysis or drafts of write-up. We call this 'formative feedback' because it is designed to help you develop your existing work (in contrast to feedback at the end of your thesis which is mostly designed to explain your mark). Staff often spend a lot of time on formative feedback, so read it carefully as they are giving you directions for how to develop your work. Some institutions may give you a deadline for formative feedback on a full draft of your thesis. This is a valuable opportunity to (1) identify and fix any problems and (2) identify how and where to enhance your work for maximum marks, so do take advantage of it. By looking at a full draft, your supervisor can not only see the strengths and weaknesses of individual sections, they can also get an idea of how the dissertation works as a whole. Don't worry if you know some sections are at a much earlier stage of development than others. Your supervisor will take that into account in their feedback.

You may sometimes feel that the formative feedback you receive is overly harsh, or even unfair. It's usually a good idea when you feel this way to come back to it later once you have got over the initial upset or disappointment. Often, we need a day or two before we can read critical feedback neutrally enough to recognise its usefulness. If you don't understand the feedback, or don't know how to translate it into doing things differently in future, ask your supervisor. When you are writing your next piece of work for your thesis, go back to the comments you received last time and double-check that you've acted on it; supervisors can feel frustrated if they think you're not taking in their feedback.

Supervision and data analysis

One of the great things about qualitative projects is the data. You'll probably have loads of it and it will all be interesting. But trying to identify patterns in your data or move your analysis from descriptive to conceptual analyses are significant challenges. The best way to meet these challenges successfully is to talk to your supervisor about your data, and to do this you need to be familiar with it. This may sound obvious, but often students aren't as familiar with their data as they think they are.

To be familiar with your data you need to listen to the recordings and read through your transcripts (or other forms of data that you're using) several times. Make sure you can talk confidently about what's in them and try to outline some codes or patterns in the data that you can take to your supervisor. If you're struggling with the analysis in some way, try to reflect on what it is that you're finding difficult. Does it all seem relevant? Or none of it relevant? Or you don't know how to start? Talking to your supervisor about the exact nature of your difficulty will help them find solutions that work for you. (Also see Chapter 8 for advice on troubleshooting common problems with your analysis.) Your supervisor may offer to look at a sample of data for you; this can be really helpful, so do take them up on that.

Supervisory relationships in group supervision

Universities often organise project supervision on a group basis, rather than one-to-one. There are two main models of this. It may involve a true group project in which each student collects data on the same topic and then all the data are shared among the group. Data are then analysed and the research project written up on an individual basis. Alternatively, students may be conducting separate individual projects, but with a common broad topic and/or methodology. Usually where group supervision is used there may be some one-to-one contact with the supervisor in the latter stages of the project, but most (if not all) sessions are held with the whole group.

Top tips

Getting the most from group supervision

- Make an effort to contribute to sessions. If you sit quietly in the corner, you will not gain all you could from supervision. In particular, don't worry that your question or comment seems silly – in all likelihood if it is an issue for you, it will be for the others. They will probably be grateful to you for raising it.

(Continued)

- Learn from your fellow students. Meet outside of the supervision sessions to share your thoughts, ideas or concerns. The opportunity to gain from peer interaction is a real bonus of group supervision. Students can benefit from group work in terms of sharing the work load - such as identifying relevant readings or reducing the amount of transcription you need to do. Group projects can also create the kinds of benefits students get from study groups, such as being able to develop, explore and share ideas. But be careful if sharing the details of your analysis and write-up. Although fruitful synergies can occur doing this, it can also lead to intentional or inadvertent plagiarism, so in general we would recommend that when it comes to writing up you do this individually.
- Do not put up with free-riding from other members of the group. By this we mean cases where one person makes little or no contribution to the group, but then expects other members to help them out. If you feel this is happening, talk to your fellow supervisees and together explain to the person involved why you are not happy with their behaviour. Should the problem persist, talk to your supervisor about it.

Want to know more about supervisor relationships?

www.vitae.ac.uk
This is a website for postgraduate students, but with information on the supervisor-supervisee relationship that is relevant for both undergraduate and postgraduates.

Dynamics Between You and Your Participants

The other relationship you have to think about in your research is the one you have with your participants. And, as with your supervisor, this relationship is a two-way process – who you are will affect how your participants engage with you. And in turn, your participants – and perhaps the project topic itself – may affect you, sometimes in unexpected ways.

Top tips

Researcher-participant relationships

All relationships - however positive - contain power relationships, and it is important for researchers to reflect on how power may manifest itself in their projects. Researchers are usually considered to hold more power (reversing your situation with your supervisor).

As researchers we are powerful because we are in charge of the project (we ask the interview questions, for example) and because we represent institutions (such as a university or an academic discipline such as psychology). These institutions are loaded with social power, so although you may see yourself as 'just a student', you need to be sensitive to participants who may see you as representing something much more powerful.

It must be recognised, though, that power in research relationships is a complicated thing, and can work in the other direction to that we've just described. You may find yourself in a position where you feel your participants are in a more powerful position than you, such as when interviewing people in high-status jobs, or who are significantly older than you. It is important in such circumstances that you are confident about your own knowledge as a researcher and about the value of your research. If you feel nervous, talk to your supervisor about practical steps you can take to make you feel surer of yourself. For instance, they may suggest you do a practice interview with them role-playing the type of participant you will be working with.

Characteristics such as your age, ethnicity, gendered or racialised position, and other aspects of what you look or sound like might also affect how participants engage with you. For example, Beth ran a series of focus groups with women significantly older than herself about their experiences of contemporary beauty ideals. Tensions emerged in the process because it was apparent that the participants were comparing themselves to her and finding themselves lacking (in their eyes she was young and beautiful, and they were older and less beautiful). Beth considered herself normal and with her own appearance issues that are (unfortunately) also normal for many young women, and she hadn't really considered how cultural norms that devalue older women might impact on the dynamics between her and her participants. So, she hadn't prepared for how her appearance was viewed (and resented) by her participants.

What if participants do things that worry or offend you? You should always try to plan for the things that might arise in your research project, but sometimes things happen that are unanticipated. This can include participants saying things that you find offensive, or things that you feel need to be challenged because of their harmful implications in a wider sense. Although this is unusual, things also might happen between you and your participants that you find intimidating or frightening. We discuss these issues in more detail in Chapter 4.

It's useful to consider how you differ from your participants and how that might impact on their responses to you (this is part of a wider issue called 'reflexivity', which is discussed in more detail in Chapter 9). How you as a person may affect the way that participants respond to you is an issue to discuss with your supervisor before you start collecting data. To make the most of your discussion we recommend that you read up on the subject (see, for example, King et al., 2019).

Sometimes it may feel that the participants have more power than you, as we discuss above. After all, you usually need them more than they need you. You may experience participants who at first were apparently very supportive of the project now acting in ways that seem to be sabotaging it. And you'll almost certainly be 'stood up' or 'ghosted' on occasion, which is frustrating. Alternatively, there may be cross-overs with other power structures, such as gender, that make you feel vulnerable or wrong footed – see, for example, Riley et al. (2003) for an analysis of such examples. It's important to talk to your supervisor if you have any of these feelings or if these experiences are troubling you. Remember, though, that although interaction with your participants can create challenges, in the majority of cases it is one of the most rewarding aspects of doing a qualitative project.

Cautionary tale

The researcher–participant relationship

While Suzy enjoyed interviewing her participants, her fourth interview raised some difficult issues for her. The participant was Lastri, a first-year female student from Indonesia. Lastri was 19 years old and had only had one brief trip to England before coming to study there. While there are many Indonesian students at the university, Lastri was the only one on her course and in the student accommodation block where she lives. She told Suzy that she felt very isolated and lonely, and was too shy to try and get to know British students, whose interests and lifestyles often felt very different from hers. After the interview, she emailed Suzy several times, saying how nice it was to talk to someone who was interested in her story, and asking whether Suzy could call round and see her some time. Suzy was worried about Lastri's well-being, and also felt uncomfortable that she was trying to develop their relationship into a friendship that Suzy didn't want.

Suzy took her concerns to her supervisor, Dr Hilton, who reassured her they were legitimate. He talked about how researchers' perspectives on relationships with participants differed, but that sometimes researchers feel that more is being asked of them than they can give. He also noted that it was important that Lastri wasn't negatively affected by her participation in the project. So together they worked out a plan for finding support for Lastri that didn't rely on an unwanted emotional relationship with Suzy.

They decided that Suzy should identify appropriate sources of support for Lastri and make contact with them to help facilitate the development of Lastri's social network. After some email communication with the overseas students support officer, Suzy met with Lastri and introduced her to two students who had volunteered for a student buddy system where established students provide social support for new students. Suzy also sent Lastri an email with links to some clubs and societies that matched interests she had mentioned in the interview. At this point she carefully explained that her research perspective meant that she needed to keep a bit of distance between herself and her participants and so wouldn't be able to meet up with Lastri, but would love to hear from her with an occasional email. From her response, Lastri seemed happy with this. At the end of the term Lastri sent Suzy an email saying she now felt she was settling in much better to university life.

The nature of qualitative work means that you may emotionally connect with your participants, particularly if your project involves repeated meetings or sensitive questions. Even apparently 'safe' questions such as asking about a music collection can elicit powerful emotions and stories from participants (see Chapter 4's cautionary tale 'unexpected revelations'). You need to plan strategies for dealing with these situations and for how your research may 'spill over' into other aspects of your life. For example, is there a chance that in your social life you could bump into a participant? Do participants have a right to think of you as a friend if you've met them several times and they've told you intimate details about their life? Alternatively, if you recruit friends or family members as participants, how might the research process impact on your subsequent relationships with them? It is useful to reflect on these issues as you plan your study, so that you can best protect and support yourself and your participants. Sometimes the decision should be not to recruit these people.

An important way that research can spill over into researchers' lives is when you respond emotionally to what participants have told you or what you have found out about vulnerable people's lives (this can happen even if you are working with secondary data or data produced without interacting with participants, such as Internet archives). If you are dealing with sensitive issues or feel upset by your data make sure you speak with your supervisor, and if necessary organise other forms of support such as those offered by your university counselling service. See Chapter 4 for more on this.

Our last comment on how research can affect the researcher is to note that knowledge is a powerful thing. It can change you. And with any change there is a loss of the old self. With one project, for example, Sarah enjoyed watching some of her students gain a feminist political consciousness through their project, only to realise that this process was double-edged when they also become alienated from some of their friends who didn't share their concerns about the inequalities they cared about.

Conclusion

A well-run project is one that is thoughtfully conceived, where the researcher regularly refers to and updates their plan as necessary, and where the supervisory relationship is used effectively. We hope we have given you some useful guidance as to how you might achieve this. All projects have their ups and downs, but if you can plan ahead so that you have a sense of the activities you need to do to successfully bring together this significant piece of work, then you are in a good position to ride through any difficult patches. While we have focused on potential problems in this chapter, remember that completing your own research project, and developing a good working relationship with your supervisor, and fellow students if you're doing a group project, can be among the most satisfying aspects of your student career. Next, we consider in detail how to search for and review literature for your project.

References

Arnold, J., Silvester, J., Patterson, F., Robertson, I., Cooper, C. and Burnes, B. (2005) *Work Psychology: Understanding Human Behaviour in the Workplace*. Harlow: Pearson.

Charmaz, K. (1995) Grounded theory. In J.A. Smith, R. Harré and L. Van Langerhowe (eds), *Rethinking Methods in Psychology*. London: Sage. pp. 27–49.

King, N., Horrocks, C. and Brooks, J. (2019) *Interviews in Qualitative Research*, 2nd edition. London: Sage.

Locke, E.A. and Latham, G.P. (2002) Building a practically useful theory of goal setting and task motivation: A 35-year odyssey. *American Psychologist*, 57, 705–17.

Riley, S., Schouten, W. and Cahill, S. (2003) Exploring the dynamics of subjectivity and power between researcher and researched. *Forum for Qualitative Social Research*, 4(2). Online journal available at: www.qualitative-research.net/fqs-texte/2–03/2rileyetal-e.htm (accessed 3 September 2010).

Sullivan, C. and Forrester, M. (eds) (2019). *Doing Qualitative Research in Psychology: A Practical Guide*. Sage.

6

DOING A LITERATURE REVIEW

Jo Bryce and Michael Forrester

An excellent research project requires you to be familiar with other research and theories relating to your topic. This is why one of the key tasks associated with your project is a literature review.

Literature reviews usually happen at three key points in a project:

- during the development of your research question(s);
- during the planning stages, as you work out the rationale for the steps you will take to complete your project; and
- towards the end of the project, either because:
  - o preliminary analysis points you towards literature you had not previously considered, or
  - o to check for relevant studies published since your previous literature searches, or
  - o because you are doing a grounded theory project (see Chapter 8).

In this chapter we provide guidance on how to carry out a literature review for your project. Usually, this will help to inform the development of your research question(s) (see Chapter 2). If you plan to use grounded theory (see Chapter 8), then your review would be delayed and carried out after some initial data collection. Assuming that you are not using grounded theory, you need to carry out a thorough literature review early on in your project so that you can:

- find out what has already been done and how;
- understand the kinds of questions people interested in your general topic area have already been asking; and
- get to grips with the issues that are relevant to your area of interest.

To help you with this task, this chapter is divided into four main sections representing key components of a literature review. In this chapter we assume that you are doing your literature review at the research question development stage, but our advice will be relevant to a literature review done at any stage.

········ **·In a nutshell**··· ·· ···········

Key literature review components

- Finding suitable material: Searching for, and locating, research, journals, books and related information sources.
- Establishing relevance: Identifying and categorising literature in a given area (including establishing what constitutes 'relevant' material).
- Constructing an account: Telling a story about the research, which can be chronological, thematic and/or discipline focused.
- Linking to your research questions: Understanding the relationship between your literature review and research question(s).

· ·

Throughout the chapter, we will illustrate how these four components relate to each other by using a literature review of conversation analysis (CA) research (see Chapter 8) on pre-school children's conversational skills as an example. The selected example is deliberate because the topic is of interest to a range of researchers, but the method is a specialist area. This meant that it was necessary to identify relevant studies from a large pool of research, much of which was not relevant. Next, a way of synthesising the relevant studies and writing a review was needed. The problems that arose along the way are similar to those that many students face when conducting a literature review, and so our example helps demonstrate some solutions to these challenges.

┌─ **Top tip**─

Wikipedia and online sources

It is increasingly common for people to use Wikipedia as a source of information. However, for academic work, you should avoid using Wikipedia (and many other Internet sources and online articles) because it is not a peer-reviewed or independently evaluated source, unlike journal articles and academic textbooks. It is also common that the entries contain incorrect information about the topic. Sometimes people look at Wikipedia to get a sense of some of the key issues regarding a topic or person, but while it can give a useful overview for some topics, you should not use it as the basis for academic research and writing. This is why literature searches using bibliographic information systems, which are available through university libraries, should be the focus for identifying references to include in your review. The sources you use should generally be peer-reviewed, although there are some situations where grey literature such as professional reports, research undertaken by government agencies and charities could be relevant to include if they have been independently reviewed.

Finding Suitable Material

There are a number of key bibliographic information systems that you can call upon when first searching (for example, ISI's Web of Knowledge, PsycINFO, EBSCOHost, PEP-Web Search). These systems hold vast databases of published research but may not contain all the studies relevant to your project. This is because these databases are associated with particular institutions or disciplines. For example, PsycINFO holds information on psychological publications, and so psychology students studying the topic of 'motherhood' might miss relevant sociological studies if they only used PsycINFO for their literature search. It's important, therefore, to think about the topic that you're studying and whether the focus of your research is within or across discipline boundaries (for example, psychology, sociology, social anthropology). This will help you decide which systems to include in your search. You will also need to check the available bibliographic information systems your institution offers. Both of these steps will help you identify which combination of databases is best suited to your needs.

By this stage it is likely you will have gained some familiarity with the various bibliographic information systems available to you and have some knowledge of the practicalities of accessing them. But, if you're unsure, speak to your library staff.

One of the difficulties in doing a literature review to develop your research question(s) is knowing what to search for when you don't yet know what might be relevant. So, to conduct your review you need to be able to search effectively and also determine relevance.

To search effectively you need to develop a strategy for searching bibliographic databases that is consistent, methodical and that works in practice. This involves:

- doing a series of searches that strategically use key words, 'wildcards' and 'Boolean operators' (discussed below) to identify studies that are relevant to your project; and,
- organising your search findings so that you can conceptually map out the thinking of previous researchers on your subject.

Bibliographic information systems work by identifying articles (and other academic outputs such as book chapters or conference proceedings) that have the key words you've entered somewhere in the article (usually the title, author or abstract). You can combine key words together in various ways to structure these searches. For example, you can ask for articles in specific journals by specific authors with a specific key word in the title. Alternatively, you could give a combination of key words to be found in the title or abstract. This is where 'wildcards' and 'Boolean operators' (for example, AND, OR, NOT, WITH) can be used. These are codes that you can use to specify your searches. For example, an asterisk (*) is a wildcard that allows you to search for different variants of the same term and can be useful if you're looking for all the work by a particular author.

For example, a search for Forrester M* would identify publications where the author is identified by their initial and also where they are referred to as Michael (or Mike).

It would also identify work by all the other Forresters whose first initial is M. So, to narrow it down further you might use the Boolean operator *and* to ask for 'Forrester M* and conversation analysis'. Asterisks are also useful if you've got a topic term that can be shortened; for example, if you were interested in research on children's talk you could type in 'children and talk*' which would pick up research with children that use either the term 'talk' or 'talking'.

There are many wildcards and Boolean operators, and not all are used across all the bibliographic information systems. Check the online help of the system you're using to find out more about this.

Want to know more about searching databases?

For an accessible and detailed discussion of how to use key words, wildcards and Boolean operators see:

Shaw, R. (2019) 'Conducting literature reviews', in C. Sullivan and M.A. Forrester (eds), *Doing Qualitative Research in Psychology: A Practical Guide*. London: Sage. pp. 78-96.

However, knowing how to combine key words is not enough if you don't know what key words to use. If you are new to an area, initially only trial and error will reveal whether words closely associated with your key terms turn out to be relevant. At the beginning of your project, one strategy is to use the most common everyday uses of words that seem relevant to your interests. Putting in these general terms and combining them with other related words will allow you to retrieve many items which may be relevant.

Top tip

Strategies for identifying relevant publications

- Start with everyday common-sense terms.
- As your search progresses start to recognise the common terms used by authors doing research relevant to your study.
- Search by author for researchers active in your area (ask your supervisor for suggestions).
- Combine your key word searches with wildcards and Boolean operators.
- Use citation searches: if there is a key study in your area, you can use 'citation search' to identify all the papers that reference this key study. This gives you a way of identifying publications that might not use the key words you're searching with but are relevant to your work because you share the need to cite this key study.

To identify which of these returns are relevant to your study you need a way of systematically analysing the kinds of studies being identified by these key words. Adopting a consistent and careful procedure to searching allows you to:

- create searches that pick up relevant studies;
- 'sift' though the output so you can ignore irrelevant articles; and
- create summaries to describe the studies you find.

By developing a systematic way to search the literature and keeping a record of your findings, you can quickly gain a good idea of how many relevant studies there are in a field. Before long you will have a good sense of what previous researchers have found out or established, and some of the gaps in their knowledge that you might be able to address with your study.

Top tip

Systematically analysing search results

Shaw (2019) provides a set of accessible conceptual tools for systematic searching. Her procedure is to create a mind map of all relevant search terms and use these terms with the 'CHIP' tool (below) to help structure your search terms and to create a summary description of the literature in the field. The CHIP tool requires you to consider the articles you've identified in terms of:

1   the Context of the particular study;
2   How the study was conducted;
3   the Issues examined; and
4   the People involved in the study.

In our literature review, the relevant terms were 'child', 'conversation' and 'analysis'. Notice immediately the numerous other possibilities associated with each of these terms given below:

- **Child:** infant, schoolchild, youngster, kid, development (and more)
- **Conversation:** talk, talking, dialogue, discourse, communication, converse, chat, speaking, speech, rhetoric, communicative (and more)
- **Analysis:** examine, scrutiny, enquiry, break-down, examination, interpretation

A search using all these terms would identify relevant studies with children that didn't use our specific term of 'child' (for example, those that used 'infant' or 'development'). But using all these terms would also create an overwhelming number of studies, which it wouldn't be possible to sift through in a reasonable amount of time, and which, for many different reasons, would not be relevant to our search. We therefore needed to further refine the search strategy.

When refining your search strategy, you need to strike a balance between finding everything ever published about a topic and having a focus that is so specific that you miss important work within your topic of interest. In a project you are not expected to include and review all possible material. Rather, you should review a selected set of work that is relevant to your research topic area.

Top tip

Refining the search procedure

Our aim was to find studies of children that have involved research using the methodology of CA (which is influenced by a theory known as 'ethnomethodology'). Consider the results of the following searches:

1   Child* = > 100,000 items found
2   Child* and conversation = 1015 items found
3   Child and conversation analysis = 289 items found
4   Child and ethnomethodology = 16 items found

Notice the gradual 'funnelling' of the search and the corresponding reduction of found items. The relatively large number returned for the first three searches is misleadingly high and is likely to include a lot of irrelevant material. Reasons for this include that in search 3, for example, the database will search for anything that includes either 'child and conversation' or 'child and analysis'. We could have chosen to search 'child and conversation with analysis', which may have narrowed the search in the right direction, but instead we relied on our knowledge of the area. 'Conversation analysis' is often described as a form of ethnomethodology and introducing this term immediately constrained the number of returns. We were therefore able to refine our search using this knowledge of the area. Somebody who didn't have this knowledge may have had to use Boolean operators differently or sift through the titles or abstracts of the 289 articles until they got a sense of the key words being used for articles relevant to their research.

The actual number of articles you need to review will depend on the specific topic area you are working in and the question you are asking. If you find you have either many more, or significantly fewer, items than you would expect from looking at other review articles, then it is likely that your focus is too general or has not become fine-grained enough. In the latter instance it may be that that your searching procedures are possibly missing potentially relevant material. When in doubt ask your supervisor for guidance on this point.

Top tip

Read your supervisor

If your supervisor is actively researching in the area of your project, look up their work and include it in your review if it is relevant to your review and helps strengthen your rationale for your study.

Establishing Relevance

Alongside the practicalities of actually searching for material, doing your literature review also develops other important skills. In particular, you need to begin evaluating whether a piece of work is relevant or not, and, related to this, whether the research is likely to be of greater or lesser value to your research aims. Relevance and value depend on a variety of factors.

· · · · · · ·In a nutshell· ·

Relevance and value

Ask yourself:

1   What are the main theoretical ideas in the area and does the study I'm looking at explicitly or implicitly orient towards these ideas?
2   How relevant does the study I'm looking at seem to the research area? You can see how other authors refer to specific studies, particularly those who are seen as important in the development of understanding the topic area.
3   What different methodologies are used in this area and are they appropriate for the questions asked? Think about this in relation to the methodology of the studies you review. Look at the strengths and weaknesses identified by the study authors in the discussion section of the paper to help you with this.
4   What is the new knowledge developed by the study and how does it contribute to theory in your topic area? How important is this knowledge?
5   What are the knowledge gaps identified by the study results? Looking in the discussion of the papers you are reviewing will be useful here as researchers should make it clear what the contribution of the study is to the area, but also identify knowledge gaps and areas for future research.

Don't forget to build up a set of detailed notes that categorise your studies with reference to these questions!

· ·

As you begin your search, it will quickly become apparent what kinds of questions researchers in any given area have been asking; the kinds of methods they tend to use in their investigations; and, either implicitly or explicitly, the theoretical orientations that are prevalent in a particular area.

One of the most important sources of information to you during your initial searching are the abstracts (or summaries) of papers or research studies, which are often provided through commonly used information systems (sometimes referred to as 'abstracting' systems). Let us turn to some examples from the search stage of our example review and consider two different studies. Doing so will help you to understand why one paper was included in our review, while the other wasn't deemed to be relevant. This will help you to work out strategies you might use in your own project (see Table 6.1).

Table 6.1 Example abstracts examined during review

Paper 1: Ensor, R. & Hughes, C. (2008). Content or connectedness? Mother-child talk and early social understanding. *Child Development*, 79(1), 201-16.	**Paper 2:** de Leon, L. (2007). Parallelism, metalinguistic play, and the interactive emergence of Zinacantec Mayan siblings' culture. *Research on Language and Social Interaction*, 40(4), 405-36.
Abstract 1: 'Despite much research into individual differences in social understanding among preschoolers, little is known about corresponding individual differences within younger children.	**Abstract 2:** 'In this article, I investigate how two young Tzotzil Mayan siblings playfully manipulate the sequential structure of adjacency pairs to align, to confront each other, and to challenge family roles and hierarchies.
Likewise, although studies of preschoolers highlight the importance of mental-state references, other aspects of talk have received less attention. The current study involved 120 families with 2-year-olds; video-based transcripts of observations of family interaction were coded for quantity, connectedness, and content of mothers' and children's talk. At 2, 3, and 4 years of age, children completed social understanding and verbal ability tests. Mothers' connected turns and mental-state reference within connected turns showed independent associations with children's social understanding (as did children's mental-state references, both overall and within connected turns). Connected conversations provide a fertile context for children's developing social understanding.'	The young learners' intentional disruption reveals the early control of dialogic repetition typical of Mayan languages. More important, it illustrates the children's development of communicative competence as they reorganize greeting structures or reauthorize messages through frame shifts. In the case of a greeting game, the siblings disrupt its inherent sequential structure using semantic counterpointing with different address terms. When conveying a question sent by an adult, the 4-year-old playfully repeats it and recycles it across several turns in alignment with his younger brother and his grandfather. The subversion of the social organization of talk shows how the children interactively construct an emergent sibling culture that contests the social organization of the age-graded structure of the extended family.'

There are a number of strategies that can be used in combination to help decide about the relevance and value of an article for your review. Below we outline two strategies and show you how we can use them to help us determine the relevance and value of the two studies in Table 6.1.

····In a nutshell····

Identifying relevance

Strategy 1: Consider (a) the words used, (b) the source of the publication and (c) the authors.

Strategy 2: Being clear about what you are looking for when analysing abstracts.

Strategy 1: Consider (a) the words used, (b) the source of the publication and (c) the authors

Being methodical is key to completing a literature review. So, try to be consistent in your approach to each item you examine. As you begin to identify possible papers and chapters, you will quickly start to develop an expertise on the key words, relevant journals and names of the authors who are publishing in your area.

With paper 1, we find 'mother–child talk' and 'early social understanding' as two typical examples of terms generally related to child conversation. With paper 2, we find a somewhat different set of phrases or terms, including 'metalinguistic play', 'interactive emergence' and 'siblings'. Our knowledge of CA meant that we knew that the terms in paper 2 are more usually associated with the topic area of our review. Less experienced researchers could make these judgements by researching the terms a little further. You could use other information about the subject that you have gleaned from lectures, from other reading or through discussions with your supervisor.

It is important to remember that you are learning on the job. So, neither you nor your supervisor should expect you to be an expert in the area. It is inevitable that with your first searches a number of publications that could be relevant might escape your attention. Similarly, you might include publications that are not very relevant. Don't worry – your skills and expertise will improve with practice.

As you develop your literature searching abilities, you will be able to tell how likely it is that a paper will be relevant by looking at the journal a paper is published in. For example, although on the face of it, *Child Development* would seem to be a more directly appropriate publication for research on language in children, it is actually the journal that paper 2 is published in, *Research on Language and Social Interaction*, that has a history of publishing CA papers.

As for the authors of papers and chapters, the more you search the more likely it is that you will discover researchers who have published a lot in one specific area, and this will give you a clue to the potential relevance of the publication. Again, it can help a great deal if you have already discussed with your supervisor what journals and authors are more likely to publish relevant material for your study.

Strategy 2: Being clear about what you are looking for when analysing abstracts

When it comes to reading and assessing abstracts, we can go through a process similar to CHIP (see above) in order to establish whether an article is worth obtaining and reading in full. There are several specific questions you can ask which will help guide your assessment:

1   Who are the people being researched in this study and are they likely to be relevant to my specific review?
2   What kind of methodology was used? If there is a tendency to use a specific qualitative method for the kind of project you're interested in, this question may be relevant. But note that many topics are studied using different methods, so studies that use a range of methods may be relevant for you.
3   What is this research about?
4   What are the main findings? And what does this contribute to the topic?
5   How likely is it that this research will be relevant to my review?

Below, we have addressed these questions by comparing the two abstracts provided in Table 6.1 (above). For our review, we were interested in conversation analytic work on children's conversational skills during the pre-school years. This meant looking for papers that used a specific method (CA) to investigate a specific topic (young children's conversational skills).

The processes we used to assess the relevance of these papers are similar to those that you need to use for your project, although your study may require a less focused review. For example, you may not want to limit yourself to research that only used one method. Typically, a review of an area includes research that has used a range of different methodologies. Table 6.2 compares the two abstracts.

The example in Table 6.2 shows you the benefit of developing expertise in recognising technical terms or terms more associated with particular kinds of research. You can see that care should be taken during the early phase when you are becoming familiar with an area, and it may be that at first you want to be over-inclusive to compensate for a lack of expertise. Over time, you will start to recognise certain phrases and terms that serve as important clues to relevance. Reading about your subject and speaking to your supervisor about the most relevant key words, journals, authors, and technical terms will also help.

Constructing an Account

Once you have found the various journal articles, chapters, books, conference reports or any other relevant publication relevant for your review (for example, government reports) you will then begin the process of writing the actual review. Given that your

Table 6.2 Key questions for summarising research papers and evaluating their relevance

	Paper 1	Paper 2
Q1: Who?	120 children in three age groups	Two pre-school siblings
Evaluating the relevance	Irrelevant. CA studies rarely use such large samples	Relevant. The intensive work done in CA means CA studies often focus on only a small number of participants
Q2: Methodology?	Quantitative (Coding and correlations)	Qualitative – CA
Evaluating the relevance	Irrelevant. CA does not usually employ a coding procedure or statistical analysis	Relevant. Although CA not mentioned explicitly, CA terms are (e.g. 'adjacency pairs')
Q3: Research Question?	Individual differences in social understanding across ages	What constitutes sibling culture and its emergence?
Evaluating the relevance	Unclear. Terms used are ambiguous and could be relevant (e.g. social understanding)	Relevant. Technical terms used in CA are evident in the abstract
Q4: Findings?	Association between mother's words and children's social understanding	Demonstration of children's conversational skills in use of turn-taking structures
Evaluating the relevance	Irrelevant. No terms evident that a CA researcher would use	Relevant. Technical terms used in CA are evident (e.g. 'turn-taking')
Q5: Relevance?	Unlikely to be relevant	Likely to be highly relevant

review might summarise anywhere between 10 and 100 studies, it really helps if, from the outset, you have decided what kind of review you will carry out. The number of studies you review will depend very much on the question you are asking and whether other researchers have addressed similar issues or questions to yours.

It is important for you to recognise that a literature review is not simply some kind of list of every relevant study carried out to date. Once you've got a big pile of relevant studies it can be hard to resist the temptation to describe one study after another, but this creates an overly descriptive list without elements of evaluation, critique or narrative structure.

To make sure your literature review isn't overly descriptive try and do the following things:

- explain why the studies are of interest;
- clearly highlight the focus of the studies;
- show how the studies you are reviewing fit into a more general picture of the emerging or existent literature;
- critically evaluate the literature you are reviewing; and
- offer a coherent narrative.

─Top tip─

Writing an excellent review

Two key ingredients of a well-written review are as follows:

- a critical evaluation of the literature you are reviewing; and
- a narrative that flows logically and is coherent.

For more information on critical evaluation see Chapter 1, and for writing styles see Chapter 10.

─Top tip─

Avoid writing your review as a list

The following paragraph illustrates the descriptive and list-like style of reviewing literature that you should avoid:

Anderson, Smith and Jones (1998) conducted a qualitative study of mother-child talk which they analysed using CA and found out that connected conversations were important for the development of children's understanding of social situations. Brightlight et al. (1999) tested adults using the Mill Hill Vocabulary Test, the Perceived Social Competence Scale and perceptions of the quality of mother-child interactions. They found that participants with higher perceived quality of interactions showed higher levels of social competence and scores on the vocabulary test. Tolstoy and Bekaerman (2001) investigated children aged 3 and 5 and replicated the results of Jones and Solder (1993). Another study that looked at the quality of mother-child interactions was Zentner (1994) who found that connected conversations were very important for child development.

Activity 6.1: See if you can try rewriting this paragraph based on the advice provided in this section. An example rewrite is provided at the end of the chapter.

You need to develop your own narrative. This does not mean writing a fictional creative story. But it is a creative act to bring together the research relevant to your study in a way that shows your reader the patterns in that research in an evaluative and coherent way. In this way, you should tell a good story that highlights the issues, findings, and debates in the field and which links clearly to a relevant and interesting research question or set of research questions.

Reviews that have a good narrative:

- offer a coherent, logical story that is written in your own words;
- include relevant studies and interpret them;

- set out a framework so that the reader can gain a good idea of how one study is related to another;
- use these studies to develop a conceptual understanding of the topic; and
- draw out the significance of these studies for our understanding of the topic.

For more ideas on how to write your literature review see Chapter 10.

··· ···**In a nutshell**··· ···

Telling a good story

A good literature review should include the following key characteristics:

- Starts with a clear introduction outlining the structure and content of the review.
- Provides a critical overview of previous research work that is concise, coherent and understandable to the reader. This should avoid being a simple list of different studies.
- Uses a clear framework to help structure the narrative (see below).
- At the end of your review, as well as at key points throughout, it is very important to draw out the rationale behind the question(s) you are going to ask for your project. This will be related to the review in specific ways and the reader will recognise why it makes sense to ask the questions you pose given the background literature.

· ·

Top tip

Writing a review with interpretation

The following paragraph shows the interpretive style that you should try and strive for:

> In charting key aspects of the child's conversational skills and understandings, Wootton (1997) comments that intersubjective 'understandings' have three important properties: they are local, public and moral. For example, these understandings are public in that the child's conduct is systematically sensitive to agreements and preferences which have been overtly established within earlier talk. Detailing and examining intersubjective understandings is central to the work of Tarplee (2010), who addresses the inherent difficulties of using concepts such as 'feedback' to explain language development. Looking at displays of understanding, on a turn-by-turn basis, Tarplee (2010) highlights the child's orientation to sequential implicativeness and makes the point that the particular kind of parent–child interaction where linguistic pedagogy is relevant is constituted by the structure of the talk itself.

This paragraph introduces two studies, explains how they relate to one another and provides some evaluative commentary. By writing in this way, you are able to highlight the important questions you want to address and identify key issues in the field.

Review frameworks

There are various frameworks that can be used to help you structure your review and below we examine four of them: chronological; thematic; cross-disciplinary; and theoretical. We encourage you to pick one of these frameworks and use it.

Chronological reviews

With this approach your aim is to provide an overview, history or chronology of the literature that you have selected for inclusion in your review. Here you must be careful that your overview doesn't just simply fall into the trap of being a rather boring descriptive list as discussed above. Instead, try to tell a story about the literature from your notes collated from the articles that you selected as being relevant to your project.

So, for example, after your introduction, which will tell the reader how your review is structured and why it is structured the way it is, you could begin by highlighting how an early study in the area turned out to be one of the most influential. Alternatively, it might be the case that the early studies in an area quickly changed focus and researchers began to pick up on ideas that did not at first seem related directly to what had gone before.

From here you would then go through each study or preferably, a group of studies (in order to avoid writing in a list-like manner as described above), focusing on telling the reader (1) what the main findings of the article(s) are, (2) why these findings are of interest to the area and (3) what implications this finding or set of findings has for your developing argument, which forms the rationale for your study.

It is also very important to link each main paragraph of your review together. You need to keep the reader interested and in touch with the emerging story. So, at the end of one section or subsection, you might conclude by saying:

> It is therefore apparent that the main findings established by the 1990s were (x, y and z) and these ideas continued to have some influence into the 2000s, particularly through the work of Jones et al. (2001).

Then, having introduced your reader to the idea that the work of Jones is especially important to your narrative (that is, 'signposted' this), you would move on to discuss Jones et al.'s work. So, your next paragraph might go something like this:

> The most significant element that began to emerge around the turn of the century was related to the work of Jones et al. (2001), who alongside Brown's work (2002) established that x, and z were only indicative of a, b and c ...

Reminding your reader what you've said and what you may be about to say is called 'signposting' because it allows you to tell them the structure of your review and how your arguments fit together. This allows your reader to follow the flow of your review more easily. (For further discussion on 'signposting' see Chapter 10 on writing up.)

At the end of your chronological review, you need to summarise the key points you've made, particularly in terms of how they form an argument or rationale for your study and its aims. We will consider this in more detail in the final section of this chapter below.

Thematic reviews

In any specific area of study, it is possible to identify patterns of research and to group the studies according to these patterns or themes. These can be presented under different headings to give an overview of the relevant research for your project. In our review, we identified approximately 40 studies as relevant, which could be classified under five themes or headings: pre-linguistic communication; repair; competencies and understandings; grammar; and childhood.

This could be used to create a thematic structure to the narrative written as part of the review. After an introductory paragraph, this thematic structure could be introduced by writing something like this:

> Child conversation analysis (CA) research can be classified into five general areas: (a) pre-linguistic communication, (b) repair, (c) competencies and understandings, (d) grammar and (e) childhood. Such a differentiation is to some extent arbitrary and employed solely for overview purposes. While there may be some link between these sub-themes and disciplinary agendas there is not always a correspondence between discipline and topic areas. Furthermore, although there may be an implicit trans-disciplinary orientation to describing and explaining the development of children's conversational skills and abilities, this is not necessarily a shared aspect of child CA work. This overview does not cover CA based studies with older-aged children or child language impairment. (Forrester, forthcoming: xxx)

From there it is relatively straightforward to go on and set out each theme. At the beginning of a theme, remember to use signposting to remind the reader what it is about. Similarly, at the end of a theme, summarise the key points, draw out the relevance to your own developing argument and include a linking sentence to the next paragraph. Again, you would want to finish the thematic review with an overall summary of the key points.

Advantages of doing a thematic review include:

- You have less concern with who did what and when and in what order. This is especially useful if research developments in your area of interest occurred in parallel rather than linearly, which often happens in areas that employ qualitative methods such as in health psychology, clinical psychology and critical/discursive psychology.

- This structure encourages analysis and interpretation of the material, since identifying your themes requires you to think analytically about the topic.
- This style of writing also makes it much harder to fall into the trap of writing in a list-like manner.
- Identifying and drawing out themes facilitates the production of a coherent account of a body of literature and critical discussion of the material from a particular theoretical or methodological perspective. This is often a hallmark of an excellent project.

Cross-disciplinary review

Topics which are well suited to qualitative research methods also tend to often be studied by researchers from more than one discipline. Our example review is a good illustration of this, since several different disciplines employ this qualitative method when looking at children's early conversational competencies. When carrying out our review we found at least five, including: linguistics; sociology; psychology; social anthropology; and education.

Rather than a thematic organisation one could provide a cross-disciplinary framework where studies within a particular discipline are described and interpreted in a way that highlights how that discipline tends to approach the topic. For example, within research using CA to look at children's language there are several studies that look in detail at particular linguistic elements of the child's early talk – such as phonetics (Tarplee, 1996). In contrast, in the sociology of childhood researchers have considered how children's conversational participation might be subject to specific discursive formulations provided by adults (Hutchby, 2010). When going through the various studies relevant to your project you could firstly locate where each study sits and then, when summarising the work, provide some background to the distinct disciplinary orientation these studies tend to have. This will also help you identify issues yet to be addressed from the perspective that you are coming from.

Cross-disciplinary reviews are usually written with a bias towards your own discipline. For example, you might highlight the work carried out by researchers in your own discipline or evaluate work in other disciplines in the light of what it can offer to your own. If you are unsure about whether material from a discipline other than your own is appropriate for inclusion you should check this with your supervisor.

Theoretical framework reviews

Excellent project work tends to have a clear theoretical viewpoint. Using a theoretical framework for the literature review can help to introduce your theoretical framework and justify why you are using it. Doing this involves using a particular theoretical approach as a lens so that studies are not only described and evaluated in general terms but are evaluated specifically in relation to how they relate to the assumptions of a particular approach. Students who are drawing on a standpoint that contrasts with the more dominant perspectives in the discipline often use this kind of review, for example, if they're taking a critical psychology, social constructionist or psychodynamic approach. Alternatively, students might use this type of review when they are using a very specific approach, and they want to focus their project (and hence literature review) on engaging in detail with the debates and issues within this approach. Our review would be such an example, as it was exploring pre-school conversation skills from within an ethnomethodological theoretical framework.

Taking up of a particular viewpoint, and then providing a review that offers a critical account, is a skill that is acquired through the process of doing literature reviews and gradually gaining a deeper understanding of an area. As you develop your skills you will also begin to develop your own theoretical allegiances and orientations, which may influence how you want to write your review.

Top tip

Try out different frameworks

Although you will see from the above that we have our preferences in terms of the available frameworks, you still need to choose one for yourself that you feel will work for you. Why not try writing a small section of your narrative using more than one of these frameworks so that you can compare them and pick the one that you think will work best for you.

Linking to your Research Question(s)

The final and key element of a literature review is the relationship between the review and the research question(s) you are addressing in your project. We said earlier that as you write your narrative you will need to keep making links between the literature you are reviewing and the rationale for your own project. Towards the end of your literature review it is important to draw out and summarise this rationale. Whatever framework you use for organising your review, the final section should be written especially carefully. Here, make sure that what you write makes your review and critical commentary lead logically onto your own specific question or questions.

Often a review is described as a process of gradually funnelling down from the bigger, more general issues down to sub-themes, and then onto the specific issues or areas you want to address. In experimental studies, it is at this point that specific hypotheses are outlined (again, ones that make sense given prior studies and the issues identified). However, in qualitative methodological approaches, specific hypotheses are not typically set out. So, the production of a literature review, which highlights the main issues and themes, serves as the background for the reasons why the question(s) you are going to ask makes sense. You haven't simply dreamt up a question on the spur of the moment – instead you have provided a reasoned and defensible background to the question(s) you are now going to address in your project. The reader should be able to guess the kind of research question you are likely to ask from the commentary and rationale that the review has provided. See Figure 6.1 as an example from our review.

CA research on children, adult–child talk and topics germane to understanding how children learn to talk are gathering momentum. There are a number of identifiable themes in the literature that linguists and child language researchers might subsume under the term 'developmental pragmatics'. We have seen, for example, the problems and issues that have arisen with the analysis of prelinguistic communication, the questions surrounding identifying repair skills and the perplexing question of what exactly constitutes a participant skill during the child's early years.	Shows the topic is relevant and interesting. Reminds the reader what they have been told. Reminds the reader there's more to know and what the big questions are. Reminds the reader of the approach being used, its aims and why it's useful. Introduces main areas for research questions. States main research question and rationale (filling gap in literature). States how this main question will be addressed through interrelated sub-questions.
However, what is distinct about child-CA is the careful focus on how, why and under what conditions younger members of any culture gradually attain the skill necessary for producing the reflexively accountable sense-making practices that constitute talk-in-interaction. Ethnomethodologically informed child-CA extends the boundaries of traditional language acquisition research and reminds us that this is, first and foremost, a social-discursive practice. It is because of this that this project is going to focus on the question of how children gradually learn to close a conversation, an issue which has yet to be addressed in the literature. The answer to this main question will be gained through asking two related subsidiary questions: Under what conditions and at what age do children first recognise the end of conversation? What particular structures are utilised in their own first attempts at endings?	

Figure 6.1   Example of review conclusion and research questions

Other Approaches to Literature Reviews

'Systematic reviews' are becoming an increasingly common method for reviewing literature in a specific area. This approach allows the integration of results from multiple studies focusing on the same topic as each other and using similar samples of data.

This involves a critical evaluation of findings, and of the similarities and differences between different studies. Systematic reviews share the same basic principles as the methods described above, but use a formal methodology which, arguably, increases the trustworthiness of the results. A series of specific steps (i.e. searching, screening, quality assessment, reporting) are used, which make the review process transparent and verifiable. It also helps us to minimise the extent to which our own perspectives influence the way in which we select literature for review (for example, in determining what counts as 'relevant', as discussed above). It is well documented that people have psychological biases that lead them to pay more attention to, or see as more believable, information that fits with their existing views (e.g. Johnson and Eagly, 1989). Researchers (including you!) are no exception to this and being more systematic in the literature review process can be a helpful way to take this into account.

However, using this approach is very involved and can take a considerable amount of time. A somewhat less time-consuming approach, which is similar to a systematic review but can be completed in a shorter period of time (commonly three to six months), is a rapid evidence assessment (REA) (Davies, 2003). It uses the same stages as a systematic review for identifying relevant literature to answer specific research question(s) and to assess the quality of the available evidence. However, specific limits are included in the methodology (e.g. inclusion/exclusion criteria, number of databases searched, number of search terms) to ensure the work can be completed within the specified timeframe.

These systematic methods are becoming more common, and have some advantages, and it is therefore useful for you to know that they exist. But they take more time than is generally available for undergraduate projects (although REA might be more feasible in a postgraduate project). So, the literature reviews for projects are still usually done using methods that are somewhat less systematic (as we have described in the bulk of this chapter). But there is nothing to stop you from trying to find ways to introduce some more systematic elements to your review to help improve its quality. You can discuss this with your supervisor. Also, there are other techniques that you can use in your project to demonstrate awareness of how your own views on the topic you are researching, and your research methods, may have impacted on your project research (see the discussion of 'reflexivity' in Chapter 9 for more on this). Engaging with these will be a feasible way for you to show your awareness of these issues within your project work.

Want to know about rapid evidence assessments (RAEs) and systematic reviews?

You can find out more information about conducting RAEs and systematic reviews here:

Barends, E., Rousseau, D.M. and Briner, R.B. (eds) (2017) CEBMa Guideline for Rapid Evidence Assessments in Management and Organizations, Version 1.0. Center for Evidence Based Management, Amsterdam. Available from www.cebma.org/guidelines/

(Continued)

Denyer, D. (2014) The stages of a systematic review. Retrieved from: www.restore.ac.uk/logicof
    enquiry/logicofenquiry/gst/SR/stages/Pages/default.html
Dehkordi, A.H., Mazaheri, E., Ibrahim, H.A., Dalvand, S. and Ghanei Gheshlagh, R. (2021) How to
    write a systematic review: A narrative review. *International Journal of Preventive Medicine*,
    12, 27. https://doi.org/10.4103/ijpvm.IJPVM_60_20

Examples of REAs conducted by the UK government can be found here:

www.gov.uk/government/collections/rapid-evidence-assessments

You can also find examples of systematic reviews in psychology and related disciplines by searching a topic of your interest in PsychInfo and including 'systematic review' in the search term.

Want to know more about writing reviews?

See Chapter 10 in this volume. Also:

Fink, A. (2019). *Conducting Research Literature Reviews: From Paper to the Internet* (5th edition).
    Thousand Oaks, CA: Sage.
Shaw, R. (2019). Conducting literature reviews. In C. Sullivan and M.A. Forrester (eds), *Doing
    Qualitative Research in Psychology: A Practical Guide*. London: Sage. pp. 78–96.

Some good examples of literature reviews include:

Bloch, S. and Leydon, G. (2019). Conversation analysis and telephone helplines for health and
    illness: A narrative review. *Research on Language and Social Interaction*, 52(3), 193–211.
Deckx, L., van den Akker, M., Buntinx, F. and van Driel, M. (2018). A systematic literature
    review on the association between loneliness and coping strategies. *Psychology, Health &
    Medicine*, 23(8), 899–916.
Ong, B., Barnes, S. and Buus, N. (2020). Conversation analysis and family therapy: A narrative
    review. *Journal of Family Therapy*, 42(2), 169–203.

Conclusion

When you first set out to think through what you might examine in your project it might seem a straightforward task to review what has been done before in whatever area you are interested in. Hopefully by now you can see that it is important to be methodical in your search procedures and your analysis of prior work. Similarly, it should be apparent that when you report your literature review you should write a coherent, critical and engaging account of the field, which logically links to and provides a rationale for your research question(s). The following presents our overall top tips to summarise the process of literature reviewing and keep you focused on the most important elements of the task.

Top tips

Make your literature review excellent

1 Spend enough time developing suitable search strategies and familiarising yourself with the information systems available to you (e.g. Web of Knowledge; PsycINFO).
2 Be consistent and methodical when reading and evaluating abstracts and other summaries; this will really help you decide whether a piece of research is worth following up.
3 Don't be put off by obscure words and phrases. Familiarity with technical terms grows as you become immersed in the literature. Look up unfamiliar terms or ask your supervisor.
4 When writing your review avoid descriptively listing studies. Instead, focus on developing a critical narrative of the research.
5 Use a clear framework to structure your literature review, and explain this structure at the start so the reader knows what to expect.
6 Link the different sections and paragraphs in your review. Use brief summaries as you go along to remind the reader where you're up to and how the material fits in with your overall rationale and project aims.
7 Finish the review with a critically informed summary; sum up with a focus on the arguments you've made rather than on the material you've included.
8 End your summary by clearly stating your research question(s).

In this chapter we gave you the tools to carry out a full review of the literature for your project, and you can draw upon this at various points in the project. In the next chapter, we turn to the topic of data collection methods.

Answers to Activity 6.1

The following is a rewrite of the list-like review presented earlier in the chapter that instead combines the studies into a narrative created by the person who is writing. How similar was it to your own rewrite?

(Continued)

Research has examined the importance of mother-child interaction for children's social development. For example, a qualitative study by Anderson, Smith and Jones (1998) found that connected mother-child conversations were important for the development of children's understanding of social situations. This is consistent with the results of other studies conducted with young children (e.g. Jones and Solder, 1993; Tolstoy and Bekaerman, 2001; Zenter, 1994). The importance of mother-child talk on social functioning is also supported by a retrospective study of adults which found that higher perceived quality of maternal interactions was related to higher levels of social competence and verbal intelligence (Brightlight et al., 1999). Overall, these studies highlight that the quality of mother-child interactions and connectedness have an important influence on social functioning in both childhood and adulthood.

You should also note that this is just a small excerpt of what a review would look like - it needs further development, e.g. the addition of critical evaluation and a specific rationale for the study.

References

Barends, E., Rousseau, D.M. and Briner, R.B. (eds) (2017) *CEBMa Guideline for Rapid Evidence Assessments in Management and Organizations, Version 1.0.* Center for Evidence Based Management, Amsterdam. Available from www.cebma.org/guidelines/

Davies, P. (2003) *The Magenta Book. Guidance Notes for Policy Evaluation and Analysis* 25, Chapter 2. What do we already know? London: Cabinet Office.

Dehkordi, A.H., Mazaheri, E., Ibrahim, H.A., Dalvand, S. and Ghanei Gheshlagh, R. (2021) How to write a systematic review: A narrative review. *International Journal of Preventive Medicine*, 12, 27.

Hutchby, I. (2010) Feelings-talk and therapeutic vision in child–counsellor interaction. In H. Gardner and M.A. Forrester (eds), *Analysing Interactions in Childhood: Insights from Conversation Analysis*. Chichester: Wiley-Blackwell. pp. 146–62.

Johnson, B.T., and Eagly, A.H. (1989) Effects of involvement on persuasion: Meta-analysis. *Psychological Bulletin*, 106, 290–314.

Shaw, R. (2019) 'Conducting literature reviews', in C. Sullivan and M.A. Forrester (eds), *Doing Qualitative Research in Psychology: A Practical Guide*. London: Sage. pp. 78–96.

Tarplee, C. (1996) Working on young children's utterances: Prosodic aspects of repetition during picture labelling. In E. Couper-Kuhlen and M. Selting (eds), *Prosody in Conversation: Interactional Studies*. Cambridge: Cambridge University Press. pp. 406–435.

7
COLLECTING YOUR DATA

Siobhan Hugh-Jones and Stephen Gibson

One of the most exciting and attractive aspects of doing qualitative research is the availability of diverse and intriguing sources of data, and ways of collecting it. Yet this open-endedness can also be a hazard, particularly when researchers do not give enough attention to the relationships between what they want to know (the research questions), the best way(s) of getting data to help answer that question (data collection), how they will go about making sense of that data (data analysis) and the conclusions that can be drawn from their analysis. So, in this chapter, we help you to ask the right questions about data collection so that you can do an excellent project.

··· ···In a nutshell··· ··

Key questions about data collection

- What do I want to know? (or, what is my research question?)
- Who or what could help me answer/understand that?
- Is one source of data enough or do I need to look at others also?
- How much data should I collect?
- What equipment/resources do I need?

· ·

This chapter is structured around the following key issues:

1   Understanding the importance of epistemology and ontology: We begin by briefly reminding you of the importance of these issues, which were introduced in our discussion of the 'methodological kite' in Chapter 1. We return to them throughout this chapter in order to emphasise that remaining aware of the

assumptions you make about your data will help you to produce research of the highest quality.

2   Deciding what data to collect and how to collect it: We take you through some key decisions you'll need to make.

3   Approaches to data collection: We then spend the bulk of the chapter providing snapshots of some of the methods of data collection you might want to use and provide references to key sources for exploring these in more detail.

4   Practical issues: We finish off by dealing with a series of practical issues that you need to consider, such as recording and data storage.

Epistemological and Ontological Assumptions

Over the course of this chapter and the next, we will be outlining various ways of collecting and analysing your data. However, as we have indicated in earlier chapters, it is important to recognise at the outset that it is not always possible to simply 'mix and match' approaches to data collection and analysis. Instead, your method of data collection and your analytic approach should be consistent with each other, with the research question(s) you are addressing, and – ultimately – with the epistemological and ontological assumptions you are making about your data. Are you treating your data as a route – however partial and imperfect – to underlying 'thoughts', 'beliefs' or 'experiences'? Or are you treating your data as action-oriented accounts constructed to perform a particular function in a particular context? The various approaches to qualitative research (see Chapter 8) involve sometimes quite different assumptions about the nature of the world (ontology) and the nature of knowledge (epistemology) and these have important implications for how you view your data and its relationship with 'reality' (see Chapter 1). In this respect, there can be as much – if not more – of a divergence between different qualitative approaches as there is between qualitative and quantitative approaches.

How do I Decide What Data to Collect?

Often when we start a piece of research, we already have in mind where, or from whom, we might collect data. However, it is worth pausing at this stage to really think through whether you have thought of all possible sources of data and have decided upon the optimal data source(s). Think about the potential of various types of data to answer your research question(s), the practical access you have to either participants, or to existing data, and the time you have available (see Chapter 3 for more on these planning issues). You should also think about how you will deal with tricky issues like generalisability (see Chapter 3) when you discuss your results and whether this might impact on your data collection.

In qualitative psychology, there are relatively few dictates about what method of data collection must be used for a particular research agenda. Rather, the quality and rigour of the research is judged on the appropriateness of the data for answering the research question, which will in turn be informed by the analytic approach you intend to adopt. The best way of getting to grips with this is to read around so you can see how data collection is typically done in your chosen methodological approach. This raises the issue of the relationship between method and methodology (see Chapter 1) with the former simply referring to the way in which you collect your data (for example, interviews, focus groups, diaries), and the latter involving a broader range of decisions regarding the assumptions you will be making about your data, what sort of questions you will be asking of it and how you will analyse it. Methodology thus links your epistemological and ontological assumptions, your research question(s), and your methods of data collection and analysis (see the 'methodological kite' in Chapter 1). These need to be consistent with one another for your work to make sense and 'hang together'. In this chapter we focus on questions of method, and in the next chapter turn to questions of analysis. However, both method and analysis should be viewed within the overall framework of your methodology.

The question of how you are going to analyse your data is particularly important – as with any form of research, whether qualitative or quantitative, you must have a clear idea of how you are going to analyse your data before you collect it. Chapter 8 deals in more detail with analysis and Chapter 3 with planning.

Top tip

Flexible research questions

Don't worry too much if you find yourself tweaking your research question as data collection progresses. As long as the relationship between them remains consistent, you're okay (see Chapter 2 for more on research questions).

In a nutshell

Collection or generation?

Although we've followed convention and called this chapter 'Collecting your data', we might instead have called it 'Generating your data'. This is because many qualitative researchers emphasise that the idea of data existing independently of our research is problematic (see, for example, Speer, 2002). Rather than being something already in existence that we collect, we might therefore think of data as being created or generated by our research activity. You might want to consider what this means in relation to your choice of language when writing up your research.

Approaches to Data Collection

In this section, we present overviews of eight of the most widely used approaches to data collection for qualitative projects in psychology: semi-structured interviews, narrative interviews, focus groups, diaries, naturalistic data, archival data, Internet data and visual data. We provide snapshots of these approaches, highlighting their key features and indicating useful resources where you can find fresh ideas and more details on how to use these methods. We also outline some key points about mixing methods.

Semi-structured interviews

Semi-structured interviews (SSIs) are a particularly popular form of data collection in qualitative research for many reasons. SSIs are popular because interviews are:

- relatively inexpensive and easy to arrange;
- flexible, and can be used to address almost any subject matter;
- able to generate rich data that is suitable for different forms of analysis.

In addition, for many people in the West, interviews are a familiar form of interaction (Atkinson and Silverman, 1997), although you should think about the cultural appropriateness of your method. For instance, Lawrence (2022) notes the particular importance of the concept of *guanxi* (a term denoting the harmonious quality of interpersonal relationships) in establishing trust and rapport with her participants from China.

SSIs involve direct questions but with freedom for either the interviewer or interviewee to raise issues not previously anticipated or to dismiss questions deemed less relevant to particular participants. This allows a balance in the process between researcher-led questions (based on topics relevant to theory) and participant-led issues (that may help the researcher identify important issues that they would not otherwise have considered).

Interviewers and interviewees draw upon everyday conversational skills during interviewing (Hester and Francis, 1994), but the SSI is a particular type of conversation that is driven by a research agenda and that involves the assumption that the interviewee will disclose things while the interviewer does not (see Madill, 2011). Interviews are usually recorded and transcribed for analysis (see below and Chapter 8 for more on transcription).

Importantly, there are some conceptual differences in the ways that SSIs can be understood. These relate to debates on ontology, epistemology, context, co-construction and autobiographical memory (for example, Potter and Hepburn, 2005; Thomsen and Brinkman, 2009). For example, the SSI can be viewed as a means to access and explore subjective experience (e.g. Horner et al., 2022), as a co-constructed version of reality (e.g. Hugh-Jones et al., 2021) or as a discursive performance (King and Hugh-Jones, 2019). To be able to use SSIs competently you will need to have an understanding of where your research fits into these debates. If you're not sure turn to Chapter 1, and also speak to your supervisor.

Interview research begins with a set of questions and probes (called an interview schedule or guide) that relate to your research question in a way that bears your intended method of analysis in mind. Interview questions can be difficult to produce, particularly as the use of leading and directive questions, for example, should be avoided (see Madill, 2023, for interview techniques and useful examples). Conducting the interview is always harder than novice researchers anticipate, and the importance of piloting, practice and reflecting on completed interviews should not be underestimated. Additionally, in recent years, researchers have increasingly turned to online video-conferencing tools (e.g. Zoom) as a means through which to conduct semi-structured interviews (see the section Internet data below, and Chapter 4).

Top tip

Transcribe your pilot

Enhance your interviewing skills – and your analysis – by taking time to conduct and transcribe a pilot interview before embarking on your main round of interviewing. Examine the transcript to see how your role as the interviewer has shaped and constrained the sorts of responses provided by the participant, as well as to get a sense for which questions and prompts seemed to work and which didn't. This can form a crucial part of your approach to reflexivity (see Chapter 9 for more on reflexivity, and Chapter 5 for an example of how a pilot interview allowed a student, 'Suzy', to develop her research).

Want to know more about semi-structured interviews?

King, N. and Hugh-Jones, S. (2019) The interview in qualitative research. In C. Sullivan and M.A. Forrester (eds), *Doing Qualitative Research in Psychology: A Practical Guide* (2nd edn). London: Sage. pp. 121–44.

King, N., Horrocks, C. and Brooks, J. (2019) *Interviews in Qualitative Research* (2nd edn). London: Sage.

Brinkmann, S. and Kvale, S. (2015) *InterViews: Learning the Craft of Qualitative Research Interviewing* (3rd edn). London: Sage.

Madill, A. (2023) Interviews and interviewing techniques. In A.T. Panter (ed.), *APA Handbook of Research Methods in Psychology*. Washington, DC: APA.

Narrative interviews

Narrative interviews are associated with an approach to psychology which emerged following a 'turn to narrative' in the mid-1980s. Narrative psychologists have argued that psychology should explore the 'story' as a metaphor for human experience (instead of, for example, humans as information processors; Sarbin, 1986). Although there are divergent forms of narrative psychology, they share an understanding that stories play a crucial role in almost every human activity because as we tell stories about ourselves, we make sense of our experiences and our lives.

··· ···In a nutshell··· ··

The function of narratives

Narratives:

- organise and structure action and experience;
- are central in the formation, maintenance, development and renegotiation of identity.

···

Although narratives can be found within many types of data collection (such as interviews, focus groups and diaries), narrative psychology has been developed to study narrative form and function in its own right (Hiles et al., 2017). Narrative approaches can be used to examine specific events or life histories, and the construction of meaning-making, self and identity within them (see the dedicated journal *Narrative Inquiry* for examples).

Although there are many ways to explore narratives (such as in diaries or autobiographies), the life-history narrative interview is particularly prominent, aiming to elicit a detailed narrative from the participant (McAdams, 1993). It explores seven areas: i) life chapters (assigned and described by the participant), ii) key events/nuclear episodes (for example, peak experiences, earliest memories and turning points, and their meaning), iii) significant people and their impact, iv) future script (goals, dreams, plans), v) stresses and problems, vi) personal ideology (fundamental beliefs and values) and vii) life theme(s).

Life-history interviews often begin with a single question designed to elicit narratives. For example, in a study of women's experiences of anorexia nervosa, O'Shaughnessy et al. (2013: 47) used the following question:

> I am interested in hearing about the life experiences of women living with anorexia. I would like you to tell me the story of your life, all the events and experiences which are important to you; start wherever you like. Please take as much time as you need, I'll listen and I won't interrupt.

The researchers then followed up on these interviews with a second, semi-structured interview with each participant, enabling them to explore particular aspects of the narrative in more detail, and clarify any areas where further detail was required.

Want to know more about narrative interviews?

Andrews, M., Squire, C. and Tamboukou, M. (eds) (2013) *Doing narrative research* (2nd edn) London: Sage.

Hollway, W. and Jefferson, T. (2013) *Doing Qualitative Research Differently: A Psychosocial Approach* (2nd edn). London: Sage.

McAdams, D.P., Josselson, R. and Lieblich, A. (eds) (2006) *Identity and Story: Creating Self in Narrative*. Washington, DC: APA.

Focus groups

Focus groups typically involve 6–10 participants talking about a particular phenomenon (for example, neighbourhood crime) or shared experience (for example, marriage in later life). Due to the semi-public nature of focus groups, overtly sensitive and private subject matter are not always appropriate for focus group research.

Focus groups are not one-to-one interviews with many people, but function to promote and encourage collaborative responses. Often, hearing other people's accounts, experiences or opinions can prompt and help others to reflect on, and articulate, their own perspective. Focus groups can therefore offer something more than what we glean in individual interviews (see, for example, Flowers et al., 2000). Focus groups are therefore often used to examine group interaction itself (Puchta and Potter, 2004), and can also be used to explore participants' perspectives, or their responses to an intervention or to your research findings. As well as being a sole method to explore an issue, focus groups can also be used to identify a range of prominent issues that can then be further examined with different methods.

As the group dynamic is fundamental in focus groups, they need to be planned (in relation to the selection of participants and questions, for example) so that the potential for dialogue and debate is enhanced. For this reason, focus groups typically feature participants deemed to be similar on some key variable(s) (for example, status, gender or ethnicity), but who are not so homogeneous that they have no difference of opinion or experience. Focus-group participants are not usually known to each other, and – to encourage them to speak freely – ideally will not be likely to meet again in the future. In focus groups the interviewer is known as the moderator and their role is to facilitate the group's discussion, and to optimise each participant's potential for contribution; this also means there is less researcher control than there may be in other methods.

─Top tip─

Encouraging interaction

One of the main advantages of focus groups over one-on-one interviews is that they allow for interaction between participants. You therefore need to ensure that the way in which you run your focus group encourages your participants to talk to each other, rather than simply taking it in turns to talk to you. To facilitate this, it can be useful to explicitly state in your introduction to the focus group that you value participants discussing issues with each other. Running one or two pilot focus groups will also help you get a feel for how best to facilitate this process.

Thematic analysis and discourse analysis (DA) can easily be applied to focus group data, and interpretative phenomenological analysis (IPA) has also been used with focus group data (see Palmer et al., 2010). Conversation analysis (CA) can, in principle, be used to analyse focus groups as well, although given CA's interest in analysing the structure of interaction, it would be best to consider it only when you are interested in how focus groups themselves work (as opposed to when you are using focus groups to find out about some other topic). Methods of analysis are discussed in Chapter 8.

─Want to know more about focus groups?─

Barbour, R. (2018) *Doing Focus Groups* (2nd edn). London: Sage.
Krueger, R.A. and Casey, M.A. (2015) *Focus groups: A Practical Guide for Applied Research* (5th edn). London: Sage.
Morgan, D. (2018) *Basic and Advanced Focus Groups*. London: Sage.

Diary methods

Diary methods have been prominent in recording patient experiences in health research since the 1930s and are now popular across a range of sub-fields of psychology. Diary methods are particularly attractive to those interested in daily experience because they allow sensations, thoughts and emotions to be recorded with little retrospection, and are relatively unobtrusive in individuals' natural settings (Bolger et al., 2003). Furthermore, the flexibility of diary methods allows participants to be given a choice in how best to capture their experiences, such as in Scott et al.'s (2021) study of adolescents' experience of the Covid-19 pandemic, in which participants recorded their diary entries using various combinations of audio and video recordings, text, email, photos and social media messages. Given the range of possible objectives of diary-based studies, diary data can be subjected to a range of analytic methods, including DA, IPA and narrative analysis.

Diary records can either be interval-contingent (at specified times) or event-contingent (following certain events, which can be conceptualised as objective and/or subjective, such as having anxious thoughts or feelings). Diary studies can also be used as a preliminary stage of data collection to inform subsequent stages, for example, in the development of interview schedules (see Carter, 2002). Reporting periods typically last between one day and four weeks (Keleher and Verrinder, 2003).

Limitations of (solicited) diary methods include high rates of attrition (Kaun, 2010) and the reliance on participants to complete entries; there is thus a need to balance immediacy of recordings with the need to avoid being overly intrusive. In addition, participants may not complete entries in the level of detail anticipated by researchers (although see Green et al., 2006), and the extent of entries can vary considerably from participant to participant (Bolger et al., 2003).

Top tip

Think about the audience

Whether you use solicited or unsolicited diary data, remember that it is always written to someone (even if only to the self). Consider carefully how this may shape the resulting diary entries, bearing in mind your methodological approach.

Completing diary entries may also impact upon the thoughts and feelings being reported (Day and Thatcher, 2009) or upon future behaviour or diary entries (Finley, 2010; Merrilees et al., 2008). This is not necessarily problematic (diary keeping can be a positive experience for participants (Peel et al., 2006), but you should show awareness of these complexities in your use of diary data and the claims you make about it in your analysis. See Chapter 4 for more on ethics and the effects on participants, and Chapter 5 for more on relationships with participants.

Until relatively recently, participants would have completed diary entries in paper-and-pen form, but there are now a range of technological tools available that enable audio (e.g. Cottingham and Erickson, 2020; Monrouxe, 2009), video (Taylor et al., 2019), online and app-based methods (Rudrum et al., 2022) for recording participants' diary entries. Ethical issues related to online diaries include identifying what are public and private domains, data storage and the fact that participants may disclose more online than they might do in other contexts (Kaun, 2010). See Chapter 4 for more discussion of ethical issues and online settings.

Want to know more about diaries?

Bartlett, R. and Milligan, C. (2021) *Diary Method*. London: Bloomsbury.

Bolger, N., Davis, A. and Rafaeli, E. (2003) Diary methods: Capturing life as it is lived. *Annual Review of Psychology*, 54, 579–616.

Hyers, L. L. (2018) *Diary Methods*. Oxford: Oxford University Press.

Kaun, A. (2010) Open-ended online diaries: Capturing life as it is narrated. *International Journal of Qualitative Methods*, 9, 133–148. http://ejournals.library.ualberta.ca/index.php/IJQM/article/view/7165/7022

Naturalistic data

Data that exist independently of the researcher can be described as naturalistic, or naturally occurring. As used in CA and DA, it typically refers to talk-in-interaction, although other types of data can be naturalistic in form (for example, diaries, media, Internet data).

· · · · ·· **In a nutshell** ·

Identifying naturally occurring data

Potter (2004) suggested the 'dead social scientist test' to discern whether data is naturalistic; the test involves asking 'if the researcher got run over on the way to the university that morning, would the interaction nevertheless have taken place, and in the way that it did?' (p. 612). This contrasts with data that has come into being only because of the active involvement of the researcher (as in interviews and focus groups).

· ·

There has been lively debate around the nature and importance of naturalistic data, and it is sometimes viewed as a much-needed antidote to limitations that are inherent in interview research, such as lack of attention to context and the impact of the inter-viewer. Potter and Hepburn (2005) argue that naturalistic data has several commendable features:

- It can represent live interaction and experience, reducing the reliance on retrospective accounts.
- It reflects the participants' priorities more than the researcher's and avoids 'flooding' participant accounts with the concerns of the researcher.
- It avoids positioning participants as disinterested experts on their own and others' practices and thoughts.

- Problematic inferences about the data are avoided as the topic itself is studied directly.
- It may bring up novel insights that were beyond the boundaries set by the researcher.

In response to calls for more (or exclusive) reliance on naturally occurring data, it has been argued that interviews are important instances of interaction in their own right and can be used in ways that acknowledge that they are not simplistic reflections of 'reality' (Speer, 2002: 512). Furthermore, it is important to remember that even naturalistic talk always has to be selected, recorded, transcribed and processed by the researcher. Indeed, some authors have questioned whether the researcher can ever be removed from any data (Ashmore and Reed, 2000). At the very least, dealing with naturalistic talk must involve a sensitivity to who is talking and why, and to what might be at stake in the interaction.

Conversation and discourse analysts have conducted research on data from a variety of naturalistic settings, including telephone conversations (Humă et al., 2019), family mealtime talk (Hepburn, 2020), workplace meetings (Smart and Auburn, 2018), police interrogations (Jol and Stommel, 2021), meetings between politicians and members of the public (Hofstetter and Stokoe, 2018) and therapy sessions (Peräkylä et al., 2008). A range of techniques have been developed to study online interactions (Meredith et al., 2021), such as those conducted via social media (Meredith, 2016), video calling platforms (e.g. Licoppe and Morel, 2012) and mobile phones (Hutchby and Barnett, 2005).

As with all methods of data collection, there are ethical considerations specific to the collection of naturalistic data, particularly around informed consent. This may apply even if the data are publicly available, given that the originator of the data may not have had an opportunity to consent. See the British Psychological Society's (2021a) Code of Human Research Ethics, and Chapter 4, for more on these issues.

Want to know more about naturalistic data?

Potter, J. and Hepburn, A. (2005) Qualitative interviews in psychology: Problems and possibilities. *Qualitative Research in Psychology*, 2, 281-307. (Also see the commentaries published in response to this.)

Rapley, T. (2018) *Doing Conversation, Discourse and Document Analysis* (2nd edn). London: Sage.

Wiggins, S. (2017) *Discursive Psychology: Theory, Method and Applications*. London: Sage.

Archival data

When academics carry out a research study, there is often an expectation that the data generated will be deposited in an archive on completion of the study. This has become more prevalent in the last decade, as psychology and other disciplines have sought to address concerns over the transparency and trustworthiness of their research practices (Branney et al., 2019). While it is still less common to archive qualitative data than quantitative data, there is nevertheless a growing body of publicly available data that provides a range of fascinating opportunities for student research projects.

Broadly speaking, there are four principal ways in which data are archived: 1) global repositories such as the Open Science Framework (https://osf.io), which any researcher can register with to deposit data (and a range of other material from research projects); 2) national repositories such as the UK Data Service (https://ukdataservice.ac.uk), which maintains archives from a range of projects funded by the UK research councils; 3) journal websites, which often include data from published papers as part of a collection of online supplementary material (e.g. the audio files used in Shaw and Kitzinger's [2012] conversation analytic study of a home birth helpline are available by clicking on the 'supplemental' tab on the online version of the article); 4) institutional repositories operated by individual universities (e.g. see Murray's [2022] interview transcripts on the Open University's research portal). The wealth of archived data provides a rich resource for researchers to carry out secondary analysis (Largan and Morris, 2019).

One of the key advantages of archival data is that it can enable your investigation to take on a historical perspective (Tileagă and Byford, 2017). As an example, the last decade has seen a number of studies explore various aspects of Stanley Milgram's (1974) obedience experiments by drawing on archived material held at Yale University's Manuscripts and Archives Service, which houses the Stanley Milgram Papers collection. Oppenheimer (2015) used the notes and sketches from the archive to explore how Milgram designed his shock machine. Oppenheimer highlights the key role of the machine's unusual layout in eliciting obedience from participants. In a slightly different vein, several researchers (e.g. Gibson, 2013; Hollander, 2015; Kaposi, 2020) have used recordings and transcripts of the obedience experiments to explore *how* the experiments worked as social interactions.

Top tips

Archival data

- Make sure you're aware of the permissions required - the researcher who collected the data may need to give their approval, or the participants may need to be contacted to give additional consent (see Chapter 4). The data may also be protected by copyright. The archive holding the data will be able to tell you this information and assist you in securing relevant permissions.
- Be aware of the limitations of the data - for example, you may have access to interview transcripts but not to the audio recordings. More generally, make sure you remain aware that you don't have access to the 'insider' knowledge about a dataset that one has when analysing one's own data.

- Make sure you consider the purpose for which the data were originally collected – this forms a key part of a reflexive approach to archival data (see Chapter 9 for more on reflexivity).
- Make sure you're familiar with your department's regulations on the use of archival data in student projects. Your supervisor will be able to advise on this.

Want to know more about archival data?

Corti, L. and Thompson, P. (2004) Secondary analysis of archived data. In C. Seale, G. Gobo, J.F. Gubrium and D. Silverman (eds), *Qualitative Research Practice*. London: Sage. pp. 327–43.

Fielding, N. (2004). Getting the most from archived qualitative data: Epistemological, practical and professional obstacles. *International Journal of Social Research Methodology*, 7, 97–104.

Largan, C. and Morris, T. (2019) *Qualitative Secondary Research: A Step-by-Step Guide*. London: Sage.

Parry, O. and Mauthner, N. (2004) Whose data are they anyway? Practical, legal and ethical issues in archiving qualitative research data. *Sociology*, 38, 139–52.

Ruggiano, N. and Perry, T.E. (2019) Conducting secondary analysis of qualitative data: Should we, can we, and how? *Qualitative Social Work*, 18, 81–97.

Internet data

The rapid development of online technology, such as social media, video conferencing platforms and smartphones, has created a range of opportunities for qualitative researchers. These technologies are an important focus for psychological enquiry because many aspects of our lives, especially in the industrialised West, are mediated by smart technology of one kind or another. This has psychological implications (e.g. how we manage our online identities and interactions), and thus is an important object of study in its own right. However, the pervasiveness of this technology also creates opportunities for researchers who are interested in a whole range of topics to reach a wider sample of participants who may otherwise be hard to reach.

·····In a nutshell·····

Internet data

Internet data suitable for qualitative analysis can be divided into two types:

- Solicited data: Online interviews, focus groups, diaries and other forms of data collection that involve the researcher actively seeking to engage with participants for the purposes of data collection.

(Continued)

- Unsolicited data: The collection of pre-existing material, such as social media posts, YouTube videos, blogs or other forms of online content that exist regardless of their use as data (see also the section 'Naturalistic data' above).

. . . .

Online interviews and focus groups have become particularly common in recent years as a result of the Covid-19 pandemic, which meant that researchers had no choice but to use online platforms such as Zoom, Teams and Skype if they wanted to continue their work during the various 'lockdowns' imposed by governments around the world in 2020–21 (e.g. Carter et al., 2021; Lobe et al., 2020). Online interviewing can be used for:

- accessing participants unable to attend a face-to-face interview;
- where people may feel uncomfortable sharing their perspectives on sensitive matters in a face-to-face setting (see, for example, Madill et al., 2023);
- when Internet activity is itself the focus of your enquiry (for example, in understanding cyber sub-cultures, see Williams, 2006).

Considerable thought must be given, though, to the many ethical (see Chapter 4) and practical (see Chapter 3) issues surrounding online interviewing. For example, it will be important to ensure that participants' technical set-up (e.g. Internet connection, software, webcam) is adequate for the purposes of the research; and consideration should be given to the security of any data that may be stored on third-party servers (see British Psychological Society, 2021b; Lobe et al., 2020). Moreover, despite the increasing pervasiveness of these technologies in our lives, they will be less appropriate for accessing participants who are less likely to have ready access to, or familiarity with, these technologies.

Pre-existing Internet data sources suitable for qualitative analysis are extensive, and include web pages themselves, blogs, discussion forums, video-sharing sites (e.g. YouTube) and other forms of social media. Qualitative researchers have analysed unsolicited Internet data to explore a range of topics, such as racism (Rowe and Goodman, 2014), domestic abuse (Leitão, 2021), immigration (Gibson et al., 2018), mental health (Dempsey et al., 2022), gender (Nesbitt-Larking, 2022) and autism (Angulo-Jiménez and DeThorne, 2019).

Use of pre-existing Internet data requires considerable thought around methods of sampling (see Chapter 3). For instance, will you select data at random from a defined set or do you have specific criteria for selecting data? Similarly, it is important to consider what type of – and how much – data you will include and exclude (see Smedley and Coulson, 2021, for useful advice). Ethical issues are also prominent with the use of pre-existing Internet data, particularly around what constitutes public or private domains (see Chapter 4; British Psychological Society, 2021b; Burles and Bally, 2018; Roberts, 2015).

─Want to know more about Internet data?─

Bouvier, G. and Rasmussen, J. (2022) *Qualitative Research Using Social Media*. Abingdon: Routledge.

Coulson, N. (2015) *Online Research Methods For Psychologists*. London: Palgrave.

Morison, T., Farren Gibson, A., Wigginton, B. & Crabb, S. (2015) Online research methods in psychology: Methodological opportunities for critical qualitative research. Special issue of *Qualitative Research in Psychology*, 12(3).

Salmons, J.E. (2022) *Doing Qualitative Research Online* (2nd ed.). London: Sage.

Visual data

Since the 'turn to language' in the 1970s and 1980s (Reavey and Johnson, 2017), qualitative researchers in psychology have largely been concerned with talk or text as the primary means of conveying or constructing meaning. Yet communication is multi-modal – not only do people speak, but they experience and view their world in material (or cyber) space.

When adopting the definition of 'discourse' as being 'wherever there is meaning' (Parker, 1999: 1), it is apparent that analysis of data in other modalities (most commonly visual and auditory data) can constitute a valuable contribution to our understanding of psychological and social phenomena (Lynn and Lea, 2005). Moving beyond the spoken or written word may involve a particularly ethical and inclusive form of data collection, especially where articulation on the topic may be difficult for participants or researchers (see, for example, Duara et al., 2018; Liebenberg, 2009; Pini et al., 2018; Wright et al., 2010).

To date, where qualitative researchers in psychology have considered non-textual forms of data, they have focused mostly on visual data. Visual data can be collected in a range of ways; researchers can:

- solicit visual data from participants, using drawings, maps, performance, video diaries, photo-elicitation or photovoice (e.g. Bates et al., 2017; Donnelly et al., 2021; McGrath et al., 2020; Melvin et al., 2021);
- examine unsolicited/pre-existing data, such as photographs, books, paintings, film/video, graffiti, advertisements (e.g. Byford, 2018; Kilby and Lennon, 2018; Pownall et al., 2022);
- combine data from varying modalities (such as Anderson's (2004) 'walking interview' and Guijarro and Sanz's (2008) study of text and imagery in children's books).

---Top tips---

Visual data

If you are considering using visual data, ask yourself these important questions:

- What role will it play in your research; for example, will it be used to facilitate discussion and/or will it be analysed in its own right?
- Will you carry out analysis alone or will it be a collaborative venture with your participants?

In addition, it is worth bearing in mind that there are some ethical issues (see Chapter 4) which are particularly relevant to visual data. Ethical guidance on the use of visual data is likely to be harder to find than guidance on other methods. For example, in the UK, the BPS Code of Human Research Ethics (2021a) does not offer extensive guidance on the collection or use of visual data, other than stating that audio, video or photographic recordings of participants can only be done with their permission. However, you will need to consider issues around privacy, unintended identification of others, re-presentation and ownership of the images (see Warr et al., 2016).

---Want to know more about visual data?---

Reavey, P. (ed.) (2021) *A Handbook of Visual Methods in Psychology: Using and Interpreting Images in Qualitative Research* (2nd edn). London: Routledge.

Reavey, P. and Johnson, K. (2017) Visual approaches: Using and interpreting images. In C. Willig and W. Stainton-Rogers (eds), *The Sage Handbook of Qualitative Research in Psychology* (2nd edn) (pp. 354-73). London: Sage.

Warr, D., Guillemin, M., Cox, S. and Waycott, J. (eds) (2016) *Ethics and Visual Research Methods: Theory, Methodology and Practice*. New York: Palgrave Macmillan.

Mixing Methods

Having introduced a range of methods of data collection, it is important to highlight that these need not necessarily be thought of as mutually exclusive alternatives but can be combined to form a mixed methods approach. Often when researchers talk about mixed methods they mean the use of qualitative and quantitative methods in the same project, although it is just as possible to use different qualitative methods together. One of the key advantages of mixing methods is to enable you to gather data from a range of different sources and to consider how it does, or does not, converge – something known as *triangulation*.

·······In a nutshell···

Triangulation

Triangulation refers to the combined use of different datasets collected by more than one method or from different participant groups. Triangulation can be thought of as a form of quality check on your data; for example, does data from different methods point to similar findings? However, how you think about triangulation does depend on the epistemological and ontological features of your research (see Madill et al., 2000).

··

Activity 7.1

The challenges of triangulation

Consider the following research scenario. How might you respond to these challenges?

A researcher is interested in the ways that primary school classroom teaching assistants promote the social and emotional development of children with particular needs. Schools, and individual assistants, have agreed to take part on the basis that multiple data sources will be examined, including interview data from parents, pupils and other staff. However, some classroom assistants are concerned that the study might not adequately capture the depth of their engagement with pupils as this develops over long periods of time. They are also concerned that the study might not identify what value they bring to pupils, particularly as no objective measures of academic development are being used.

How might a researcher manage potentially competing interests of different participants in a way that does not diminish the benefits of triangulation? Some suggested solutions to this problem are identified at the end of the chapter.

Regardless of whether you mix different methods of qualitative data collection, or qualitative and quantitative methods, the crucial point is to be consistent in the sorts of assumptions you make about your data. So, although you can relatively easily mix *methods* of data collection, mixing methodologies is more challenging for the novice researcher, though it is possible (Frost, 2021). If you are planning to mix methods, the recommendation is to have a clear understanding of the ontological and epistemological frameworks that underlie the methods you're using and aim for consistency throughout the project. Remember that epistemological and ontological coherence is one of the hallmarks of an excellent qualitative study. If you're not sure what we mean by this, see Chapter 1 for further discussion on ontology and epistemology, and Chapter 9 on quality criteria.

―――― Cautionary tale ――――――――――――――――――――――――――――――

Methodological mix-ups

Karen was interested in finding out about people's attitudes to the prison system. She initially planned to use a questionnaire with standard Likert response scales in order to determine people's attitudes on a number of relevant issues. She then intended to conduct follow-up interviews with a small number of participants and analyse them using discourse analysis in order to see if people with different types of attitudes constructed the prison system in different ways. However, after reading around discourse analysis (see Chapter 8) and discussing her ideas with her supervisor, she realised that her ideas were problematic insofar as discourse analysis challenges the whole idea of people having identifiable 'attitudes' as conventionally understood. Once she grasped this, she adapted the study to use discourse analysis to show how even people with apparently strong attitudes towards the prison system may display the sorts of variability in their discourse that analysts such as Potter and Wetherell (1987) and Billig (1989) have identified.

The key lessons from this tale: Read up on your chosen approaches in advance, and always discuss your ideas with your supervisor.

―――― Want to know more about mixing methods? ――――――――――――――

Flick, U. (2018). *Doing Triangulation and Mixed Methods*. London: Sage.

Todd, Z., Nerlich, B., McKeown, S. and Clarke, D.D. (2004). *Mixing Methods in Psychology: The Integration of Qualitative and Quantitative Methods in Theory and Practice*. Hove: Psychology Press.

Yardley, L. and Bishop, F.L. (2017). Mixing qualitative and quantitative methods: A pragmatic approach. In C. Willig and W. Stainton-Rogers (eds), *The Sage Handbook of Qualitative Research in Psychology*. London: Sage. pp. 398–414.

Practical Issues in Data Collection

How much data do I need?

Students frequently ask this question, but it is a tricky one to answer. There are no hard-and-fast rules, and it is crucial that you are guided by your supervisor who will be able to tailor advice to your specific project. As a general rule, fewer participants are involved in qualitative projects than would be in experimental or survey studies. This is because qualitative studies typically collect more data from individual participants. Having said that, some forms of qualitative data collection would challenge the notion that research involves 'participants' at all, at least in the conventional sense of that term. If you are collecting data from social media or other Internet or media-based sources, in what sense can we talk about a specific number of participants? Far better, therefore, to think in terms simply of the *amount of* data. This will also depend on the particular approach you take, and of course you will need to consider what is feasible to do in the time allocated to your project. It might also be useful to draw on specific guidelines concerning matters such as saturation (Guest et al., 2006), the idea that you know when you have collected enough data when no new material of analytic interest appears; or information power (Malterud et al., 2016), the idea that the greater the information gathered from each individual participant, the fewer participants you need in total. All of these issues need to be fully discussed with your supervisor. As a starting point, however, we offer the general guidelines below for final year undergraduate projects, based on the recommendations of Gough et al. (2003).

·····In a nutshell···

How much data do I need?

Method of analysis:	Recommended (minimum) hours of data:
Thematic analysis	5 hours (inc. pilot work)
IPA	5 hours (inc. pilot work)
Grounded theory	5 hours (inc. pilot work)
Conversation analysis	1-2 hours
Discourse analysis	3-4 hours
Narrative analysis	3-4 hours

Adapted from Gough et al. (2003: 12)

So, if you're conducting interviews that each last around an hour, you would look to collect data from five participants for thematic analysis, IPA and grounded theory, and three or four for narrative and discourse analysis (see Chapter 8 for more on these analysis methods). It is worth noting that although the difference between undergraduate and postgraduate research is more about the conceptual level of the work than the size of the dataset, it is also likely that postgraduate research would require more data than the minimum figures given here.

If your data consist of written documents (such as media reports, diary methods or Internet discussion forums) then you will need to adapt these guidelines somewhat. In terms of the extent of printed material, five hours' worth of interview transcript could run to something like 100–25 pages of A4 paper (single-line spacing, 12-point font size). This should give you a rough idea of how much data from written documents would be roughly equivalent. However, if you are using unsolicited data from the

Internet (for example, discussion forums), then given that you don't need to recruit participants, conduct interviews and then transcribe them, it is reasonable to assume that you should be analysing a more extensive dataset. Again, your supervisor should be in a position to advise you on what is likely to work best in your specific project.

Recording

If you are using interviews, focus groups or want to analyse 'naturalistic' conversational data (see above), then you will need to make recordings using either audio or video technology. Audio recording is easy and relatively cheap, with many researchers opting to use a mobile phone or similar device to capture audio, although you should check with your institution's ethics guidelines to ensure that you are abiding by any requirements concerning secure data storage.

Top tip

Know your device!

Always make sure you know how your recording device works, and that it is fully charged before use. This sounds obvious, but it is easy to forget, and you will kick yourself if you lose data simply because you can't record it. Technical problems do happen, but you can prepare for them - if possible, you could even take a spare recording device with you in case one doesn't work. Check your institution's rules about using your own device to record.

If you are using Internet or social media data, you should make sure that you save copies of material you want to analyse. Because of the rapidly changing nature of online material, it can be useful to set a particular date and time on which to sample your materials and save them to your device. Make sure that you then use the stored data rather than returning to the website/social media feed, as the material on it might have changed.

Cautionary tale

The disappearing webpage

Umit was interested in the way in which fans of a television science fiction programme, *Farscape*, displayed their identity as fans of the show, and how they defined what counted as committed or 'genuine' fan behaviour. He planned to use data from an Internet discussion forum devoted to discussion amongst *Farscape* fans, and he spent quite a bit of time reading around topics such as identity, as well as methodological literature on discourse analysis - the approach he was planning to use. However, he didn't print out or save copies of the actual discussions themselves when he first decided to pursue the project, assuming that they would be available online when he came to do his analysis. When he returned to the website several weeks later he found that the site was no longer online. The lesson here is to be aware that data on the Internet can disappear as quickly as it can appear, so make sure you save a copy of any webpages you think might be useful as data.

Transcription

If you are using audio or video data then you will need to transcribe your data. Although at first glance it might seem that transcription is a routine technical matter, it is actually better thought of as a preliminary part of the analysis. Transcription is theory-laden and the way in which you transcribe your data reflects a range of ontological and epistemological assumptions (see Chapter 1). For this reason we deal with it more extensively in Chapter 8 (where you will also find some useful references on transcription), but note here that there are some concrete practical tips that can simplify the process of transcription.

Top tips

Transcription practicalities

- The better the sound quality of your data the easier it will be to transcribe. Try to bear this in mind when selecting recording equipment and arranging locations for interviews or focus groups.
- Use a foot pedal for transcription - this allows you to control the playback of your recording using a foot pedal which connects to your computer to allow you to transcribe digital sound files using a word processing programme. Ask your departmental technician if you have access to one.
- Allow plenty of time for transcription. For a relatively basic transcription you will probably need around five or six hours to transcribe every hour of recorded data. For a more detailed transcription (as used in conversation analysis and some forms of discourse analysis) it might be closer to 20 hours!

Storing

An issue which is sometimes neglected is how you store your data. It is vitally important that participants' data is stored securely in accordance with relevant legal frameworks, and in accordance with your institution's own requirements. In the UK and many other

European countries, the General Data Protection Regulation (GDPR) applies, and data which might be used to identify participants should not be stored in a way that contravenes this regulation.

Top tips

Data storage and data protection

- Store data that might be used to identify participants securely.
- Don't retain data that might be used to identify participants longer than strictly necessary for your project. Indicate on your consent form how long information will be retained, and after this date destroy it.
- Anonymised data can be retained. In principle, this could be indefinite if you were depositing your data in a repository (see above), though this is not typically expected for student projects. The most important consideration is that retention of any data should be in line with your university's policies, and should always be on the basis of informed consent from your participants.
- Check the relevant legal framework in your country. You should have someone at your university who can advise you – in the UK, institutions should have data protection officers, and information on ethics and data protection should be provided as part of your dissertation course handbook (or a similar document). If in doubt, ask your supervisor.

Data protection and data security are discussed further in Chapter 4.

Note also that the issue of how you store your data is more than simply a matter of data protection. Organising and managing your data effectively will help you to conduct your analysis much more effectively and make it far simpler when it comes to selecting material to include in your write-up.

Want to know more about data storage?

Howitt, D. (2019). *Introduction to Qualitative Research Methods in Psychology: Putting Theory into Practice* (4th edn). Harlow: Pearson. [Chapter 17 discusses these issues in the context of research ethics.]

The UK Data Service website has a useful guide to the key issues of data protection for social researchers in the UK: https://ukdataservice.ac.uk/learning-hub/research-data-management/data-protection/data-protection-legislation/data-protection-act-and-gdpr/

Conclusion

In this chapter we have introduced some of the major considerations around data collection. To conclude, let us return to the key questions we posed at the beginning of the chapter to show you how we have addressed them:

- What do I want to know? (or, what is my research question?)

  We have seen how your method of data collection should enable you to answer your research question, as well as being consistent with the other key elements of your methodology – your epistemological and ontological position, and your analytic approach.

- Who or what could help me answer/understand that?

  You should now appreciate that the range of potential data sources in qualitative research are multiple. Interviews are still the most common method of data collection, but the past couple of decades have seen an explosion in the use of online data in particular, as well as other sources, such as visual and archival data.

- Is one source of data enough or do I need to look at others also?

  For many projects, one is likely to be ideal; however, we have seen that it is perfectly possible for student projects to combine data from different sources (and to combine qualitative and quantitative data), provided that they don't lead you into epistemological confusions!

- How much data should I collect?

  We've seen how different amounts of data may be appropriate for different qualitative approaches, and emphasised the importance of discussing this issue in detail with your supervisor.

- What equipment/resources do I need?

  Recording and transcription equipment are the two most common pieces of kit needed by students doing qualitative projects. The best advice is to think about this early and plan ahead – you don't want to leave it too late and find that all the equipment in your department has been booked out by other students! For more on planning see Chapter 3.

- How am I going to analyse my data?

  You'll by now appreciate that how you collect your data depends in large part upon how you plan to analyse it, and in the next chapter we'll take you through a range of approaches to analysis.

──Answers to Activity 7.1──

This is a complex problem, and not one an undergraduate student is likely to encounter. However, it shows how tricky it can be to triangulate in qualitative research, especially when participants are feeling anxious about what the study might mean for them. In this scenario, it might work to interview classroom assistants first, and have them involved in the design of other data collection methods to be used in the study. This would capitalise on their insider knowledge of classrooms and pupils, and might generate some new ways of capturing the impact that they have with particular children.

References

Anderson, J. (2004) Talking whilst walking: A geographical archaeology of knowledge. *Area*, 36, 254–61.

Angulo-Jiménez, H. and DeThorne, L. (2019) Narratives about autism: An analysis of YouTube videos by individuals who self-identify as autistic. *American Journal of Speech-Language Pathology*, 28, 569–90.

Ashmore, M. and Reed, D. (2000) Innocence and nostalgia in conversation analysis: The dynamic relations of tape and transcript. *Forum: Qualitative Social Research*, 1, Art. 3. http://nbn-resolving.de/urn:nbn:de:0114-fqs000335.

Atkinson, P. and Silverman, D. (1997) Kundera's Immortality: The interview society and the invention of the self. *Qualitative Inquiry*, 3, 304–25.

Bates, E.A., McCann, J.J., Kaye, L.K. and Taylor, J.C. (2017) 'Beyond words': A researcher's guide to using photo elicitation in psychology. *Qualitative Research in Psychology*, 14, 459–81.

Billig, M. (1989) The argumentative nature of holding strong views: A case study. *European Journal of Social Psychology*, 19, 203–33.

Bolger, N., Davis, A. and Rafaeli, E. (2003) Diary methods: Capturing life as it is lived. *Annual Review of Psychology*, 54, 579–616.

Bouvier, G. and Rasmussen, J. (2022) *Qualitative Research Using Social Media*. Abingdon: Routledge.

Branney, P., Reid, K., Frost, N., Coan, S., Mathieson, A. & Woolhouse, M. (2019) A context-consent meta-framework for designing open (qualitative) data studies. *Qualitative Research in Psychology*, 16, 483–502.

British Psychological Society (2021a) *BPS Code of Human Research Ethics*. Leicester: British Psychological Society.

British Psychological Society (2021b) *Ethics Guidelines for Internet-Mediated Research*. Leicester: British Psychological Society.

Burles, M.C. and Bally, J.M.G. (2018) Ethical, practical, and methodological considerations for unobtrusive qualitative research about personal narratives shared on the internet. *International Journal of Qualitative Methods*, 17, 1–9.

Byford, J. (2018) The emotional and political power of images of suffering: Discursive psychology and the study of visual rhetoric. In S. Gibson (ed.), *Discourse, Peace and Conflict: Discursive Psychology Perspectives* Cham: Springer. pp. 285–302.

Carter, B. (2002) Chronic pain in childhood and the medical encounter: Professional ventriloquism and hidden voices. *Qualitative Health Research*, 12, 28–41.

Carter, S.M., Shih, S., Williams, J., Degeling, C. and Mooney-Somers, J. (2021) Conducting qualitative research online: Challenges and solutions. *The Patient – Patient-Centred Outcomes Research*, 14, 711–18.

Corti, L. and Thompson, P. (2004) Secondary analysis of archived data. In C. Seale, G. Gobo, J.F. Gubrium and D. Silverman (eds), *Qualitative Research Practice*. London: Sage. pp. 327–43.

Cottingham, M.D. and Erickson, R.J. (2020) Capturing emotion with audio diaries. *Qualitative Research*, 20, 549–64.

Day, M. and Thatcher, J. (2009) 'I'm really embarrassed that you're going to read this…': Reflections on using diaries in qualitative research. *Qualitative Research in Psychology*, 6, 249–59.

Dempsey, M., Foley, S., Frost, N., Murphy, R., Willis, N., Robinson, S., Dunn-Galvin, A., Veale, A., Linehan, C., Pantidi, N. & McCarthy, J. (2022) Am I lazy, a drama queen or depressed? A journey through a pluralistic approach to analysing accounts of depression. *Qualitative Research in Psychology*, 19, 473–93.

Donnelly, S., Wilson, A.G., Mannan, H., Dix, C., Whitehill, L. & Kroll, T. (2021) (In)visible illness: A provocative study of the lived experience of self-managing rheumatoid arthritis. *PLoS One*, 16(4), e0250451.

Duara, R., Hugh-Jones, S. and Madill, A. (2018) Photo-elicitation and time-lining to enhance the research interview: Exploring the quarterlife crisis of young adults in India and the United Kingdom. *Qualitative Research in Psychology*, 19, 131–54.

Fielding, N. (2004) Getting the most from archived qualitative data: Epistemological, practical and professional obstacles. *International Journal of Social Research Methodology*, 7, 97–104.

Finley, N. (2010) Skating femininity: Gender maneuvering in women's roller derby. *Journal of Contemporary Ethnography*, 39, 359–87.

Flowers, P., Knussen C. and Duncan, B. (2000) Community, responsibility and culpability: HIV risk-management amongst Scottish gay men. *Journal of Community and Applied Social Psychology*, 10, 285–300.

Frost, N. (2021) *Qualitative Research Methods in Psychology: Combining Core Approaches* (2nd edn) London: Open University Press.

Gibson, S. (2013) Milgram's obedience experiments: A rhetorical analysis. *British Journal of Social Psychology*, 52, 290–309.

Gibson, S., Crossland, M. & Hamilton, J. (2018) Social citizenship and immigration: Employment, welfare, and effortfulness in online discourse concerning migration to the United Kingdom. *Qualitative Psychology*, 5, 99–116.

Gough, B., Lawton, R., Madill, A. & Stratton, P. (2003) *Guidelines for the Supervision of Undergraduate Qualitative Research in Psychology*. York: LTSN Psychology.

Green, A.S., Rafaeli, E., Bolger, N., Shrout, P.E. & Reis, H.T. (2006) Paper or plastic? Data equivalence in paper and electronic diaries. *Psychological Methods*, 11, 87–105.

Guijarro, J.M. and Sanz, M.J.P. (2008) Compositional, interpersonal and representational meanings in a children's narrative: A multimodal discourse analysis. *Journal of Pragmatics*, 40, 1601–19.

Hepburn, A. (2020) Managing embodied misconduct: Burping and spitting in family mealtime interactions. In S. Wiggins and K. Osvaldsson Cromdal (eds), *Discursive Psychology and Embodiment: Beyond Subject–Object Binaries*. Cham: Palgrave Macmillan. pp. 57–80.

Hester, S. & Francis, D. (1994) Doing data: The local organization of a sociological interview. *British Journal of Sociology*, 45, 675–95.

Hiles, D., Čermák, I. & Chrz, V. (2017) Narrative inquiry. In C. Willig and W. Stainton-Rogers (eds), *The Sage Handbook of Qualitative Research in Psychology* (2nd edn). London: Sage. pp. 157–75.

Hine, C. (2000) *Virtual Ethnography*. London: Sage.

Hofstetter, E. and Stokoe, E. (2018) Getting service at the constituency office: Analysing citizens' encounters with their Member of Parliament. *Text & Talk*, 38, 551–73.

Hollander, M.M. (2015) The repertoire of resistance: Non-compliance with directives in Milgram's 'obedience' experiments. *British Journal of Social Psychology*, 54, 425–44.

Hollway, W. & Jefferson, T. (2000) *Doing Qualitative Research Differently: Free Association, Narrative and The Interview Method*. London: Sage.

Horner, C.R., Hugh-Jones, S., Sutherland, E., Brennan, C. and Sadler-Smith, C. (2022) 'This doesn't feel like living': How the COVID-19 pandemic affected the mental health of vulnerable university students in the United Kingdom. *European Journal of Mental Health*, 17, 52–64.

Howitt, D. (2010) *Introduction to Qualitative Methods in Psychology*. Harlow: Pearson.

Hugh-Jones, S., Burke, S. and Stubbs, J. (2021) 'I didn't want to do it on my own': A qualitative study of women's perceptions of facilitating and risk factors for weight control on a UK commercial community program. *Appetite*, 165, 105308.

Humă, B., Stokoe, E. and Sikveland, R.O. (2019) Persuasive conduct: Alignment and resistance in prospecting 'cold' calls. *Journal of Language and Social Psychology*, 38, 33–60.

Hussain, Z. and Griffiths, M.D. (2009) The attitudes, feelings and experiences of online gamers: A qualitative analysis. *CyberPsychology and Behavior*, 12, 747–53.

Hutchby, I. & Barnett, S. (2005) Aspects of the sequential organization of mobile phone conversation. *Discourse Studies*, 7, 147–71.

Jol, G. and Stommel, W. (2021) The interactional costs of 'neutrality' in police interviews with child witnesses. *Research on Language and Social Interaction*, 54, 299–318.

Kaposi, D. (2020) Saving a victim from himself: The rhetoric of the learner's presence and absence in the Milgram experiments. *British Journal of Social Psychology*, 59, 900–21.

Kaun, A. (2010) Open-ended online diaries: Capturing life as it is narrated. *International Journal of Qualitative Methods*, 9, 133–48.

Keleher, H.M. and Verrinder, G.K. (2003) Health diaries in a rural Australian Study. *Qualitative Health Research*, 13, 435–43.

Kilby, L. and Lennon, H. (2018) Charlie Hebdo and the Prophet Muhammad: A multimodal critical discourse analysis of peace and violence in a satirical cartoon. In S. Gibson (ed.), *Discourse, Peace and Conflict: Discursive Psychology Perspectives*. Cham: Springer. pp. 303–21.

King, N. and Hugh-Jones, S. (2019) The interview in qualitative research. In C. Sullivan and M.A. Forrester (eds), *Doing Qualitative Research in Psychology: A Practical Guide* (2nd edn). London: Sage. pp. 121–44.

Krueger, R.A. and Casey, M.A. (2009) *Focus Groups: A Practical Guide for Applied Research* (4th edn). London: Sage.

Largan, C. and Morris, T. (2019) *Qualitative Secondary Research: A Step-by-Step Guide*. London: Sage.

Lawrence, L. (2022) Conducting cross-cultural qualitative interviews with mainland Chinese participants during COVID: Lessons from the field. *Qualitative Research*, 22, 154–65.

Leitão, R. (2021) Technology-facilitated intimate partner abuse: A qualitative analysis of data from online domestic abuse forums. *Human–Computer Interaction*, 36, 203–42.

Licoppe, C. and Morel, J. (2012) Video-in-interaction: 'Talking heads' and the multimodal organization of mobile and Skype video calls. *Research on Language and Social Interaction*, 45, 399–429.

Liebenberg, L. (2009) The visual image as discussion point: Increasing validity in boundary crossing research. *Qualitative Research*, 9, 441–67.

Lobe, B., Morgan, D. and Hoffman, K.A. (2020) Qualitative data collection in an era of social distancing. *International Journal of Qualitative Methods*, 19, 1–8.

Lynn, N. and Lea, S.J. (2005) Through the looking glass: Considering the challenges visual methodologies raise for qualitative research. *Qualitative Research in Psychology*, 2, 213–25.

Madill, A. (2011) Interaction in the semi-structured interview: Comparative analysis of the use of and response to indirect complaints. *Qualitative Research in Psychology*, 8, 333–53.

Madill, A. (2023) Interviews and interviewing techniques. In H. Cooper, M.N. Coutanche, L.K. McMullen and A.T. Panter (eds), *APA Handbook of Research Methods in Psychology*. Washington, DC: APA.

Madill, A., Duara, R., Goswami, S., Graber, R. and Hugh-Jones, S. (2023). Pathways to recovery model of youth substance misuse in Assam, India. *Health Expectations*, 26(1), 318–328.

Madill, A., Jordan, A. and Shirley, C. (2000) Objectivity and reliability in qualitative analysis: Realist, contextualist and radical constructionist epistemologies. *British Journal of Psychology*, 91, 1–20.

Malterud, K., Siersma, V.D. and Guassora, A.D. (2016) Sample size in qualitative interview studies: Guided by information power. *Qualitative Health Research*, 26, 1753–760.

McAdams, D.P. (1993) *The stories We Live By: Personal Myths and the Making of the Self*. New York: Guilford.

McAdams, D.P., Josselson, R. and Lieblich, A. (eds) (2006) *Identity and Story: Creating Self in Narrative*. Washington, DC: APA.

McGrath, L., Mullarkey, S. and Reavey, P. (2020) Building visual worlds: Using maps in qualitative psychological research in affect and emotion. *Qualitative Research in Psychology*, 17, 75–97.

Melvin, K., Rollins, C.P.E., Cromby, J., Crossley, J., Garrison, J.R., Murray, G.K. and Suckling, J. (2021) Arts-based methods for hallucination research. *Cognitive Neuropsychiatry*, 27, 199–218.

Meredith, J. (2016) Transcribing screen-capture data: The process of developing a transcription system for multi-modal text-based data. *International Journal of Social Research Methodology*, 19, 663–76.

Meredith, J., Giles, D. and Stommel, W. (eds) (2021) *Analysing Digital Interaction*. Cham: Palgrave Macmillan.

Merrilees, C.E., Goeke-Morey, M. and Cummings, E.M. (2008) Do event-contingent diaries about marital conflict change marital interactions? *Behaviour Research and Therapy*, 46, 253–62.

Milgram, S. (1974) *Obedience to Authority: An Experimental View*. New York: Harper & Row.

Monrouxe, L.V. (2009) Solicited audio diaries in longitudinal research: A view from inside. *Qualitative Research*, 9, 81–103.

Murray, A. (2022) Qualitative data for amplifying disabled identities: Invisible disabilities in Personal Independence Payment assessments and appeals (PhD thesis), The Open University. *Dataset.* https://doi.org/10.21954/ou.rd.19714552.v1

Nesbitt-Larking, P. (2022) Constructing narratives of masculinity: Online followers of Jordan B. Peterson. *Psychology of Men & Masculinity*, 23, 309–20.

Oppenheimer, M. (2015) Designing obedience in the lab: Milgram's shock simulator and human factors engineering. *Theory & Psychology*, 25, 599–621.

O'Shaughnessy, R., Dallos, R. and Gough, A. (2013) A narrative study of the lives of women who experience anorexia nervosa. *Qualitative Research in Psychology*, 10, 42–62.

Palmer, M., Larkin, M., de Visser, R. and Fadden, G. (2010) Developing an interpretative phenomenological approach to focus group data. *Qualitative Research in Psychology*, 7, 99–121.

Parry, O. and Mauthner, N. (2004) Whose data are they anyway? Practical, legal and ethical issues in archiving qualitative research data. *Sociology*, 38, 139–52.

Parker, I. (1999) Introduction: Varieties of discourse and analysis. In I. Parker and the Bolton Discourse Network, *Critical Textwork: An Introduction to Varieties of Discourse and Analysis*. Buckingham: Open University Press. pp. 1–12.

Peel, E., Parry, O., Douglas, M. and Lawton, J. (2006) 'It's no skin off my nose': Why people take part in qualitative research. *Qualitative Health Research*, 16, 1335–49.

Peräkylä, A., Antaki, C., Vehviläinen, S. and Leudar, I. (eds) (2008) *Conversation Analysis and Psychotherapy*. Cambridge: Cambridge University Press.

Potter, J. (2004) Discourse analysis. In M. Hardy and A. Bryman (eds), *Handbook of Data Analysis*. London: Sage. pp. 607–24.

Potter, J. and Hepburn, A. (2005) Qualitative interviews in psychology: Problems and possibilities. *Qualitative Research in Psychology*, 2(4), 281–307

Potter, J. and Wetherell, M. (1987) *Discourse and Social Psychology: Beyond Attitudes and Behaviour*. London: Sage.

Pownall, M., Eyles-Smith, E. and Talbot, C.V. (2022) Constructions of family relationships in a COVID Christmas: An analysis of television advertisements on YouTube. *Feminism and Psychology*, 32, 357–75.

Pini, S., Gardner, P. and Hugh-Jones, S. (2018) How and why school is important to teenagers with cancer: Outcomes from a photo-elicitation study. *Journal of Adolescent and Young Adult Oncology*, 8, 157–64.

Puchta, C. and Potter, J. (2004) *Focus Group Practice*. London: Sage.

Rapley, T. (2007) *Doing Conversation, Discourse and Document Analysis*. London: Sage.

Reavey, P. (ed.) (2021) *A Handbook of Visual Methods in Psychology: Using and Interpreting Images in Qualitative Research* (2nd edn). London: Routledge.

Reavey, P. and Johnson, K. (2017) Visual approaches: Using and interpreting images. In C. Willig and W. Stainton-Rogers (eds), *The Sage Handbook of Qualitative Research in Psychology* (2nd edn). London: Sage. pp 354–73.

Roberts, L.D. (2015) Ethical issues in conducting qualitative research in online communities. *Qualitative Research in Psychology*, 12, 314–25.

Rowe, L. and Goodman, S. (2014) 'A stinking filthy race of people inbred with criminality': A discourse analysis of prejudicial talk about Gypsies in discussion forums. *Romani Studies*, 24, 25–42.

Rudrum, S., Casey, R., Frank, L., Brickner, R. K., MacKenzie, S., Carlson, J. and Rondinelli, E. (2022) Qualitative research studies online: Using prompted weekly journal entries during the COVID-19 pandemic. *International Journal of Qualitative Methods*, 21, 1–12.

Sarbin, T.R. (1986) *Narrative Psychology: The Storied Nature of Human Conduct*. New York: Praeger.

Scott, S., McGowan, V.J. and Visram, S. (2021) 'I'm gonna tell you about how Mrs Rona has affected me'. Exploring young people's experiences of the COVID-19 pandemic in north east England: A qualitative diary-based study. *International Journal of Environmental Research and Public Health*, 18, 3837.

Shaw, R. and Kitzinger, C. (2012) Compliments on a home birth helpline. *Research on Language & Social Interaction*, 45, 213–44.

Smart, C. and Auburn, Y. (eds) (2018) *Interprofessional Care and Mental Health: A Discursive Exploration of Team Meeting Practices*. Cham: Palgrave Macmillan.

Smedley, R.M. and Coulson, N.S. (2021) A practical guide to analysing online support forums. *Qualitative Research in Psychology*, 18, 76–103.

Speer, S.A. (2002) 'Natural' and 'contrived' data: A sustainable distinction? *Discourse Studies*, 4, 511–25.

Taylor, A.M., van Teijlingen, E.V., Ryan, K.M. and Alexander, J. (2019) 'Scrutinised, judged and sabotaged': A qualitative video diary study of first-time breastfeeding mothers. *Midwifery*, 75, 16–23.

Thomsen, D.K. and Brinkmann, S. (2009) An interviewer's guide to autobiographical memory: Ways to elicit concrete experiences and to avoid pitfalls in interpreting them. *Qualitative Research in Psychology*, 6, 294–312.

Tileagă, C. and Byford, J. (2017) Qualitative psychology and the archive. *Qualitative Psychology*, 4, 55–7.

Todd, Z., Nerlich, B., McKeown, S. and Clarke, D.D. (2004) *Mixing Methods in Psychology: The Integration of Qualitative and Quantitative Methods in Theory and Practice*. Hove: Psychology Press.

Warr, D., Guillemin, M., Cox, S. and Waycott, J. (eds) (2016) *Ethics and Visual Research Methods: Theory, Methodology and Practice*. New York: Palgrave Macmillan.

Williams, J.P. (2006) Authentic identities: Straightedge subculture, music and the Internet. *Journal of Contemporary Ethnography*, 35, 173–200.

Wright, C.Y., Darko, N., Standen, P.J. & Patel, T.G. (2010) Visual research methods: Using cameras to empower socially excluded black youth. *Sociology*, 44, 541–58.

Yardley, L. and Bishop, F. (2008) Mixing qualitative and quantitative methods: A pragmatic approach. In C. Willig and W. Stainton-Rogers (eds), *The Sage Handbook of Qualitative Research In Psychology*. London: Sage. pp. 352–69.

8

ANALYSING YOUR DATA

Stephen Gibson and Siobhan Hugh-Jones

Deciding which analytic approach is most appropriate for your project is a central task of doing qualitative research. In this chapter, we help you with your decision making about your data analysis by giving you an overview of:

- what is available to you in terms of the most prominent qualitative analytic approaches; and
- principles and practices of data analysis that are shared by qualitative approaches.

We expect this to be especially useful to you at two stages of your project: when you are planning your project and when you start to analyse your data.

In the planning stage, this chapter should be useful for you as you develop your research questions (see Chapter 2). In Chapter 1, we introduced the 'methodological kite', which emphasises the importance of coherence between your philosophical perspective, research question, method of data collection and analytic approach. As you are developing your research question you will need to know several things about data analysis, which are considered in this chapter:

- What approaches are available that you could use to answer your question(s).
- Whether these approaches come with any conceptual 'baggage' that needs to be coherent with other aspects of your project (for example, their epistemological assumptions, preference for a specific kind of data collection method, or the way that they would phrase a research question).
- Where you can turn for a deeper understanding of the method that you think you're going to use.
- General principles of qualitative analysis that you should know about before embarking on your study.

You may also find this chapter useful when you start your analysis. Doing an excellent project will mean that you've read more widely on your chosen method of analysis.

But this chapter's focus on the principles and practices of data analysis that are shared by many qualitative approaches will help locate your specific reading within a wider understanding of how to do high-quality analysis. Our 'top tips' sections should help you here too.

·······In a nutshell···

Analysing your data

Focusing on these three key questions will help you to plan and do your analysis:

1   What different approaches to data analysis are there?

     There are many to choose from. We discuss six of the most popular: thematic analysis; interpretative phenomenological analysis; grounded theory; narrative analysis; discourse analysis; and conversation analysis.

2   How do I decide which approach to take?

     Different approaches are better suited to different sorts of questions, and which you choose will depend on your interests and what you want to find out. This chapter includes a decision-making flow-chart to help you decide on an approach that's appropriate for your project.

3   How do I do qualitative analysis?

     Exactly how you do your analysis will depend on the approach you select. However, there are some principles and practices that are common to all approaches: remaining 'anchored' to your research question; ensuring an appropriate form of transcription; the importance of careful reading; and conducting a systematic analysis.

· ·

Approaches to Data Analysis

Although qualitative methods have had a place in psychology since its origins, the last 30–40 years has seen an upsurge of interest in qualitative methods in the discipline. This has generated an array of exciting, useful and practical approaches to qualitative analysis (Willig and Stainton-Rogers, 2017). The field is constantly progressing and evolving, with researchers using methods in fresh, flexible ways, applying them to novel areas and to different types of data. For the novice researcher (and even for those more experienced) the considerable number of options available for qualitative analysis can be confusing, if not overwhelming, and the reluctance to specify 'how to do' analysis that occurs with some approaches can create anxieties about whether one's analysis is legitimate.

To try to overcome some of these anxieties, we provide overviews of six of the most widely used approaches below. These are thematic analysis, interpretative phenomenological analysis, grounded theory, narrative analysis, discourse analysis and conversation analysis. As we go through these approaches, we will refer to a number of concepts introduced in Chapter 1 (e.g. phenomenology, constructionism, critical realism). We will describe the fundamentals of each method and direct you to resources to help with the 'nuts and bolts' of analysis. In addition to the texts listed after each approach, there are several excellent introductory textbooks on qualitative approaches in psychology (e.g. Howitt, 2019; Lyons and Coyle, 2021; Smith, 2015; Sullivan and Forrester, 2019; Willig, 2022). Most of these cover the core approaches summarised in the present chapter and can get you started with finding out more about them. But to do well in your project you will need to use additional publications which give in-depth coverage of your chosen method of analysis.

Top tip

Read widely around your chosen approach

The best projects will display evidence of wider reading beyond standard introductory research methods texts. Consult some of the more in-depth sources listed in the further reading boxes below and use databases such as PsycINFO to look for the latest research (see Chapter 6) that has used your method of analysis. These published papers can help you to justify your approach.

Thematic analysis

In a hugely influential paper, Braun and Clarke (2006) argued that thematic analysis should be seen as a foundational approach for qualitative analysis. By this they meant that it provides the foundations upon which many other approaches are built. In particular, the process of thematic *coding* underpins IPA, grounded theory and narrative analysis (see below). However, Braun and Clarke also suggested that thematic analysis should be seen as an approach in its own right, which may be particularly suited to research questions concerned primarily with the *content* of what people say. Central to thematic analysis is the identification of *themes* in data.

There are two broad varieties of thematic analysis: data-driven and theory-driven. Data-driven thematic analysis involves trying to avoid starting with any predetermined theoretical ideas and being as open-minded as possible about what you might find in the data. Note, however, that it is impossible to cast off completely all of our many and varied preconceptions and assumptions about the world, so the best we can usually aim for is to be aware of how these preconceived ideas shape such things as the topic we choose to study, the questions we ask of our participants, and the areas we choose to focus on in analysis and writing up. This idea is at the heart of the concept of reflexivity, which is central to all approaches to qualitative research (see Chapter 9). This has recently been foregrounded by Braun and Clarke (2022) who now explicitly label their approach as *reflexive* thematic analysis in order to highlight the importance of critical reflection on researcher subjectivity in the analytic process.

············In a nutshell···· ···

Coding and themes

Coding: An analytic technique used in many qualitative approaches, coding involves working through a transcript and noting down short comments on segments (for example, a line, or whole speaking turn) of your data, usually in the margins of your transcript.

Theme: An analytic unit that describes some level of patterning in a dataset, in relation to a research question. Themes are identified by sorting codes into categories.

Theory-driven thematic analysis is particularly useful when you have a set of theoretical concepts you want to apply or test in a novel context. The aim is not to 'test' them in the statistical sense of seeing if they can withstand falsification. Instead, the aim is to see if these theoretical concepts help you make sense of the situation you are interested in, and whether your data are consistent with the theory, or whether it might need to be modified in order to better explain the data. When doing this type of thematic analysis, you might actually begin with a series of codes or themes and look for them in your data – see Heathcote et al. (2021) for an example of such an approach. If you are interested in exploring theory-driven thematic analysis further, a particularly useful form of this approach is template analysis (King, 2012).

Thematic analysis is flexible in a number of ways. It can be used with a range of philosophical perspectives (e.g. constructionism, realism, interpretivism, critical realism; see Chapter 1). But you do need to make sure that you are clear on your philosophical position or you risk the sort of incoherence that we discussed in Chapter 1 when we introduced the methodological kite (see Chapter 2 for more on this too). It is similarly flexible in the range of approaches to data collection that it can be used with, and while – as with many approaches – it is often used with interview data, there are more and more examples of work that looks at a wider range of data. Indeed, in their recent textbook on thematic analysis, Braun and Clarke (2022) use an extended example from a social media dataset to illustrate the approach.

Want to know more about thematic analysis?

Braun, V. and Clarke, V. (2006) Using thematic analysis in psychology. *Qualitative Research in Psychology*, 3, 77-101.

Braun, V. and Clarke, V. (2022) *Thematic Analysis: A Practical Guide*. London: Sage.

King, N. (2012). Doing template analysis. In G. Symon and C. Cassell (eds), *Qualitative Organizational Research: Core Methods and Current Challenges* (pp. 426-50). London: Sage.

Interpretative phenomenological analysis

Interpretative phenomenological analysis (IPA) focuses on individual experience and the meanings that such experience has for people. It adopts an idiographic approach to research where the aim is to arrive at a rich description of individual cases. This is in contrast to the nomothetic approach which attempts to uncover universal laws. Thus, IPA research tends to work with either case studies or very small sample sizes. This is appropriate as the aim of IPA is not to make generalisable claims in the same way that you might want to do if you were conducting a survey or experiment (see Chapter 3). However, this does not mean that the approach is any less detailed. IPA typically involves the use of semi-structured one-to-one interviews. Analysis proceeds on transcripts presented in a broadly playscript format (see section on transcription later in this chapter) and involves a process of coding similar to that used in thematic analysis.

The key distinguishing feature of IPA is, as its name suggests, its emphasis on phenomenology and interpretation. It can be seen as a critical realist approach insofar as it takes a cautious view of the relationship between what is said in an interview and a participant's actual experiences, but nevertheless takes the position that such experience is real and can be made sense of by the analyst through a process of careful analysis (Shaw, 2019). This is at the heart of IPA's engagement with the concept of reflexivity, which emphasises the researcher's active role in interpreting participants' experiences.

IPA stresses the role of interpretation in two respects: i) as people, we make sense of our phenomenological experiences; and ii) as researchers, we seek to make sense of other people who are trying to make sense of their own experiences. This two-sided approach to interpretation is known as the *double hermeneutic*.

In a nutshell

The double hermeneutic

A process of interpretation which stresses that in the same way that people seek to make sense of (interpret) their experience, so the researcher needs to interpret people's own interpretations of those experiences.

Keeping a research diary is useful for all research (see Chapter 9), but is particularly important for IPA (and grounded theory). In IPA a reflective diary is used to record impressions, hunches and other notes on the analytic process (see Shaw, 2019). This helps to remind you that you are yourself engaged in a process of interpreting what the participant has said, something which is central to the idea of the double hermeneutic.

Want to know more about IPA?

Smith, J.A., Flowers, P. and Larkin, M. (2022) *Interpretative Phenomenological Analysis: Theory, Method and Research* (2nd edn). London: Sage. (A comprehensive introduction to IPA.)

Smith, J.A. and Nizza, I.E. (2021) *Essentials of Interpretative Phenomenological Analysis.* Washington, DC: American Psychological Association.

Smith, J.A. and Shinebourne, P. (2012) Interpretative phenomenological analysis. In H. Cooper, P. M. Camic, D.L. Long, A.T. Panter, D. Rindskopf and K.J. Sher (eds), *APA Handbook of Research Methods in Psychology, Vol. 2. Research Designs: Quantitative, Qualitative, Neuropsychological, and Biological.* Washington, DC: American Psychological Association. pp. 73–82.

Grounded theory

Grounded theory was developed by the sociologists Glaser and Strauss (1967) as a way of developing theory inductively. By this, grounded theorists mean that, rather than starting with a theory and testing it (as is the case with hypothetico-deductivism, which underpins the experimental method) we can start with data and develop theory from it.

The central aim of grounded theory is to develop theory that is grounded in the data. Grounded theorists go as far as to suggest that you should avoid a literature review at the start of your project in case this predetermines your course and limits the capacity for the data to truly drive theory development. Instead, a grounded theory project ideally features a delayed literature review (see Chapter 6). In this respect, grounded theory differs from approaches such as thematic analysis and IPA because of its emphasis on developing theory in order to understand processes and causal relations. Given its emphasis on theory development, it is often characterised as a realist perspective (see Chapter 1), but an increasingly popular form of grounded theory takes a social construc-tionist approach (see Charmaz, 2014).

Grounded theory makes use of an extended process of coding, beginning with open coding and working through focused coding, axial coding and theoretical coding

(Gordon-Finlayson, 2019, provides a particularly good explanation of the distinctions between these). At any point in this process you might find yourself returning to an earlier stage in the analysis, which means that different stages of the analysis feed back into each other and can be repeated several times if necessary. In this sense, grounded theory is not a straightforward linear process of analysis, but is cyclical. For example, grounded theorists emphasise the importance of continuing the process of data collection once analysis is under way. This allows you to test out hunches on cases which might provide a challenge to your emerging theory. For example, Payne (2021) provides an extended example of a study of older Chinese people living in the UK who had been treated for cancer. She describes how initially the research involved sampling participants who were members of community groups, but as the study developed the researchers began to wonder if their emerging theory would be equally applicable to people who had not joined such groups, and so conducted interviews with a sample of participants who were not members of community groups. This process is called theoretical sampling (see Chapter 3 for more on sampling).

An important process in grounded theory is memo writing, which involves frequent and systematic recording of your thoughts, ideas and reflections on your data at every stage of analysis. This forms the basis of a research diary in grounded theory. It is separate from coding, although it can (and should) expand upon things that you notice during coding. Gordon-Finlayson (2019: 296) describes memo writing as 'the engine of grounded theory' because it is in your memos that you will develop and refine your initial ideas that may lead you ultimately to your theory. As noted above, the grounded theory process is not linear and therefore does not have an obvious end point. However, grounded theorists recommend that you should stop your analysis when you reach the point of theoretical saturation; that is, when further data collection and analysis no longer adds anything to your theory.

Want to know more about grounded theory?

Corbin, J. and Strauss, A. (2014) *Basics of Qualitative Research: Techniques and Procedures for Developing Grounded Theory* (4th edn). London: Sage.

Charmaz, K. (2015) *Constructing Grounded Theory* (2nd edn). London: Sage. (Outlines Charmaz's social constructionist version of grounded theory.)

Bryant, A. and Charmaz, K. (2012) Grounded theory and psychological research. In H. Cooper, P. M. Camic, D.L. Long, A.T. Panter, D. Rindskopf and K.J. Sher (eds), *APA Handbook of Research Methods in Psychology, Vol. 2. Research Designs: Quantitative, Qualitative, Neuropsychological, and Biological.* Washington, DC: American Psychological Association. pp. 39–56.

Narrative analysis

Narrative analysis, or narrative psychology, is an approach which emphasises the storied nature of our attempts to make sense of our lives. In particular, the approach focuses on how people construct a sense of self through *narrative*, and involves asking people for extended accounts of their lives, or some aspect of their lives.

······**···In a nutshell···**···

Narrative

A narrative is a story which organises some aspect of experience into a meaningful whole, usually with a beginning, a middle and an end.

···

Narrative analysis frequently involves the use of interviews, typically making use of open-ended questions designed to encourage participants to tell the story of their life, or of some aspect of their life in which the researcher is interested. A particularly useful form of interviewing is biographical or life-story interviewing, in which the interviewer asks the interviewee to tell them the story of their lives (see Chapter 7 for more detail). These tend to be useful in producing the level of detail needed for an in-depth narrative analysis. In principle, however, the approach can be used with a much wider range of data; for example, there is an established tradition of work exploring narrative in therapeutic consultations (see Payne, 2006). Hiles et al. (2017) present a useful model of what they call narrative oriented inquiry (NOI). They outline a series of steps in the research process (such as designing the interview schedule and conducting the interview), and provide illustrations of how different types of narrative analysis can be used within this framework.

In analysing narratives, it can often be useful to briefly summarise the beginning, middle and end of the narrative, as well as drawing attention to any other key features (see Murray, 2015). This process often helps to draw attention to the way in which many narratives reflect a standard form, such as a heroic or progressive narrative in which the protagonist proceeds towards their ultimate goal; or a tragedy, in which obstacles along the way impede progress, leading to a failure to achieve the goal. This helps you to begin to understand the form of the narrative you are working with, but you will also want to deal with the specific content of the narrative. In this respect, you might explore the tone of the narrative (for example, optimistic or pessimistic), the images or metaphors used to construct it, the broader themes recurring throughout the narrative, and the underlying values and principles present in the narrative (McAdams, 1993). These are only a selection of the sorts of analytic tools available in narrative analysis; there are many more subtle concepts and distinctions which you will be able to explore using the further reading below.

Want to know more about narrative analysis?

Andrews, M., Squire, C. and Tamboukou, M. (eds) (2013) *Doing Narrative Research* (2nd edn). London: Sage.

Bailey-Rodriguez, D., Frost, N. and Elichaoff, F. (2019) Narrative analysis. In C. Sullivan and M.A. Forrester (eds), *Doing Qualitative Research in Psychology: A Practical Guide* (2nd edn) (pp. 209-32). London: Sage.

Josselson, R. and Hammack, P.L. (2021) *Essentials of Narrative Analysis*. Washington, DC: American Psychological Association.

Discourse analysis

Discourse analysis (DA) is the study of language (or *discourse*), and the ways in which it can be used by speakers or writers to formulate versions of 'reality'. It assumes that language can never neutrally represent 'reality' and that it is always action-oriented, by which we mean that words do things. As language users, we are all aware of how we can present different versions of things that happen depending on what impression we want to offer our listener. There are variations in the ways that discourse can be analysed, and Wiggins (2017) provides a good explanation of the key distinctions between these. Riley and Wiggins (2019) show how they contrast by analysing the same data with two different types of DA.

·····In a nutshell·····

Discourse

Any textual or linguistic material, either in spoken or written form.

Despite the wide variation in approaches to DA, it is useful to begin your exploration of this approach with Potter and Wetherell (1987). They outlined three key components of DA: construction, function and variation.

·····In a nutshell·····

Construction, function and variation

Discourse analysts are interested in how, through language, people construct versions of objects, events and other phenomena. We can think of this, metaphorically, as being like

(Continued)

house-building. In the same way that a builder would use bricks, mortar, wood and steel to construct a house, we are constantly engaged in constructing reality through the use of language. However, in place of bricks and mortar, we use raw materials such as descriptions, clichés, arguments, questions and answers to build versions of our worlds. Importantly, we have at our disposal a range of raw materials that we can put together in different ways, depending on what kind of structure we want to build. Similarly, as a house would be constructed by many builders working together – and sometimes disagreeing on how the house should be built – so we construct our world jointly with others, sometimes arguing about how best to construct it. As a result, discourse analysts emphasise that raw materials such as descriptions (for example, 'it's a bit cold in here') are not neutral statements of reality but perform some function in the context in which they are used. For example, if someone responds to the above statement by moving to close a window, we might suggest that what was apparently a description actually functioned as a request for a window to be closed. Finally, if people use discursive raw materials to perform a range of different functions, we should expect their constructions of the world to vary depending on the function they are performing.

. . . .

Taken together, these principles of DA have epistemological implications, notably challenging the notion of a singular truth or reality, and so DA can be seen as a highly relativist social constructionist perspective (see Potter and Hepburn, 2008). However, this is a source of debate as other researchers have developed alternative versions of DA which adopt a critical realist approach (see Sims-Schouten and Riley, 2019; and see Chapter 1 for more discussion of these ideas). As with any qualitative approach, it is important to understand these epistemological issues *before* you begin your project – and indeed before you decide which version of DA to adopt.

Want to know more about discourse analysis?

Potter, J. and Wetherell, M. (1987) *Discourse and Social Psychology: Beyond Attitudes and Behaviour*. London: Sage. (The book that introduced DA to psychology, and still one of the best starting points for exploring the approach in depth.)

Taylor, S. (2013) *What Is Discourse Analysis?* London: Bloomsbury.

Wiggins, S. (2017) *Discursive Psychology: Theory, Method and Applications*. London: Sage.

Conversation analysis

Conversation analysis (CA) was developed in the 1960s by the sociologist Harvey Sacks. It is used by a growing number of psychologists interested in the dynamics of conversational interaction. In contrast to many other qualitative approaches, CA stresses the importance of transcripts of 'naturalistic' interactions, such as telephone calls, and everyday conversations (see Chapter 7). Where interviews have been the subject of conversation analysis, it has been with a view to exploring how the interview works as a particular kind of interaction (see Forrester, 2019 for an example), rather than using it as a way of understanding people's views, experiences or life histories. A key analytic tool in CA is the notion of participant orientation.

········In a nutshell ··

Participant orientation

Essentially this means that any claims you make about your data should be justifiable with reference to the way in which participants in the interaction(s) you are studying themselves treat the interaction. For example, a conversation analyst would not typically seek to suggest that gender was relevant in an interaction unless it could be demonstrated that the participants in that interaction themselves treated gender as relevant. See Stokoe and Smithson (2001) for a useful critical discussion of this issue.

···

Instead of coding data as would be done in, for example, thematic analysis, CA involves close attention to the details of interaction (see Drew, 2015, pp. 111–12, for an explanation of why coding is not appropriate in CA). In order to facilitate this, a notable feature of conversation analytic work is the level of detail included in its transcripts, which ensures that minute details of intonation, overlap, timings and other features of speech delivery are included (see below). This allows conversation analysts to explore the delicate choreography of social interaction, and has led to many insights on the orderliness of conversation in a variety of informal and formal settings.

──Want to know more about CA?──────────────

Hepburn, A. and Potter, J. (2021) *Essentials of Conversation Analysis*. Washington, DC: American Psychological Association.

Hutchby, I. and Wooffit, R. (2008) *Conversation Analysis* (2nd edn). Cambridge: Polity. (A highly accessible introduction to CA.)

Wooffitt, R. (2005) *Conversation and Discourse Analysis: A Comparative and Critical Introduction*. London: Sage. (As the title implies, this book discusses both DA and CA, and as well as including readable introductions to both, it develops a series of arguments in favour of CA's attention to the minute details of interaction over some more broad-brushed DA approaches.)

Deciding Which Approach to Take

Now that you know a little about some of the key approaches available to you, it's time to think about how you might go about deciding which to use in your project. In Figure 8.1, we offer some guidance in decision making about which method of analysis might be most appropriate for your work. Although presented as a flow-chart, what really matters is the fit between your philosophical perspective, research question(s), data collection method and analytic approach (see Chapter 1), rather than the order in which these are selected. However, there is an important caveat here, namely that no formula should supersede a considered and personal judgement about the appropriateness of your analytic choices, and you should discuss these issues with your supervisor. Equally, practical criteria such as what approaches you have been taught during your degree programme and the supervisory expertise available to you are important.

···· ···In a nutshell··· ·······································

Experience or discourse?

A useful way to begin making your decision is to think about whether or not you are primarily interested in people's experiences, or whether you are interested in the form and function of discourse. Do you value a focus on experience, or are you sceptical about treating language as reflective of experience? Whereas DA and CA involve a rejection of notions of 'experience' as a focus of enquiry, the other approaches can each be used within epistemological frameworks which assume access to experience is possible.

· ·

A related consideration concerns epistemology. Different methods of analysis take up certain epistemological positions, so your choice of method should be consistent with your epistemological stance as a researcher and with your decisions around data collection or selection. For example, if you were working with interview data you would need to consider whether you were treating language as fundamentally constructive and functional (a position sympathetic to DA or CA), or as a window to the psychological world of the participant (a position sympathetic to IPA, NA and some forms of TA and GT), or possibly as a straightforward recounting of an event or phenomena (a position sympathetic to realist approaches in TA and GT). For more on epistemology, see Chapter 1.

You might also consider whether your research question is best presented as a 'what' or a 'how' question, although often wording it either way does not alter the fundamental concern (for example, how do adoptees tell the story of their lives? What are the key themes in adoptees' accounts of their lives?). The form of data you are going to work with is also an important consideration, primarily whether it is individual or group, naturalistic or solicited, large or small. Whilst most methods of analysis can be used

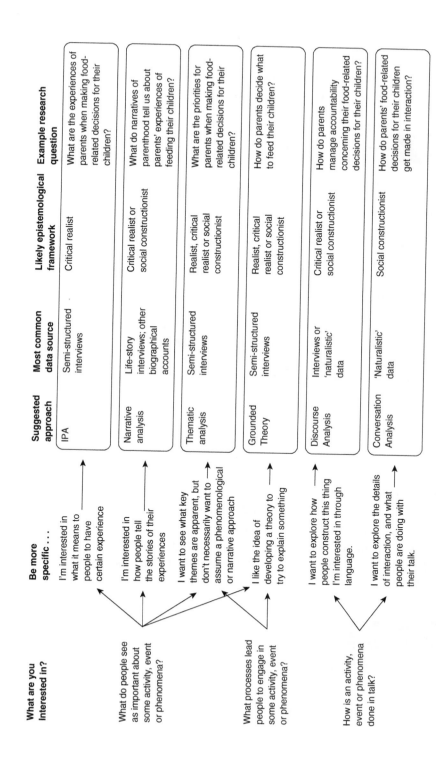

The chart below maps research interests to suggested approaches, data sources, epistemological frameworks, and example research questions.

What are you Interested in?	Be more specific . . .	Suggested approach	Most common data source	Likely epistemological framework	Example research question
What do people see as important about some activity, event or phenomena?	I'm interested in what it means to people to have certain experience	IPA	Semi-structured interviews	Critical realist	What are the experiences of parents when making food-related decisions for their children?
	I'm interested in how people tell the stories of their experiences	Narrative analysis	Life-story interviews; other biographical accounts	Critical realist or social constructionist	What do narratives of parenthood tell us about parents' experiences of feeding their children?
	I want to see what key themes are apparent, but don't necessarily want to assume a phenomenological or narrative approach	Thematic analysis	Semi-structured interviews	Realist, critical realist or social constructionist	What are the priorities for parents when making food-related decisions for their children?
What processes lead people to engage in some activity, event or phenomena?	I like the idea of developing a theory to try to explain something	Grounded Theory	Semi-structured interviews	Realist, critical realist or social constructionist	How do parents decide what to feed their children?
How is an activity, event or phenomena done in talk?	I want to explore how people construct this thing I'm interested in through language.	Discourse Analysis	Interviews or 'naturalistic' data	Critical realist or social constructionist	How do parents manage accountability concerning their food-related decisions for their children?
	I want to explore the details of interaction, and what people are doing with their talk.	Conversation Analysis	'Naturalistic' data	Social constructionist	How do parents' food-related decisions for their children get made in interaction?

Figure 8.1 Decision-making chart

with a range of data types, some are more restricted; for example, CA is so intensive that smaller amounts of data are typically examined (Forrester, 2019), narrative analysis requires a personal narrative around isolated or life-span events (Howitt, 2019), and there is debate around the appropriateness of subjecting interview data to a discourse analysis (see, for example, Potter and Hepburn, 2005).

Top tip

Take a position

Before beginning your analysis, make sure you have a clear epistemological position on what you consider your data to be (or to represent), and ensure you analyse it and write about it in a way that is consistent with that position. So, if you were using DA, you would not make claims about participants' thoughts, attitudes and feelings, but would instead attend to the nature and function of the talk. Alternatively, if you were using IPA, you would avoid writing about what the participants said as purely functional or entirely constructed, and would instead treat it as a way to understand their emotional and psychological world.

So, be clear about your epistemological position during your analysis, and write up your findings in a way that is entirely consistent with this, thus evidencing a sound understanding of these important features of qualitative research (see Chapter 1 for more on epistemology; Chapter 9 on coherence as a measure of quality and Chapter 10 for writing up).

How to Analyse Qualitative Data

As indicated in the overviews above, there are important differences between approaches to qualitative analysis. These are not simply differences in how the analysis is done, but also involve different research questions and often different forms of data. However, it is possible to identify some broad similarities across methods, and in the rest of this chapter we review some generic analytic processes that will help you with whatever form of qualitative analysis you are doing. This will help to make the analytic process more concrete and will facilitate the delivery of a sound, rigorous analysis (see Chapter 9).

In a nutshell

Key analytic processes

The following are important processes in qualitative analysis:

- anchoring to your research question;
- transcription;

- initial readings; and
- systematic analysis.

These are inter-related, and early stages drive successive ones, like cogs in a system.

· ·

Anchoring to your research question

It is important that your analysis addresses your specific research question(s). However, research questions can change over the course of a project as new and unexpected findings emerge (see Chapter 2 for a discussion of the cyclical nature of research question development).

In principle, any dataset can be used to address a range of research questions. For example, if you have a series of interviews with people who have chronic fatigue syndrome (CFS), you might examine the data for the way in which interviewees construct their condition in medicalised terms, or with a view to exploring how sufferers navigate the healthcare system, or how recovery from the syndrome is perceived and experienced. What you want to know shapes your analytic activity; if you were interested in the first of these questions about CFS, you would examine the entire corpus for medicalised language, whereas if you were interested in the second question, you would identify and analyse only those aspects of the data that related to interaction with community nurses, GPs and other health professionals, and ignore other parts of the dataset that were not relevant. Deeming some aspects of the data as more useful than others in answering the research question is a credible and viable decision, although you must report your rationale for this.

Cautionary tale

Answer the question!

Toby's research question for his final year project was: 'How do young offenders account for their offending?' He collected data from three focus groups, each with five participants who had offended. He wanted to analyse the data with discourse analysis, and phrased his research question appropriately, with the term 'accounting for' necessarily implying a focus on the function of talk. However, he encountered problems in the focus of his analysis as he was drawn to the experiential aspects of the data (for instance, some participants reported experiences of extreme boredom, frustration and lack of purpose) and so Toby progressed his analysis by attending to the emotions, experiences and psychological states which the participants reported. His final analytic output was therefore more like what would be

(Continued)

produced by IPA rather than discourse analysis, and did not answer his stated research question. Indeed, his output appeared to answer a somewhat different question, namely: 'In what ways do young offenders experience triggers to their offending?' If you find yourself following a similar path, don't worry, all is not lost! Indeed, a hallmark of a good research project is that it is flexible and can move to explore interesting findings thrown up by preliminary analysis. So, provided you recognise that your approach to the data is shifting, you may be able to switch emphasis during your project. This may involve you collecting more data, but the important thing is to:

- Recognise the shift in emphasis before you get to the writing up stage!
- Learn the principles and quality criteria of any new method you need to use.
- Revisit your research question so that your study is conceptually coherent.

Transcription

As noted in Chapter 7, transcription is more than merely a technical process – it involves making important analytic decisions. Transcription in qualitative research typically refers to the conversion of spoken talk (audio or video) into another representation of language, typically text (so you do not have to do transcription if your data is already text). Although transcription is time consuming (see Chapter 7), it serves many important functions; not only does it transform your data into a format suitable for analysis, it also familiarises you with your data, and stimulates your analytic thinking. It is in this sense that it can be seen as a preliminary stage of analysis.

In recent years, speech-recognition technology has improved to the point where it can be useful for providing a rough first-pass transcript. There are a range of specialist software packages, but the tools available through the standard Microsoft 365 suite are more than adequate. You should note, however, that if you use a speech-to-text app to aid your transcription you should always go through it in detail yourself as there will be many errors, and it won't use any particular transcription conventions that you may need for your analysis. See Chapter 5 for more on this.

Different analytic methods tend to favour different forms of transcription, typically distinguished as either *orthographic* (or playscript) or non-orthographic, and each varying according to the level of detail required for analysis (see Table 8.1). Playscript/orthographic transcription transforms audio data into a word-for-word (verbatim) representation in a way that focuses largely on what words were spoken, rather than how. In contrast, Jeffersonian transcription (named after its creator, Gail Jefferson) captures not only the words spoken, but also many *paralinguistic* features of the interaction, and sometimes *extralinguistic* features. Conversation analysts typically transcribe only a portion of the data in full Jeffersonian format, as they interrogate the data at a greater level of interactional detail.

A modified form of Jeffersonian transcription, called Jefferson-Lite (Parker, 2005) is often used, particularly in discursive work. Whilst playscript in form, it also captures some paralinguistic features that might be seen as impacting on how the talk is understood (such as lengthy silences, shouting).

···· ···In a nutshell··· ···

Transcription terminology

Paralinguistic features include aspects of speech delivery such as pauses, overlaps, emphasis, volume and intonation.

Extralinguistic features include gaze, body language and other non-verbal behaviours.

Orthography is the standard spelling and punctuation system of a written language.

As well as being fit for different analytic purposes, varying forms of transcription can be understood as representing different theoretical conceptualizations of talk, with playscript forms drawing attention to the content of what was said rather than the details of interaction, and Jeffersonian transcription doing the opposite. In this sense, transcription is theory-laden. As well as being appropriate for your analytic purpose, decisions about what form of transcription to adopt should also be compatible with your epistemological and ontological position (Lapadat and Lindsay, 1999).

Table 8.1 Forms of transcription preferred by particular analytic methods

Analytic Method	Preferred level of transcription
Thematic Analysis	Orthographic/playscript
IPA	Orthographic/playscript
Grounded Theory	Orthographic/playscript
Narrative Analysis	Orthographic/playscript
Discourse Analysis	Jeffersonian or Jefferson-Lite*
Conversation Analysis	Jeffersonian
	* depending on the level of detail required by your research question and type of discourse analysis used.

Transcription is not an uncomplicated activity. No form of transcription can deliver an exact replica of the original talk with all of its intricacies, and by its very nature transcription shapes the data. You will enhance the quality of your work if you can demonstrate an awareness of this. For guidance on how to present extracts from it in your work, see Chapter 10.

Want to know more about transcription?

Hammersley, M. (2020) Transcription of speech. In M.R.M. Ward and S. Delamon (eds), *Handbook of Qualitative Research in Education*. Cheltenham: Edward Elgar. pp. 374-9.

Bird, C.M. (2005) How I stopped dreading and learned to love transcription. *Qualitative Inquiry*, 11, 226-48 (A cautionary tale about the 'dos and don'ts' of transcription.)

Jefferson, G. (2004) Glossary of transcript symbols with an introduction. In G.H. Lerner (ed.), *Conversation Analysis: Studies from the First Generation*. Amsterdam: John Benjamins. pp. 13-31. (A guide to symbols used in Jeffersonian transcription; available online at: www.liso.ucsb.edu/Jefferson.)

For an online tutorial in Jeffersonian transcription, visit Emanuel A. Schegloff's online Jeffersonian transcription tutorial:

www.sscnet.ucla.edu/soc/faculty/schegloff/TranscriptionProject/index.html

For examples of playscript and Jeffersonian transcription of the same data, see: https://tqrmul.com

For software to assist with Jeffersonian transcription see: www.audacityteam.org

Initial readings

Reading your transcripts, in a way that builds on the familiarity established during transcription, is an important early stage of every analytic method (Smith and Osborn, 2015: 40, refer to it as *'free textual analysis'*), and, like later stages of analysis, is driven

Table 8.2 Purpose of first stage reading in different analytic methods

Analytic Method	Purpose
Thematic Analysis, Grounded Theory, IPA	Establish a holistic sense of the breadth and depth of the experiences the participant has talked about. Establish a basic sense of what appear to be the key issues, experiences or feelings that the participant reports. You may get an early sense of themes upon successive readings. Be attentive, at a preliminary level, to the way you as the interviewer are involved in shaping the data.
Narrative Analysis	Establish a sense of the entire story generated by the participant, with initial identification of what appears to be the narrative tone, key images/metaphors and themes.
Discourse Analysis	Establish a sense of the breadth of issues covered in the data. Be attentive, at a preliminary level, to what key issues or phenomena are being talked about. You may get a sense of what appear to be familiar and unusual ways of talking.
Conversation Analysis	The initial reading might be of a Jefferson-Lite or playscript transcription alongside the audio as a way to decide what to focus on and transcribe in full Jeffersonian format. A more specific research question may be developed at this point.

by your research question. However, students new to qualitative methods often feel their initial reading is directionless and are unsure that they are doing it right. Table 8.2 may help to render the purpose of this first stage more tangible.

Unless you have a specific reason to begin with one in particular, it generally does not matter which transcript you begin your analysis with. This first stage of reading is as important as later stages of analysis and it helps to loosely map out in your mind the breadth and depth of the data. Once you have established this, you may feel freer to focus on more micro aspects of the data, as these will now feel *contextualised*. At this stage, it can often be useful to read your transcripts whilst listening to the audio recordings.

·······**··In a nutshell····**···

Contextualisation

This is a term used generally in qualitative methods to acknowledge that aspects of the data should always be understood as being part of a broader dataset (such as an interview or set of extracts) which has itself been generated or collected by a researcher. In other words, nothing should be considered as existing 'in a vacuum'.

··

Systematic analysis

Analysis, by its very nature, demands dedicated and goal-directed thinking. It is more than summarising, rephrasing or regurgitating the data in a journalistic form, but at the same time it should not extend into over-interpretation (for example, making claims about the motives of a participant without evidence of this in the data). You can find the right balance by being systematic and recognising that qualitative analysis is a cyclical process, in which your ideas develop more conceptually over time. For most forms of analysis, your job is to find the big ideas in the data – broadly speaking, these could be understood to be themes or discourses. You work with the detail of what participants said in order to build up a sense of what those big ideas are. It is very normal for students to worry that they are over- or under-interpreting so seek help from your supervisor to get this balance right.

Your analysis needs to be systematic so that it doesn't slip into a chaotic, haphazard, vague process that produces any output you like. As Lyons (2021: 5, emphasis in original) states: '*no single interpretation is the "correct" or "true" one [but t]his does not mean any interpretation is a good interpretation*'. Rather, qualitative analysis is a focused and rigorous activity that seeks to impose structure on potentially quite disorganised data in ways that facilitate increasingly abstract ways of conceptualising the data in order to answer a specific question.

To facilitate this, you need a system for organising, recording and managing your analytic process. This may be in paper and pencil form, via specialist qualitative data analysis software (see below), or a mixture of the two. Good organisation is not only important for keeping you on track but will help you to evidence some markers of quality (see Chapter 9 for a detailed discussion of these issues). Whatever approach you take, recording your developing thoughts and hunches about your data is highly recommended. This is formalised in some approaches (for example, memos in grounded theory; reflective diaries in IPA), in which the record of your engagement in the analytic process can serve as part of the process of being reflexive about your data (for examples see Charmaz, 2015; Gordon-Finlayson, 2019). Students may, for example, keep a research diary (see Chapter 9) where they note what they find interesting, unusual or unexpected about what a participant said, or where there are examples of contradictory view or experiences within or across transcripts.

Analysis is an intensive process, in which you become immersed in your data. By 'immersed', we mean that you dig deep into it, try to feel it and understand it, linger with ideas and be extremely curious about what participants are conveying or experiencing. So, aim to work on your analysis in substantial chunks of time (like a half or full day), rather than an hour here and there. Otherwise, you may fail to make those conceptual insights that are the hallmark of an excellent analysis. Also, you waste time trying to get your thinking back to the point where you had left off.

Top tip

Keeping track

If you are leaving your analysis for some time, leave a note to yourself about what you were thinking and why (you might record this in a research journal). This helps you pick up faster when you come back to it.

There are some commonalities between methods. For example, thematic analysis, IPA and grounded theory all involve an early stage of preliminary, open or initial coding whereby terms (usually referred to as codes) are assigned to sections of the text in a way that represents the key point, or nature, of that portion of data, or what you notice about it. Whilst this can be done on a line-by-line basis, codes are normally applied to 'meaningful units', which are portions of data (words or paragraphs) that appear to convey something important. Such systematic scrutiny guards against haphazard or partial examination of the data and promotes a firmly evidence-based analysis (Charmaz, 1995).

Howitt and Cramer (2020) note that novice researchers can often make the mistake of reaching too far beyond the data in their initial coding. Figure 8.2 provides an example of a page of hand-coded transcript, and these codes stick pretty close to the content of the transcript, without attempts to over-interpret what is being said. In fact, some codes use the participant's own words (e.g. 'gutted'; 'stupid things') – these are known as *in vivo* codes. It is worth noting Howitt and Cramer's (2020: 412) advice that 'initial codings can be seen to be little more than a fairly mundane summary of a few lines of text'. The same codes can be assigned to portions of data that appear similar, and you can return to codes later when needed, usually to refine them. Early codes are not typically reported in the write-up, but a sample can be included in your appendices if required by your department.

Initial coding in narrative analysis might generate a 'working map' of the narrative tone, imagery and themes at a preliminary level (Crossley, 2007). Coding in discourse analysis has a different meaning and typically involves the identification of all instances where the objects or phenomena under investigation are constructed in the data (Potter and Wetherell, 1987). Conversation analysis does not use the term coding but rather, once features of the talk have been selected for study, analysis focuses specifically on the details of the interactions themselves (Drew, 2015).

Activity 8.1

Have a go at coding

Watch a segment of the video-recorded semi-structured interviews available at: https://tqrmul. com. Once you have done this, download the transcript of the relevant interview and have a go at coding. If you are working with a friend, why not both have a go? Discuss any differences and similarities between your codes.

Top tip

Deviant case analysis

Each of the approaches discussed in this chapter make use of some form of deviant case analysis (sometimes also referred to as negative case analysis). This analytic tool involves actively seeking out cases in your dataset which contradict, or otherwise cause problems for, your analytic claims. This helps you to jettison claims which are not supported by your data, and ultimately to refine your claims so that they account for each case in your dataset (see Silverman, 2020).

There are a number of computer-assissted qualitative data analysis siftware (CAQDAS) packages available. Some of the most commonly used include NVivo, Atlas.ti and MaxQDA. If you have access to one of these through your institution you may want to explore the possibility of using it to manage your project. CAQDAS packages can be useful for organising your data, as well as for helping to clarify your analytic thinking.

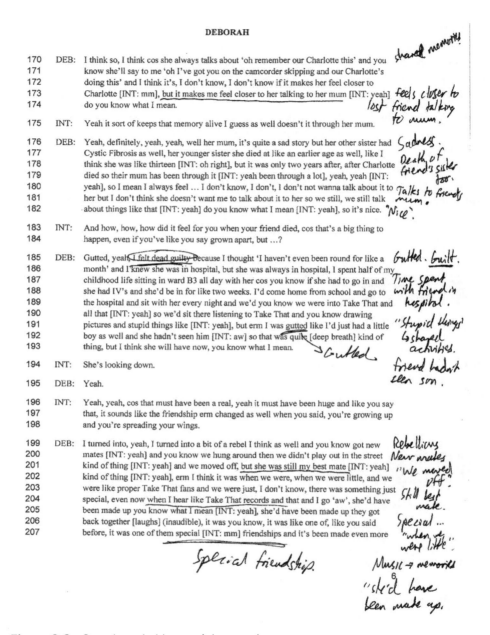

DEBORAH

170 DEB: I think so, I think cos she always talks about 'oh remember our Charlotte this' and you
171 know she'll say to me 'oh I've got you on the camcorder skipping and our Charlotte's
172 doing this' and I think it's, I don't know, I don't know if it makes her feel closer to
173 Charlotte [INT: mm], but it makes me feel closer to her talking to her mum [INT: yeah]
174 do you know what I mean.

shared memories!

feels closer to lost friend talking to mum.

175 INT: Yeah it sort of keeps that memory alive I guess as well doesn't it through her mum.

176 DEB: Yeah, definitely, yeah, yeah, well her mum, it's quite a sad story but her other sister had
177 Cystic Fibrosis as well, her younger sister she died at like an earlier age as well, like I
178 think she was like thirteen [INT: oh right], but it was only two years after, after Charlotte
179 died so their mum has been through it [INT: yeah been through a lot], yeah, yeah [INT:
180 yeah], so I mean I always feel … I don't know, I don't, I don't not wanna talk about it to
181 her but I don't think she doesn't want me to talk about it to her so we still, we still talk
182 about things like that [INT: yeah] do you know what I mean [INT: yeah], so it's nice.

Sadness.
Death of friend's sister too.
Talks to friends mum.
"Nice".

183 INT: And how, how, how did it feel for you when your friend died, cos that's a big thing to
184 happen, even if you've like you say grown apart, but …?

185 DEB: Gutted, yeah, I felt dead guilty because I thought 'I haven't even been round for like a
186 month' and I knew she was in hospital, but she was always in hospital, I spent half of my
187 childhood life sitting in ward B3 all day with her cos you know if she had to go in and
188 she had IV's and she'd be in for like two weeks. I'd come home from school and go to
189 the hospital and sit with her every night and we'd you know we were into Take That and
190 all that [INT: yeah] so we'd sit there listening to Take That and you know drawing
191 pictures and stupid things like [INT: yeah], but erm I was gutted like I'd just had a little
192 boy as well and she hadn't seen him [INT: aw] so that was quite [deep breath] kind of
193 thing, but I think she will have now, you know what I mean.

Gutted. Guilt.
Time spent with friend in hospital.
"Stupid things" & shared activities.
→ Gutted
friend hadn't seen son.

194 INT: She's looking down.

195 DEB: Yeah.

196 INT: Yeah, yeah, cos that must have been a real, yeah it must have been huge and like you say
197 that, it sounds like the friendship erm changed as well when you said, you're growing up
198 and you're spreading your wings.

199 DEB: I turned into, yeah, I turned into a bit of a rebel I think as well and you know got new
200 mates [INT: yeah] and you know we hung around then we didn't play out in the street
201 kind of thing [INT: yeah] and we moved off, but she was still my best mate [INT: yeah]
202 kind of thing [INT: yeah], erm I think it was when we were, when we were little, and we
203 were like proper Take That fans and we were just, I don't know, there was something just
204 special, even now when I hear like Take That records and that and I go 'aw', she'd have
205 been made up you know what I mean [INT: yeah], she'd have been made up they got
206 back together [laughs] (inaudible), it was you know, it was like one of, like you said
207 before, it was one of them special [INT: mm] friendships and it's been made even more

Rebellious
New mates
"We moved off"
Still best mate.
Special …
"when we were little"

Special friendship.

Music → memories
"she'd have been made up.

Figure 8.2 Sample coded transcript excerpt

However, it should be noted that the packages do not do the analysis for you, just as you wouldn't expect the paper-and-pen to do the analysis for you if you were working by hand!

If you are using CAQDAS software, make sure that you have access to some relevant training. It is perhaps still unusual for CAQDAS to be taught on undergraduate degree programmes, and if you haven't been taught how to use a CAQDAS package during your course, then it might be wise not to try and get to grips with it specifically for your project. However, if this is something you are keen to explore, you could ask your supervisor if your university runs any training sessions that you could attend. See Figure 8.3 for an example of how the coding process can work in a CAQDAS package.

Want to know more about CAQDAS?

Silver, C. and Lewins, A. (2014) *Using Software in Qualitative Research: A Step-by-Step Guide* (2nd edn). London: Sage. (A classic of its kind, dealing with a range of practical and conceptual issues around the use of CAQDAS.)

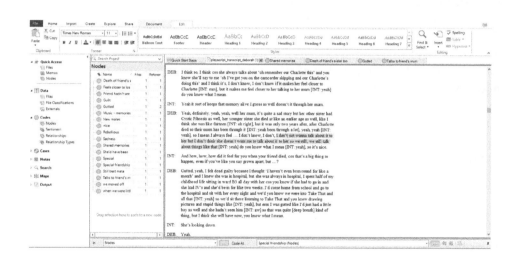

Figure 8.3 Sample coded transcript in NVivo

This is an excerpt from the same portion of transcript featured in Figure 8.2, so you can see how different the same coding process looks when comparing the paper-and-pen method to a computer-assisted approach. It has been coded using NVivo, one of the most popular CAQDAS packages. NVivo refers to codes as 'nodes', which you can see listed in the middle column. On the left is the transcript, with the text highlighted being that covered by the 'Talks to friend's mum' code. This example already gives you a sense of how the language of the software might vary from the terms used in your analytic approach, and when it comes to writing up your work you should always use the language of your chosen approach rather than relying on the terms used in the CAQDAS package.

In many approaches, initial coding would be followed by further coding stages. For example, as noted above, grounded theory involves discrete stages for open, focused, axial and theoretical coding to progress from an initial (open) form of coding to a more conceptual (theoretical) form (see Gordon-Finlayson, 2019). In fact, there are many different ways to approach coding, depending on your analytic approach (see Saldaña, 2021, for a particularly influential overview).

Help with Qualitative Analysis

Qualitative data analysis is difficult, no matter how many textbooks you read, or how clearly the stages are described. Table 8.3 details some of the most common challenges and worries, with some advice on how to overcome them. It is very useful to look at good quality previous work which has used the same method of analysis that you are interested in. Examine the analysis for level of detail, use of evidence, extent of interpretative activity and how claims about the data are justified. Be aware, though, that the requirements for a final year project (especially in terms of the amount of data) may be different to those for published work. In addition, make effective use of peers (who understand your method of analysis) and your supervisor. Very few qualitative researchers work in isolation; indeed, it is deemed good practice to bring your analytic thoughts at varying stages for discussion with others (see, for example, Storey, 2021). This helps you to assess the credibility of your analysis and to see where you could be more searching, confident or creative in your thinking about the data, or indeed where you have begun to make unjustified claims about it.

Conclusion

This chapter has introduced some of the most commonly used approaches to qualitative analysis. As will be apparent by now, however, these are not simply approaches to analysis, but provide perspectives on qualitative research in its entirety, from the type of research questions you might ask, to the type of data you collect, as well as the sorts of assumptions and claims you make about your data. Indeed, it is perhaps best to think of these approaches as providing perspectives on how we should understand psychology itself. You might now be aware that you should not approach the process of qualitative research in a piecemeal fashion; if you have a research question, you should know what approach to analysis you are going to take, what data you are going to collect, and so on. All of these things need to be decided at the start of your project. Having said that, things can, and do, change during the course of a project; new questions arise, the possibility of collecting different data might present itself, you may come across a paper that makes you think of your data in a different way. Indeed, one of the hallmarks of really good qualitative research might be said to be the extent to which it opens up

Table 8.3 Common concerns in qualitative analysis

Concern/Challenge	Ways to overcome it
Don't know where to start	For TA, IPA, GT and NA, select a transcript – any transcript – and begin with initial readings, taking it three to five lines at a time, and assigning a descriptive label. For DA, identify where the object or phenomena under investigation is talked about. For CA, select any 30-second portion of your data and begin to transcribe it in Jeffersonian conventions – this will help you to attend to the details of interaction.
Confused about what to focus on	Analysis should be rigorous and systematic to avoid cherry picking some aspects of the data and not others. Try to interrogate every aspect of the data for its detail, variation and complexity (Henwood & Pidgeon, 1994), and its contribution to understanding your research question. However, some data can be highly incoherent or fragmented (Storey, 2021). In such cases, remain attentive to the entire transcript or dataset as well as to micro aspects of it. Be prepared to exclude some aspects of the data on the grounds that it does not shed light on the research question, and actively seek out deviant cases. Make effective use of memos/notes on your analytic decisions.
Contradictions in the data	This is not problematic as human experience, behaviour and talk is replete with apparent inconsistencies. Consider the research context which prompted the data (such as the specific conversational exchange in which it occurred), and why the account might make sense to the speaker.
Feeling stuck in your analysis	Review your progress to date, and set deadlines for the completion of different stages of the work. Ask yourself what you are happy with about the analysis so far, and what appears interesting/missing/unknown/difficult to understand about the data. Try writing summaries for parts of the dataset (e.g. for each participant or data item). Be prepared to make some decisions about your analysis, which you can return to later if needed. Take the review and your questions to a peer or supervisor. Be encouraged that analysis tends to get quicker as you progress through the dataset.
Information overload	Return to the fundamental requirement of your research question. Be prepared to amalgamate some of your early analytic outputs (where there seems to be sufficient similarity of form or function), or to eliminate some of them (where they seem less relevant or insufficiently evidenced). Remember that analysis is an iterative process so be prepared to move backwards and forwards in the analytic process.
Feeling that you are biasing the analysis	Remember your job is to produce one way to 'read' the data. Most approaches to qualitative research value the subjectivity of the analyst – how else could you understand the data? You can manage this by using memos and notes to record your perceived influence on the analysis, including the decisions you are making about it. Deploy quality criteria (see Chapter 8) such as transparency, triangulation, audit trails and credibility/plausibility checks to promote rigour in your analysis.
Over-interpretation	It is exciting to pursue possible interpretations but there must always be credible evidence for those interpretations. Bring your doubts or concerns for peer or supervisor discussion. Consider whether you are applying psychological theory or frameworks to the data at too early a stage; these considerations should perhaps be applied at the discussion stage, leaving the analysis to be more data-driven (see, for example, Frosh & Young, 2017). Remain committed to credibility checks with others.
Lack of confidence	Remember that you are aiming for a credible, plausible account of the data and are working with likelihood rather than certainty (Crossley, 2007). Have you been systematic? Could you be more questioning of the data: What is the best possible interpretation of what it means? What are your intuitive thoughts about the data? Is there evidence for these? Be prepared to make some decisions about analysis that you can return to later if needed. Compare your work with published methods using the same methodology to assess their analytic level.
None of the above really helped …	Remember to ask your supervisor for advice if you are really stuck – it is always better to do this than to struggle on in silence. Be kind to yourself: you are learning something new, it is quite hard, and that is what your supervisor is there to help with.

new possibilities for enquiry. Equally, deciding on your analytic approach should not determine precisely what you will find: you should always be prepared to be surprised by the discoveries you generate as you analyse your data. Ultimately, the acid test of good qualitative research is the same as for good research in general: does it tell us something novel about the world, and does it do so in a scholarly and convincing way? In the next chapter, we turn to consider in detail how we can be sure that qualitative research has been done well.

References

Braun, V. and Clarke, V. (2006) Using thematic analysis in psychology. *Qualitative Research in Psychology*, 3, 77–101.

Charmaz, K. (1995) Grounded theory. In J.A. Smith, R. Harre and L.V. Langenhove (eds), *Rethinking Methods in Psychology*. London: Sage. pp. 27–49.

Charmaz, K. (2014) *Constructing Grounded Theory* (2nd edn). London: Sage.

Charmaz, K. (2015) Grounded theory. In J.A. Smith (ed.), *Qualitative Psychology: A Practical Guide to Research Methods* (3rd edn). London: Sage. pp. 53–84.

Crossley, M. (2007) Narrative analysis. In E. Lyons and A. Coyle (eds), *Analysing Qualitative Data in Psychology*. London: Sage. pp. 131–44.

Drew, P. (2015) Conversation analysis. In J.A. Smith (ed.), *Qualitative Psychology: A Practical Guide to Research Methods* (3rd edn). London: Sage. pp. 108–42.

Forrester, M. (2019) Conversation analysis. In C. Sullivan and M.A. Forrester (eds), *Doing Qualitative Research in Psychology: A Practical Guide* (2nd edn). London: Sage. pp. 258–83.

Frosh, S. and Young, L.S. (2017). Psychoanalytic approaches to qualitative psychology. In C. Willig and W. Stainton-Rogers (eds), *The Sage Handbook of Qualitative Research in Psychology*. London: Sage. pp. 124–40.

Glaser, B.G. and Strauss, A.L. (1967) *The Discovery of Grounded Theory: Strategies for Qualitative Research*. New York: Aldine.

Gordon-Finlayson, A. (2019) Grounded theory. In C. Sullivan and M.A. Forrester (eds), *Doing Qualitative Research in Psychology: A Practical Guide* (2nd edn). London: Sage. pp. 284–312.

Heathcote, L.C., Loecher, N., Simon, P., Spunt, S.L., Jordan, A., Tutelman, P.R., Cunningham, S., Schapira, L. and Simons, L.E. (2021) Symptom appraisal in uncertainty: A theory-driven thematic analysis with survivors of childhood cancer. *Psychology & Health*, 36, 1182–99.

Henwood, K. and Pidgeon, N. (1994) Beyond the qualitative paradigm: A framework for introducing diversity within qualitative psychology. *Journal of Community and Applied Social Psychology*, 4, 225–38.

Hiles, D., Čermák, I. and Chrz, V. (2017) Narrative inquiry. In C. Willig and W. Stainton-Rogers (eds), *The Sage Handbook of Qualitative Research in Psychology* (2nd edn). London: Sage. pp. 157–75.

Howitt, D. (2019) *Introduction to Qualitative Research Methods in Psychology: Putting Theory Into Practice* (4th edn). Harlow: Prentice Hall.

Howitt, D. and Cramer, D. (2020) *Research Methods in Psychology* (6th edn). Harlow: Pearson.

King, N. (2012) Doing template analysis. In G. Symon and C. Cassell (eds), *Qualitative Organizational Research: Core Methods and Current Challenges*. London: Sage. pp. 426–50.

Lapadat, J.C. and Lindsay, A.C. (1999) Transcription in research and practice: From standardization of technique to interpretive positioning. *Qualitative Inquiry*, 5, 64–86.

Lyons, E. (2021) Doing qualitative research: Initial questions. In E. Lyons and A. Coyle (eds), *Analysing Qualitative Data in Psychology* (3rd edn). London: Sage. pp. 3–10.

Lyons, E. and Coyle, A. (2021) *Analysing Qualitative Data in Psychology* (3rd edn). London: Sage.

McAdams, D.P. (1993) *The Stories We Live By: Personal Myths and the Making of the Self*. New York: Guilford.

Murray, M. (2015) Narrative psychology. In J.A. Smith (ed.), *Qualitative Psychology: A Practical Guide to Research Methods* (3rd edn). London: Sage. pp. 85–107.

Parker, I. (2005) *Qualitative Psychology: Introducing Radical Research*. Maidenhead: Open University Press.

Payne, M. (2006) *Narrative Therapy: An Introduction for Counsellors* (2nd edn). London: Sage.

Payne, S. (2021) Grounded theory. In E. Lyons and A. Coyle (eds), *Analysing Qualitative Data in Psychology*. London: Sage. pp. 196–222.

Potter, J. and Hepburn, A. (2005) Qualitative interviews in psychology: Problems and possibilities. *Qualitative Research in Psychology*, 2, 281–307.

Potter, J. and Hepburn, A. (2008) Discursive constructionism. In J.A. Holstein and J.F. Gubrium (eds), *Handbook of Constructionist Research*. New York: Guilford Press. pp. 275–93.

Potter, J. and Wetherell, M. (1987). *Discourse and Social Psychology: Beyond Attitudes and Behaviour*. London: Sage.

Riley, S. and Wiggins, S. (2019) Discourse analysis. In C. Sullivan and M.A. Forrester (eds), *Doing Qualitative Research in Psychology: A Practical Guide* (2nd edn). London: Sage. pp. 233–56.

Saldaña, J. (2021) *The Coding Manual for Qualitative Researchers* (4th edn). London: Sage.

Shaw, R. (2019) Interpretative phenomenological analysis. In C. Sullivan and M.A. Forrester (eds), *Doing Qualitative Research in Psychology: A Practical Guide* (2nd edn). London: Sage. pp. 185–208.

Silver, C. and Lewins, A. (2014) *Using Software in Qualitative Research: A Step-by-Step Guide* (2nd edn). London: Sage.

Silverman, D. (2020) *Interpreting Qualitative Data* (6th edn). London: Sage.

Sims-Schouten, W. and Riley, S. (2019) Presenting critical realist discourse analysis as a tool for making sense of service users' accounts of their mental health problems. *Qualitative Health Research*, 29, 1016–28.

Smith, J.A. (ed.) (2015) *Qualitative Psychology: A Practical Guide to Research Methods* (3rd edn). London: Sage.

Smith, J.A. and Osborn, M. (2015) Interpretative phenomenological analysis. In J.A. Smith (ed.), *Qualitative Psychology: A Practical Guide to Research Methods* (3rd edn). London: Sage. pp. 25–52.

Stokoe, E.H. and Smithson, J. (2001) Making gender relevant: Conversation analysis and gender categories in interaction. *Discourse and Society*, 12, 217–44.

Storey, L. (2021) Doing interpretative phenomenological analysis. In E. Lyons and A. Coyle (eds), *Analysing Qualitative Data in Psychology* (3rd edn). London: Sage. pp. 180–95.

Sullivan, C. and Forrester, M.A. (eds.) (2019) *Doing Qualitative Research in Psychology: A Practical Guide* (2nd edn). London: Sage.

Wiggins, S. (2017) *Discursive Psychology: Theory, Method and Applications*. London: Sage.

Willig, C. (2022) *Introducing Qualitative Research in Psychology* (4th edn). London: Open University Press.

Willig, C. and Stainton-Rogers, W. (2017) *The Sage Handbook of Qualitative Research in Psychology* (2nd edn). London: Sage.

9
ACHIEVING QUALITY IN YOUR PROJECT

Cath Sullivan, Nollaig Frost
and Kathryn Kinmond

Understanding what makes good research can help you do a great project in two ways. First, knowledge of what makes good research helps you to evaluate others' research and critically evaluate existing literature. This is important for building a rationale for your study in the early parts of your write-up. Second, knowing about research quality will help you to design, carry out and present your own research to a high standard. All the other chapters in this book will help you do your best research. But in this chapter we focus explicitly on methods for recognising good research and advise you on how to use these to make your project brilliant.

In this chapter we will:

- Explain why it is important for you to think about how good qualitative research is defined and recognised.
- Outline some general quality criteria that are useful for all research.
- Discuss two quality criteria that are relevant for most qualitative student projects:

  o Reflexivity;
  o good qualitative analysis.

- Offer suggestions for how you can find specific quality criteria for the methods you are using.

What is Research Quality?

Research quality is about the strengths and weakness of research. All research has limitations – for example, a small-scale case study of a particular setting tells us only about how things work in that setting. But the study should be good enough to be credible, so we can take seriously what it tells us about that setting. While limitations are inevitable in research, low quality should not be.

So how we do we work out what counts as high-quality research? Usually, we assess research quality by using a set of agreed quality criteria. This works in the same way as a marker comparing a piece of your work against a set of marking criteria. Using a set of criteria allows us to identify specific strengths and weaknesses, ensures that we are evaluating similar studies in the same way and tells us whether research meets a minimum quality standard.

···· ···In a nutshell··· ···

Quality criteria

Quality criteria are specific standards against which research can be compared in order to:

- illustrate each research study's key strengths and weaknesses;
- ensure fairness by evaluating similar studies in the same way as each other; and
- judge whether research meets minimum quality standards and can usefully tell us things.

··

Later in this chapter we offer suggestions for quality criteria that are useful for your project. But first we consider what shapes quality criteria and some debates about them.

Why Does Research Quality Matter?

Some argue that standardised quality criteria are not possible or desirable for qualitative research (see Majid and Vanstone, 2018). Others warn that attempts to assess quality can stifle methodological innovation (Parker, 2004). Our view is that methods for assessing the quality of all research are necessary. Psychology is an empirical discipline, which means using evidence to justify our claims and the actions we recommend. Most of this evidence comes from research, which is produced through social processes that are subjective and involve interpretation. Yet considering the quality of research remains important so that we can judge whether the ways in which evidence is produced and interpreted are reasonable.

Another argument is that qualitative researchers cannot work with an 'anything goes' attitude if they want their work to be taken seriously. Although this is changing, commonly used quality criteria often assume that all research is quantitative. Therefore, qualitative research is often evaluated against inappropriate standards (Levitt et al., 2018) that lead to it being seen as poor research rather than being recognised as simply not quantitative. To prevent this, qualitative researchers must challenge inappropriate ways of judging quality and be clear about how evaluation should be done.

····In a nutshell····

Why do we need 'qualitative' criteria?

Quality criteria for quantitative research are unlikely to be useful if simplistically applied to qualitative research (Frost and Bailey-Rodriguez, 2019). For example, 'reliability' means how consistently a quantitative variable is measured across different time points and settings. So, judging reliability helps us evaluate measurement in quantitative studies. Reliability is often achieved through standardisation; for example, asking all participants the same questions in the same way (Robson, 2016). In the context of qualitative data collection, such as interviews, highly standardised questions make little sense. This is because qualitative interviewing uses questioning flexibly to maximise the participants' opportunities to express what matters to them (see Chapter 7).

When it comes to your project, the idea that its quality will be assessed is more straightforward. Your project will be evaluated against marking criteria. These will be tailored to the learning outcomes of your course but will also reflect general assumptions about research quality. So, learning about this can help you get good marks.

Top tip

Know your marking criteria

Good understanding of research quality can help you to produce a great project. But most quality criteria are written with published research in mind. Although looking at published studies can help, your research will be judged differently from how we judge research for publication. The marking criteria for your project will reflect general ideas about research quality but will be tailored to fit with what you have been asked to do.

So, get familiar with the marking criteria for your project right at the start and keep referring to them as you go along. Also, remember to discuss them with your supervisor to make sure you understand them and can judge how what you are doing fits with them.

What Shapes Quality Criteria?

Definitions of quality are debated, and researchers differ in their ideas about quality, especially when they are working within differing research traditions. Various factors shape views on this.

How do theoretical assumptions influence quality criteria?

Researchers' differing theoretical and epistemological assumptions lead to variety in qualitative research (see Chapter 1). They shape how we carry out research and judge its quality.

Want to know more about epistemology?

Discussion of epistemology appears in Chapter 1. For more detail see:

Sullivan, C. (2019) Theory and method in qualitative research. In C. Sullivan and M.A. Forrester (eds), *Doing Qualitative Research in Psychology: A Practical Guide*. London: Sage. pp. 17-34.

For example, researchers using the epistemological standpoint known as realism assume that research, if done properly, can provide unbiased knowledge (Sullivan, 2019). Consequently, they view the reduction or eradication of bias as necessary for good research. In a realist interview study researchers might systematically compare their own coding of interview transcripts with that of another researcher to see whether they produce similar results. From a realist standpoint, similarity shows that the coding results are not overly influenced by the perspective of the person coding and therefore indicates quality. In contrast, from a relativist or critical realist standpoint research is viewed as always shaped by subjective perceptions (Sullivan, 2019). So, comparing coding as described above makes little sense as a way of ensuring quality. A more relativist researcher would view such a comparison as mistakenly assuming that subjectivity can be controlled or eradicated. To keep quality high, the more relativist researcher would acknowledge and explore this subjectivity in a process known as reflexivity (more on this below). If you need a reminder about realism and relativism, see Chapter 1.

Epistemological and theoretical approaches vary in qualitative research, and this influences how we evaluate it. If you are doing your project from a realist or post-positivist approach, then it is likely to be evaluated using similar criteria to a quantitative project. Many textbooks discuss such criteria (for example, Robson, 2016). If you aren't sure what approach you are taking, or wish to take, speak to your supervisor. Quality issues for the many student projects that do not take a realist approach are discussed less often. So, we will focus on this for the rest of this chapter.

Variety in qualitative research

Many quality criteria have been proposed for qualitative research (for example, Korstjens and Moser, 2018). And there are now many sets of guidelines and checklists for evaluating qualitative research. The growth of these checklists reflects the increased use and recognition of qualitative research but may not acknowledge the differences between qualitative methods.

Want to know more about published quality checklists?

- The Publication Manual of the American Psychological Association (which gives us what is commonly known as 'APA style') has for many years provided guidelines for how research should be written up. 'APA style' aims to provide a consistent way of evaluating the quality of journal articles before publication (Levitt et al., 2018). Until recently these guidelines implicitly assumed that research was quantitative. The recent publication of the 'JARS-Qual guidelines' changed this meaning that 'APA style' no longer assumes that all research is quantitative. See Levitt et al. (2018) for more on this.
- The Critical Appraisal Skills Programme (CASP) is an initiative focused on facilitating the assessment of research quality in healthcare (Long et al., 2000). This includes the creation of a specific checklist for evaluating the quality of qualitative research. You can see this tool here: https://casp-uk.net/casp-tools-checklists/ And for a critical discussion of it, see Long et al. (2000).

Qualitative projects vary because 'qualitative research' is an umbrella term for a wide range of approaches (Gibson and Riley, 2019). And these differences mean that quality criteria that are suitable for one type of qualitative study may not be suitable for others. Because published quality checklists tend to be written for published research, they can be difficult to apply to student projects. It's useful for you to know about these checklists and, used selectively, they will help you to think about quality in your project. We'd advise you not to use any of them in their entirety but instead to tailor how you think about quality to your specific project. Below we will help you do this.

Quality Criteria for Your Project

We have highlighted that research projects vary, and that how their quality is judged must also vary to some extent. But in spite of these differences, research projects also have some common ground, and this gives rise to some general quality criteria that are likely to work for all projects. These are a good place for you to start in thinking about judging the quality of your project. Some useful general criteria are:

- Coherence. Do the methods you've chosen fit with your overall methodology and with your research question(s)? Remember you need your 'methodological kite', as discussed in Chapter 1, to fly. Also, see Chapter 2 for more on research questions and coherence.

- Good use of evidence. Have you provided clear evidence from your data that supports the claims you make? Have you provided evidence for the arguments you have made that justify your research questions?
- Rigorous use of methods. Have you followed good practice guidelines for the methods that you are using? If not, have you explained clearly how and why you have chosen to do things differently?
- Transparency in the write-up. Does your report clearly lay out exactly what you did and why? Is it clear how you have interpreted what you found? See Chapter 10 for more on this.

Activity 9.1

Focus on an example

Next time you read an article related to your research topic, consider how well it meets the general criteria above. Pay particular attention to how the authors use the data as evidence. Does it work for you as a persuasive case? If so, how? Is there anything that doesn't work for you?

Although these criteria can be used in any research, the way they are used will vary with the project. For example, 'transparency' can be a challenge in qualitative research because giving full details about your data can potentially threaten participants' anonymity and confidentiality (see Chapter 4). You might think transparency in an interview project can be achieved by providing your full set of transcripts as an appendix. But doing so might make your participants identifiable in ways that they wouldn't be just from the selective quotes that you might use in your analysis section.

Top tip

Balancing confidentiality with transparency

Conflict can occur between being transparent enough that readers can judge how ethical your work is and maintaining confidentiality. In such cases you need to do more than employ the usual ways of ensuring anonymity and confidentiality (see Chapter 4). For example, you might further modify how much information you give about your participants and be more selective about which bits of data you use. We recommend that you explain your rationale for such decisions in your method section. If you're struggling between confidentiality and transparency talk to your supervisor.

In addition to general quality criteria that we can all use, you need to identify some more specific criteria for your project. Our recommended approach for doing this is shown in Figure 9.1.

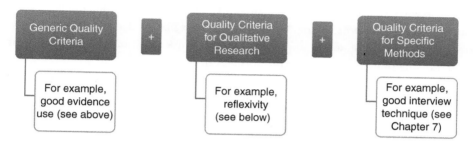

Figure 9.1 Multi-level approach to quality

Keep in mind generic quality criteria as you design and carry out your study, as they provide a basis for quality in any project. In addition, there are some quality criteria that can be used in most qualitative studies and next we suggest two that you can use. Finally, specific quality criteria for your precise methods of data collection and analysis will also exist and you should use these too. At the end of the chapter, we make suggestions for how you can locate these.

Quality Criteria for Qualitative Research

There are several quality criteria for qualitative research done using a broadly relativist or social constructionist approach (see Chapter 1). Below, drawing on our experience of supervising and marking student projects, we present two criteria that will be particularly helpful for your project.

Reflexivity

Qualitative researchers tend to view subjectivity as integral to the social process of research rather than something that can be controlled or eradicated. This is why the term 'subjectivity' is preferred to the term 'bias'. If we can't get rid of subjectivity, then how should we respond to it? To do quality research, we must employ 'reflexivity' to explore subjectivity and reflect openly about how it may have shaped our research. You are part of your project at every stage. So, a key way to be reflexive is to explicitly consider your role in shaping your research, which will help you do an excellent project. For example, you might reflect on the methodological decisions you made and what influenced them.

Reflexivity is also about showing awareness of the context in which your project was done and how this may have shaped the process and the knowledge that is produced. Various things will make up the context of your project including interpersonal dynamics and wider power relations. Universities are relatively powerful institutions and being associated with one can increase your status and power. Also, the social groups to which you and your participants belong, in relation to things like gender, ethnicity and social background, can all influence power relationships. These kinds of power relations can make it harder or easier for participants to speak honestly and to give or withdraw consent, for example. The research context is also made up of social norms and prevailing values. It may be particularly hard, for example, for a participant to be open about their experience or perspective if it is something stigmatised or socially unacceptable. Reflecting on these subjective aspects of your project is important for doing an ethical project and a thoughtful and high-quality analysis.

········ ···In a nutshell··· ···

Reflexivity

Reflexivity involves thinking about and reviewing the whole research process in terms of the context in which the research has been conducted and the researcher's own role in that process.

··

How to be reflexive

There are various ways for you to put reflexivity into practice. Reading about reflexivity develops your understanding, so by reading this chapter you are already making a start (see below for more reading suggestions). Other strategies, discussed below, are developing a reflexive approach, getting collaborative, keeping a reflexive research diary and incorporating reflexivity into your write-up.

─Top tips─

Being reflexive

- Read the literature about reflexivity to develop theoretical understanding.
- Read published work using similar methods to you and consider how reflexivity is addressed.
- Develop a reflexive approach from the beginning of your project to make reflexivity a habit.

- Talk to the people around you. Use your supervisor, your friends, your fellow students or people who share your interests to develop reflexivity in a collaborative way.
- Keep a research diary in which to record your reflections and document your reflexivity.
- Incorporate your reflections into your project write-up.

Develop a reflexive approach

From the beginning of your project try to develop and maintain a reflexive approach. This means training and reminding yourself to reflect critically on why you are doing things in particular ways and how the context might matter.

A reflexive approach means making a habit of incorporating reflexive practice throughout your project. In practice, this might involve asking yourself key reflective questions as you design, conduct and write up your project. These questions will help you to bring to the fore the ways that you see the world and how your thinking impacts on your research. At the design stage (see Chapters 2, 3 and 4), reflective questions could include:

- Why am I interested in this topic?
- What is it about me that makes me interested in this topic?
- What will I gain from researching this topic?
- Do I care what I find out in my project and why might this be so?
- How do my values, beliefs and previous experiences influence my interest in this topic?
- How does my culture influence how I approach this topic?
- What assumptions do I already have about this topic?

As your project develops and you start to collect and analyse data (see Chapters 7 and 8) you may ask yourself other questions. For example, if you have conducted an interview you might want to reflect upon that specifically. To do that you could ask yourself questions like these:

- How did I feel when I was listening to that person?
- What did I think of their answers?
- How do my own experiences and attitudes relate to what they said?
- Why did I choose those questions to ask?
- What do I think I already know about those experiences?

There is no limit to how many techniques for reflexivity you can use, and you may have others for reflecting on your project. Discuss this with your supervisor to get more ideas.

Get collaborative

You can also develop your reflexivity skills by involving the people around you in the process. For example, use supervisory meetings to discuss your decisions and the questions that arise (see Chapter 5 for more on supervision).

Another way to involve those around you is to start a peer support group with fellow students, where you can get together and discuss anything from your early ideas about the project topic to the analysis of data. Some groups like to take it in turns to discuss an aspect of a particular member's project (e.g. their ongoing analysis) in detail. Some institutions allow students to do group projects, which can provide a ready-made peer support group. You could also use the Internet to create opportunities.

Top tip

Create or join an online peer support group

You could set up a wiki or use other technologies (e.g. MS Teams or WhatsApp) to set up an online group for discussion and reflection with trusted people. This can help if meeting face to face is difficult (e.g. due to distance or availability of rooms) and it can also make it easier to keep a record of your discussions, if everyone is comfortable with that. People can meet online to discuss things together, and/or use asynchronous chat if they aren't all available at the same times. You could also join an existing online discussion group to post queries, answer questions, join discussions or just lurk and learn! For example, see Method Space by Sage Publications (www.methodspace.com).

Other friends or family can help you reflect, even if they are not fellow students. For example, why not arrange for a friend to do a mock interview with you about what it was like to be an interviewer and use this to help you reflect?

Your participants may also be able to help you put reflexivity into practice. For example, you can provide your participants with your initial interpretations of their data and ask them what they think of it. This allows you to reflect on how your findings are perceived and on your own interpretations. This technique can also be a way of establishing research quality (known as 'member checking') for studies that specifically aim to represent the perspectives of the participants.

Want to know more about member checking?

Member checking is a way to assess quality in some forms of qualitative analysis. It is only appropriate when the research aims to adequately reflect the participants' perspectives. This is not appropriate for all forms of qualitative analysis, as some methods aim to critically interpret participants' talk in ways that might not be consistent with the participants' own perspectives. Also, there are debates about how well member checking works even in those studies where it is appropriate. See these sources for further information:

Birt, L., Scott, S., Cavers, D., Campbell, C. and Walter, F. (2016) Member checking: A tool to enhance trustworthiness or merely a nod to validation? *Qualitative Health Research*, 26(13), 1802–11.

Motulsky, S.L. (2021) Is member checking the gold standard of quality in qualitative research? *Qualitative Psychology*, 8(3), 389–406.

This is related to issues about the nature and ethics of interpretation in qualitative research, and you can read more about this here:

Willig, C. (2017) Interpretation in qualitative research. In C. Willig and W. Stainton Rogers (eds), *The SAGE Handbook of Qualitative Research in Psychology*. London: Sage. pp. 274–88.

When working collaboratively you need to be mindful of rules on collaboration and collusion because your project write-up must usually be entirely your own work. For guidance on how to collaborate and reflect with others while staying firmly inside the rules of your course, speak to your supervisor. The strategies described so far can generate a lot of useful reflections, but it's also important to find a way of recording them. Research diaries can help with this.

Keep a research diary

Keeping a reflexive journal, or research diary, is a common way of recording reflections as the research process unfolds. Not only does a written record allow you keep track of your reflections but writing your diary can generate reflections because writing aids thinking.

···· ···**In a nutshell**··· ·· ···

Research diaries

In a research diary you can:

- write down what you are experiencing at different stages of the project;
- consider sticky situations or tricky decisions that arise as the research unfolds;
- record your analytic processes (e.g. how you developed coding strategies or decided which bits of data were most relevant to your aims and why);
- develop your analysis (for example memo writing in grounded theory – see Chapter 8).

· ·

Your diary can be a physical notebook, a computer file, a note in your phone or all these things. You can include text, pictures, audio recording or any other form of record that you wish. It is a useful place for comments, thoughts, ideas and hunches that you may have about the research topic and design. As you become increasingly immersed in the data collection and analysis you might note your thoughts about these parts of the process (e.g. your reflections on how interviews went and how you found yourself reacting to the data). As you carry out your project, you will encounter contradictions and questions. The diary will help you to think about ways of addressing them. It can serve to clarify your thoughts and will help you to recall aspects of the research as you progress through it. The diary provides you with a useful indicator of the parts of the research that were troubling, challenging and intriguing as well as the parts that you enjoyed or were pleased about. The diary can also be useful for you to identify questions that you may want to discuss with your supervisor or follow up in your reading. You can find useful examples of research diary entries on page 20 of Braun and Clarke (2022).

Writing a diary as you go along can help you remember what you did and why you did it, which is useful for writing up. But parts of your research diary can be private, for your eyes only. This enables you to express yourself freely, without fear of judgement. Although it is your choice in terms of what you keep private or make public, we recommend that you use your diary as a basis for including reflexivity in your project write-up.

Include reflexivity in your write-up

How you include reflexivity in your project write-up depends on which reflexive practices you use and the guidelines that you must follow when writing up. You might include a specific section in your write-up that deals with reflexivity. In this section, you will highlight the most important aspects of your own subjectivity, and of the research context, that you think readers should bear in mind when considering your findings. For example, you might mention that you were a woman interviewing men about domestic labour and gender equity. You might also discuss how these might have influenced the dynamics between you and your participants, the way data was collected and your interpretation of the data.

You can also include reflexivity throughout your project, rather than in a separate specific section. It could be argued that if you have truly developed a reflexive standpoint this should be apparent across the whole project in numerous ways. A reflexive approach may be revealed in the use of the first person to write up research, which is particularly common in qualitative studies. For more information on how to include reflexivity through your write-up see Chapter 10. Also, consult with your supervisor and refer to any institutional rules to help with this.

Want to know more about reflexivity?

Finlay, L. and Gough, B. (2003) *Reflexivity: A Practical Guide for Researchers in Health and Social Sciences.* Oxford: Blackwell

Haynes, K. (2012) Reflexivity in qualitative research. In G. Symon and C. Cassell (eds), *Qualitative Organizational Research.* London: Sage. pp. 71-89.

Lazard, L. and McAvoy, J. (2020) Doing reflexivity in psychological research: What's the point? What's the practice? *Qualitative Research in Psychology,* 17(2), 159-77.

Good qualitative analysis

Considering the quality of the analysis is another useful way to evaluate a qualitative project. How you do this will partly depend on what method of analysis you're using, but there are some general guidelines for good analysis that will be useful for most projects.

Being analytical

Qualitative research involves the analysis of data, which means making interpretations (see Willig, 2017 for a more detailed discussion of this). Also, marking criteria for student projects commonly include creating good arguments and critical evaluation, both of which involve interpretation. In practice, this means that to do a good project you will need to go beyond description of your data; you will need to be analytical. But, particularly when relatively new to qualitative research, knowing how to do this in practice can be challenging.

Top tips

Being analytical

- Make comparisons. Look for similarities and differences within your dataset. In an interview study, this might mean making comparisons between interviewees but also thinking about consistency, or lack of, within one person's interview.
- How are the things made sense of, defined and represented? If you used your data to provide a definition or description of something the research is focused on, what would that look like?

(Continued)

- Look for implicit assumptions behind talk. This can be risky, as it is easy to 'go beyond the data' here (see below) but it also provides interesting analytical insights. For example, if somebody asks you how you 'coped' in a particular situation, this implies that the situation is a difficult one. We don't ask how somebody 'copes' with something that is easy and unproblematic. So, using the word 'cope' suggests an assumption that the situation is difficult or problematic.
- Consider what participants are doing. If you have data that consist of talk, you could think about what is happening in that talk. For example, are reasons being given, or blame placed?
- Draw out the implications. What does your data mean for things in practice (e.g. if you find an intervention to enhance student well-being is experienced as stressful what might this mean for universities?) and for relevant theories (does the main theory used in this area suggest that this well-being intervention will not be stressful?).

Being analytical involves making claims about what your data means. In doing this, you need to make sure you have evidence to back those claims up. And, importantly, that you present this evidence.

Don't go beyond the data

In qualitative analysis it is important to be analytical and to present interpretations of your data. But a general hallmark of good research is good use of evidence. So, you must always ensure that your interpretations fit with the evidence in your data. This can be a fine line to tread. If you shy away from making claims about what the data means, you may end up with an analysis section that is too descriptive. On the other hand, if you get too carried away with your claims, you may fall into the trap of making claims that aren't well evidenced – sometimes known as 'going beyond the data'.

Top tips

Good qualitative evidence use

Our advice is that you try to interpret your data and avoid being too descriptive. Don't miss the chance to show your markers that you can make arguments about what your data means. These tips will help you to do this while also avoiding the trap of 'going beyond the data':

- Present relevant data extracts. Really scrutinise data extracts used as evidence to make sure they match what you're saying about them. Consciously try to find any gaps in your own evidence.

- Present multiple extracts when needed. For example, interview data often reveals differing perspectives. If pointing this out in your analysis, ensure that you include contrasting quotes to back this up.
- Think about divergent cases, which are bits of data that don't fit with your developing interpretation (e.g. Antin et al., 2015). Looking for bits of data that don't fit with the claims you are about to make is crucial for using evidence well. Make a habit of specifically seeking out contradictory evidence and adjust your claims about the data accordingly. For example, if tempted to claim that low-income families are portrayed in your media data as dysfunctional, search your data for any portrayals that challenge this. If you find any, modify your claim so that it fits with the evidence (you might say that this portrayal is common in the data but not universal).
- Think about whether your interpretation is reasonable rather than 'correct'. In qualitative analysis there is usually more than one way to interpret the evidence in our data. When trying to work out if your claims are well-evidenced, remember that what is needed is to show that your interpretation is reasonable, based on the evidence. You may need to acknowledge that other interpretations are possible (and maybe explore these, depending on your analysis method) but your claims can still be legitimate providing your interpretation is reasonable. If you feel unsure about how to judge this, use your peer support (see above) and speak to your supervisor.

We have recommended that, in addition to keeping focused on the marking criteria that will be used for your write-up, you build a set of criteria for evaluating your project. These can consist of general quality criteria, criteria for qualitative research and some specific criteria for your data collection and analysis methods. In the next section, we offer tips for finding these specific criteria.

Finding Specific Quality Criteria for Your Methods

Although some quality criteria can be used for any research, to evaluate any specific project these should be used alongside criteria that are tailored to that specific project's methodology. Detailed discussion of quality criteria for all the methods of data collection and analysis methods at your disposal is beyond the scope of this chapter. However, we offer the following advice for finding specific information on quality for your methods.

Most texts that offer descriptions of how to carry out methods of data collection and analysis include advice about how to carry them out to a high standard. Even if these are not explicitly labelled as 'quality criteria', they can be used that way. Also, in recent years it has become more common for people to write explicitly about how we might judge the quality of specific qualitative methods. Although much of what is written is aimed at research that is destined for publication, they can also provide useful tips for your project.

Top tip

Finding quality criteria for specific methods

Chapter 7 of this book provides some advice about how to collect data well with different types of interviews, diary methods, naturalistic data, archive data, data from the Internet and visual data. There are also suggestions for how to find out more about these methods, which will allow you to gather more information about they can be done well.

Chapter 8 considers various methods for analysing qualitative data – including thematic analysis, IPA, grounded theory, narrative analysis, discourse analysis and conversation analysis – and this includes information about doing them well. Again, this chapter has suggestions for further reading, which you can use to gain more knowledge about high-quality analysis.

Use the tips on literature searching in Chapter 6 to find literature on quality criteria for your chosen methods.

The journal *Qualitative Research in Psychology* published a special issue on quality in 2021 (see Lester and O'Reilly, 2021). Along with some consideration of key quality issues, this includes specific journal articles about how to assess quality in the following methods: grounded theory, thematic analysis, narrative analysis, IPA, discursive psychology, conversation analysis.

Conclusion

When thinking about what makes a good piece of research remember that your reader needs to find your project credible. That is, they need to able to believe in your study and its findings. This happens when the write-up clearly details the processes and decisions involved and shows how quality standards have been met. We have provided you with a framework that you can use to create a set of criteria that, along with your marking criteria, will make your project excellent. In the next chapter, we offer guidance for writing up your project.

Activity 9.2

Create your quality checklist

Use the contents of this chapter, along with associated reading, to create a quality checklist that is tailored to your project. Follow these steps:

1   Identify general quality criteria to use (e.g. transparency).
2   Add to this some quality criteria for qualitative methods (e.g. reflexivity).
3   Identify quality criteria for your specific methods of data collection and analysis.

You can use this checklist, alongside your other guidelines and marking criteria, to review the ongoing work on your project at any stage. You can also use this to write a list of practical steps that you will take to ensure quality (e.g. start a research diary). The checklist will also be useful for reviewing draft sections of your write-up.

References

Antin, T.M.J., Constantine, N.A. and Hunt, G. (2015) Conflicting discourses in qualitative research: The search for divergent data within cases. *Field Methods*, 27(3), 211–22.

Birt, L., Scott, S., Cavers, D., Campbell, C. and Walter, F. (2016) Member checking: A tool to enhance trustworthiness or merely a nod to validation? *Qualitative Health Research*, 26(13), 1802–11.

Braun, V. and Clarke, V. (2022) *Thematic Analysis: A Practical Guide*. London: Sage.

Finlay, L. and Gough, B. (2003) *Reflexivity: A Practical Guide for Researchers in Health and Social Sciences*. Oxford: Blackwell

Frost, N. and Bailey-Rodriguez, D. (2019) Quality in qualitative research. In C. Sullivan and M. Forrester (eds), *Doing Qualitative Research in Psychology: A Practical Guide*. London: Sage. pp. 60–77.

Gibson, S. and Riley, S.C.E. (2019) Approaches to data collection in qualitative research. In C. Sullivan and M. Forrester (eds), *Doing Qualitative Research in Psychology: A Practical Guide*. London: Sage. pp. 99–120.

Haynes, K. (2012) Reflexivity in qualitative research. In G. Symon and C. Cassell (eds), *Qualitative Organizational Research*. London: Sage. pp. 71–89.

Korstjens, I. and Moser, A. (2018) Series: Practical guidance to qualitative research. Part 4: Trustworthiness and publishing. *European Journal of General Practice*, 24(1), 120–4.

Lazard, L. and McAvoy, J. (2020) Doing reflexivity in psychological research: What's the point? What's the practice? *Qualitative Research in Psychology*, 17(2), 159–77.

Lester, J.N. and O'Reilly, M. (2021) Introduction to the special issue. Quality in qualitative approaches: celebrating heterogeneity. *Qualitative Research in Psychology*, 18(3), 295–304.

Levitt, H.M., Bamberg, M., Creswell, J.W., Forst, D.M., Josselson, R. and Suárez-Orozco, C. (2018) Journal article reporting standards for qualitative primary, qualitative meta-analytic and mixed methods research in psychology: The APA Publications and Communications Board Task Force report. *American Psychologist*, 73(1), 26–46.

Long, H.A., French, D.P. and Brooks, J.M. (2020) Optimising the value of the critical appraisal skills programme (CASP) tool for quality appraisal in qualitative evidence synthesis. *Research Methods in Medicine and Health Sciences*, 1(1), 31–42.

Majid, U. and Vanstone, M. (2018) Appraising qualitative research for evidence synthesis: A compendium of quality appraisal tools. *Qualitative Health Research*, 28(13), 2115–31.

Motulsky, S.L. (2021) Is member checking the gold standard of quality in qualitative research? *Qualitative Psychology*, 8(3), 389–406.

Parker, I. (2004) Criteria for qualitative research in psychology. *Qualitative Research in Psychology*, 1(2), 95–106.

Robson, C. (2016) *Real World Research: A Resource for Social Scientists and Practitioner- researchers.* Oxford: Blackwell.

Sullivan, C. (2019) Theory and method in qualitative psychology. In C. Sullivan and M.A Forrester (eds), *Doing Qualitative Research in Psychology: A Practical Guide.* London: Sage. pp. 17–34.

Willig, C. (2017) Interpretation in qualitative research. In C. Willig and W. Stainton Rogers (eds), *The SAGE Handbook of Qualitative Research in Psychology.* London: Sage. pp. 274–88.

10
WRITING UP A QUALITATIVE PROJECT

Sarah Riley

It makes sense for a chapter about writing up your project to come towards the end of this book. After all, you need to have done the work outlined in previous chapters to create your write-up. But when it comes to doing an excellent job of writing up, the best advice is to start writing early. It takes practice to develop your own style, and because writing forces us to put down our ideas and think about how we organise our arguments, the act of writing itself helps us think and develop those ideas. So, it pays to get in the habit of writing throughout your research project – and there are plenty of opportunities for you to write. These include writing a plan (Chapter 3), a preliminary literature review (Chapter 6), an introductory letter to participants explaining your study (Chapter 4), a research diary (Chapter 9) and the write-up itself (the topic of this chapter).

The previous chapters in this book focused on helping you make the right decisions so that you can create an excellent piece of research. But you also need to communicate this work effectively, which involves two further skills. First, you need to be able to write to your institution's requirements regarding the structure and content of a research write-up. Second, you need to develop your own style of writing – your 'voice' so to speak – so that you can write clearly, coherently and interestingly about your work (this is also a transferable skill for employability). It's often a real challenge to meet institutional requirements for content within set word counts and developing a good writing style that is both clear and concise can help you do this more easily. So, in this chapter I focus on these two aspects of writing up, taking you through the structure and content of your qualitative project write-up and discussing writing styles and techniques. The chapter will cover the following:

Write-up structure and content:

- Why research write-ups follow a particular structure.
- Outline of suggested structure and content.
- In-depth discussion of the content required for each subsection.

Writing style:

- How to write clearly and concisely.
- What kind of 'tone' to use and how to develop your own 'voice'.

Conclusion:

- Top tips for getting the job done.

Structure and Content

Although you've done them before it's probably useful to start this section by revisiting the role of a research write-up and its general structure and content. It's helpful to remind ourselves about writing up requirements because regulations may change or develop as you progress through a programme of study. Also, students might only have a partial understanding of why research write-ups follow a particular structure. So, starting with the basics is a useful way to make sure you have a clear understanding of what is expected of you – that way you won't lose easy marks.

The role of the write-up is to communicate a study, usually from one researcher to another, but a wider audience may also be considered. Journalists and students, for example, are two other groups of people who may read academic work. The main audience for your write-up is your supervisor and markers, and sometimes your supervisor will be one of your markers. Secondary audiences might be other students who read your write-up to get ideas for their own projects and external examiners who may read it as an example of the work being produced in your institution. Your potential readership is therefore likely to involve some people who know your area well, but others who may not. To meet the needs of these diverse readers, you need to write in a way that emulates the professional style of the journal articles in your area while providing enough information to be easily understood by a readership who does not have specialist knowledge of the topic being investigated (for example, your second marker).

··········**In a nutshell**··· ···

What is the write-up for?

Your write up should:

- tell your reader what you've done, why you've done it, what you've found and how this contributes to our general pool of knowledge;
- be written in a style that keeps your reader awake and interested; and

- communicate in a way that maps onto the learning outcomes and marking criteria for your project;
- fit with your institution's guidelines.

. . . .

Most institutions will have guidelines for the structure they require your write-up to follow. Look them up and either keep them with you when you're writing or make notes on what's expected and refer to those regularly instead. Many institutions, for example, require specific subheadings in method sections. If your institution doesn't have specific guidelines, then look up the American Psychological Association (APA) guidelines.

---Activity 10.1---

APA style

Most psychology students are asked to follow the structure, style and content described in the American Psychological Association (APA) guidelines. The APA offers a range of handy resources. Look up their academic writer tutorial basics on the APA style website: https://apastyle.apa.org/instructional-aids/tutorials-webinars.

Sometimes it's hard to know how to translate the generic regulations for research projects to the specifics of your own project. If you're struggling to do this, look at how other people have successfully done it. Ask your supervisor if they can recommend a couple of previous students' write-ups to read that were given good marks. You don't have to give them an in-depth read; rather, look through to get a sense of the general structure and style of presentation or focus on sections that you're having trouble with in your own write-up. Also, when you're reading journal articles, notice how they're written. If you found an article a good read, it's probably because both style and content are good. When this happens, pay attention to how it's been written as well as what it tells you about your topic. For example, as a student, I remember wondering how to start the first sentence of my method section and turning to the work of an academic I admired to see how she had done it.

At times you may find yourself in disagreement with your institution's guidelines. There is usually one of three reasons for this: students haven't fully understood the rationale behind these recommendations; the institutional guidelines haven't been updated to include requirements for qualitative as well as quantitative studies; or students are working with an unconventional method that requires a different writing style. If you're struggling to meet your institution's guidelines, either because you don't understand them fully or because you think they are inappropriate for your project, seek your supervisor's advice.

Most institutions ask for a similar structure for writing up research. This is a tried and tested way of presenting the required information in a logical way and means that a reader can easily find specific information, such as the number of participants in the study. Below, I outline a generic structure that should be appropriate for most qualitative research projects and is likely to be similar to your institution's requirements. I first present this outline as a summary table, so that you can have an overview. This serves to remind you of the structure you need to follow. It also starts to highlight areas that may be different for students new to qualitative research.

In the next section I go through the structure of a qualitative write-up in more detail by describing what is usually expected in each subsection and the rationale behind that. I also discuss where you may find differences between qualitative and quantitative write-ups and between qualitative write-ups that come from different research traditions. Students can find it hard to work out where to put information, so the aim of this section is to give you an understanding of the rationale behind the structure and offer practical suggestions for how you might translate the generic requirements for each subsection into the specifics for your qualitative research project.

···· ···In a nutshell·· ·· ·· ··············

The structure of your write-up

Title page: This contains the title of your project, your name and any other administrative information required by your institution's regulations.

Acknowledgements: An optional page where you may thank people who have helped you.

Abstract: Summary of your study between 150 and 300 words depending on your institution's regulations.

Introduction: Explains why your project is important and interesting, includes your literature review and logically leads to your research questions. This section should provide a rationale, i.e. a structured argument for your study and research questions.

Method: A description of your method, often with subsections such as: design, methodological theory, participants, procedure, reflexivity and ethics, which combined show what you did to answer your research question(s).

Analysis: The presentation of your findings, including example extracts of data, your analysis of this data and possibly links between this analysis and your literature review or research question. This section combines aspects of the 'results' and 'discussion' sections of more traditional quantitative write-ups.

Conclusion: This section is relatively short, it rounds off your write-up, summarising how your analysis answers your research questions, how it links to existing literature, limitations of the study and future research suggestions.

References: Full references for all the studies referred to in body of the write-up. Presented in a standard format, usually APA.

Appendices: Additional information about the project that it is not necessary for the reader to know to understand the project, but which adds rigour and transparency, such as consent forms. It allows your reader to follow up on an aspect of your study or to critically evaluate it.

Remember to start each of these sections on a new page.

· ·

In-depth Guidelines
Title page

Your title should be approximately 10–20 words and should describe your topic, method and possibly your participants. There is a trend to try for a catchy title, followed by a more descriptive subtitle, often with the use of a colon and a quote from a participant. Consider this example – '"I only do it because it's there": A discourse analysis of mountain climbers' talk in online message board discussions'. It follows this structure: indicative quote, type of method, type of participant, type of data. For an interesting critique of this convention for titles, see Parkin and Kimergård (2022).

Acknowledgements

Acknowledge your supervisor. It doesn't hurt to make them feel good. Even if you don't think they were that useful, they probably hoped that they were and they're likely to be the one marking your project. Other people you might want to thank include your participants, family or anyone else who has supported your studies.

Abstract

Your abstract summarises your study. Think of it as your advertisement – when looking at journal articles researchers use them to gauge if they should read the whole article – so it needs to have all the key information. What is usually required is a brief reference to the topic area, why it is important, and perhaps the literature or theoretical framework that your project builds on; your research question(s), your method (for example, design, participants, type of analysis) and key findings (e.g. main themes) described in a way that allows the reader to get a sense of what your findings were (e.g. the names of your theme names should be self-explanatory); and your conclusions drawn in relation to the project topic, possibly with reference to previous literature (e.g. if you supported or developed previous literature). You have to do this within a given word length of anything from 150 to 300 words, depending on your institution's requirements. You will also notice that some abstracts have subheadings (as in the example below) and others don't. Again, check your institution's guidelines on this point. If you're struggling, have a look at the abstracts in journal articles that are relevant to your study and see how those authors did it.

Your title and abstract set the scene for your reader, giving them an overview of what you did and what you found. This sets up a series of expectations for them that you should fulfil in the main body of the write-up. Avoid inconsistencies like reporting different numbers of participants in your abstract and method sections or emphasising a different literature in your abstract than what follows in your literature review. For this, and other reasons, although the abstract comes first, you should write it last. At that stage, you will know what's in your write-up, and you will find summarising it so much easier.

An example abstract structure

Objectives: This might include the main aim, purpose or primary objectives of the project. And the background to the project with a couple of sentences that place it in context, in terms of relevant research, key arguments and/or theoretical frameworks.

Methods: Describe the methods of data collection and analysis, and any other important methodological issues to your study (e.g. participants' inclusion/exclusion criteria) and/or key arguments or methodological theoretical positions.

Findings: Briefly describe your findings, for example listing the themes or discourses of your analysis.

Conclusions: State the conclusions that can be drawn from your study, showing how your study has developed understanding by relating your findings to previous research.

An example of this abstract structure in practice

Objectives: Menstruation tracking digital applications (MTA) are a popular technology that allows users to track for both fertility and mood management related to PMS. The objective of this study was to address a gap in knowledge of women's experiences of using of MTA for the management of PMS.

Method: A theoretical framework that focuses analytic attention on affective relationships between subjectivity, bodily sensations, digital technology and discourse was used to structure the analysis of five in-depth timeline interviews with women in Aotearoa New Zealand who experienced benefits from using MTA to manage PMS symptoms.

Results: Three themes were identified: a pedagogy of empowerment, where users learnt to control, predict and manage their PMS symptoms; a pedagogy of appreciation, where users learnt to understand their menstruating bodies as amazing, a valued part of them and awe-inspiring that radically overturned past internalised stigma; and an 'untrustworthy teacher' who eroded this affirmative learning through inaccuracy, positioning users in dis-preferred categories, or being 'creepy'.

Conclusions: MTA offers possibilities for challenging menstrual stigma that need to be nurtured, developed, and protected.

(Adapted from Riley and Paskova, 2022)

A final point about your abstract: You may want to consider how online indexing works through key words. To 'work' your key words and be more easily found, read through your write-up, and identify key terms or phrases, also think about the search terms you use in when looking for articles on your topic, map the phrases that you use and the phrases that you search for, and then make sure these terms are used systematically throughout your write-up. For example, they might occur in the abstract, subheadings of your literature review and main body of your analysis. Note, you want to use this technique to make your write-up coherent and searchable, not look like it's been written by a key-word-stuffing algorithm. When in doubt, err on the side of appearing human!

Introduction

When writing an introduction, your job is to provide a rationale for your study; this means justifying the topic of study, the theoretical approach and the broad approach to methods used. Start your introduction on a new page with a short paragraph that acts as an overall introduction to your topic and key issues of the project. You might start this section with a punchy statement or question that draws your reader in. For example, rather than start your introduction with, 'This project investigates how a group of "binge drinking" students made sense of government campaigns alcohol consumption', you could start with, 'Heavy drinking among UK undergraduate students has been a longstanding health and social issue'. You can then follow this with a short outline of the rationale of your study (for example, that the government has produced a series of health campaigns but little research has investigated how the students being targeted by these campaigns respond to the advertisements). Then tell your reader what to expect in the following literature review; this is called 'signposting' – it sets the scene for your reader, creating a better reading experience. And in the context of a student project, it's useful to remember that a happy reader is a happy marker!

Top tip

Setting the scene

By outlining what you're going to say before you say it, your reader will know what to expect and can settle into you telling them your research 'story'. This is known as 'signposting'.

Follow your introductory paragraph with a literature review of existing research on your topic in a way that presents your topic as interesting and important. Good literature reviews don't just list a series of studies and what they found, but conceptually bring this literature together, curating it for your reader. So, as discussed in Chapter 6, avoid listing a series of studies; instead map out the key ways in which previous research has addressed your topic and create a subsection for each of these. You might find a mind map or spider diagram helpful for your thinking here. For example, has the research you're reviewing focused on different sub-topics (e.g. proximity vs similarity in friendships); asked different kinds of questions (e.g. motivations or behaviours), used different theoretical frameworks (e.g. contact hypothesis vs evolutionary theories); or used different methods (e.g. observation vs interview) – note that this is where discussion of method is relevant for your literature review, any discussion of what you did in your method needs to be saved for your method section.

Once you know what the different issues are that you want to discuss, give each a subsection in your literature review in which you summarise and evaluate that issue in relation to key findings, debates, studies, or methodological approaches used. Also note any gaps in the literature (which later you can use to support your argument that your research project addresses an important gap in knowledge). When deciding how much information to give about a particular study, give more details on the studies that are most relevant to yours.

It might help to imagine your literature review as a funnel shape – starting with the broad issues and gradually developing a narrower focus that leads to your research question(s). You will need to work out a way of structuring your review so that it seems logical to go from one topic to another. When working out the structure of your introduction it can help to take a blank piece of paper and sketch out how your topics link to each other. Subheadings and 'signposting' strategies that tell your reader what they've read and what's next may help give your write-up a sense of coherence. For a more detailed discussion on how to conduct, structure and write a literature review see Chapter 6.

Finish your literature review with a clear articulation of your aims and research question(s); for example, 'How do students negotiate blame when accounting for missing lectures?' Remember to frame research questions so that they read like questions and end in a question mark. This helps you distinguish between your research question(s) and your project title, as students sometimes get these confused. Research questions are also useful when it comes to writing (and analysis) because they help you keep a focus – if you're not sure what to include or how to include it, ask yourself: how does this help me address my research question?

In summary, your literature should build a picture of the knowledge we have about your topic to date. It should be a persuasive piece of writing which concludes logically with your research question(s) and which makes a case that answering your research question would develop our knowledge of an important issue. It should tell your reader:

- Why this topic is important.
- What we know from previous work.

- What we don't know and thus what kind of work is needed that could develop our knowledge on this subject.
- Your project aims and research question(s).

Top tips

Write a great introduction

- Hypotheses are required when you are doing research that predicts an outcome; they are usually more appropriate for experimental work. Qualitative work tends to be more exploratory in trying to understand an issue better than you did before. Hence you have research questions and not hypotheses.
- When you do your literature review make sure you look for recent qualitative work on your topic; this will give you access to the most relevant literature for your project, a good idea of the kinds of research questions you might want to ask and what a good qualitative analysis on your topic may look like.
- Writing needs to get bigger before it gets smaller. So don't write to your word count to begin with; rather, write what you think needs to go in and don't worry too much about how long it gets (within reason!). Once you know what you want to say, it's much easier to then rewrite it, editing to make it clearer, more concise and within the word count.
- When considering the length of your introduction you need to find a balance between writing a persuasive argument, and having enough words left for the rest of your write-up. As a rule of thumb, your introduction is about 20 per cent of the word count of a write-up.

Writing your introduction is an iterative process. The first time you draft your introduction you may be writing it as part of a proposal, explaining and justifying what you're going to do. Towards the end of your project, when you've done your analysis, you're likely to want to re-write your introduction to highlight key areas that you now know are important to your analysis.

Method

If the job of your introduction section was to set the scene for your study and give your reader the questions that you plan to address, then the job of your method section is to show your reader what you did to answer those questions. This is often a technical section with multiple subheadings and factual statements about your method. Method sections usually account for approximately 15 per cent of the word limit. They are sometimes the easiest section to write because they are the most structured. For this reason, if you are struggling with your write-up, start with the method section.

Before you write your method, refer to your institution's requirements for this section, which often name required subheadings. Try to stick to your institution's guidelines as much as possible, but if you think they are written with quantitative studies in mind you may need to negotiate a different set of subheadings. Subheadings in qualitative projects may include: methodological principles, design, participants (or dataset), procedure, ethics, reflexivity, apparatus/materials and quality criteria. I discuss these in more detail below.

Top tips

How to do an excellent method section

- Provide enough information so that the study can be repeated or evaluated.
- Read research methods literature on your method so that you can demonstrate your understanding of why and how you used a particular method of analysis.
- Include reference to research methods literature in your method section to show how your project connects to the wider research methods knowledge, and back up your claims.
- Read up on reflexivity, validity in qualitative methods and ethics.

Methodological principles

Often qualitative write-ups include information about the broad orientation to knowledge that has been used in the research. I suggest you put this at the start of your method section, in a sub-section called 'methodological principles' (alternative names include 'theoretical framework' or 'methodology'). Start this section with epistemological issues. For example, are you framing the knowledge you're generating as something objectively real, or as creating insights into people's interpretations of reality, or producing knowledge of the discourses people use to construct their reality? Relatedly, you might discuss critical realist or social constructionist approaches to knowledge.

You can then turn to your specific method of analysis, explaining (1) how its principles align with the epistemology underpinning your project that you've just described and (2) any other key principles of that method. For example, IPA and phenomenologically informed thematic analysis are phenomenological approaches. If you've used either of these methods, you might have discussed critical realism as your epistemology, followed by some of the principles of phenomenology when applied to psychological study, such as focusing on the nature of experience and interpretation of that experience (see Chapter 1). In contrast, those using Foucauldian informed discourse analysis might discuss social constructionist epistemology followed by some of the specific principles of the discourse analysis they were using, such as a focus on the discourses constructing the object of study (see Chapter 8).

You might follow the above with a discussion of the principles of your specific method of data collection, your 'methodology of data collection'. For example, if you used semi-structured interviews, you might discuss their advantages, limitations or debates on when, why and perhaps how they should be used – relating this discussion to the principles of your method. For example, phenomenological analysis focuses on the individual, and aligns with an individualised method like one-to-one interviewing.

Discussing your broad theoretical or epistemological approach, the principles of your methods of data analysis and the principles of your method of data collection in one section allows you to show that you understand the underpinning principles of your methods and the conceptual coherence in your study (see the discussion of the 'methodological kite' in Chapter 1. Such a section is therefore relevant for your method because it's your methodology, and you can then follow it with subsections outlining your method, which describe *how* you applied those principles in practice when you did your data collection and analysis. However, some traditions prefer you to focus your method section only on the 'how' questions of what you did, and for the methodological principles discussion outlined above to be in your introduction as part of the rationale of your study. Check with your supervisor what's the best approach for your project.

When discussing your methodology and methods, reference qualitative research methods literature to justify your points. This demonstrates that you have engaged with the literature. Also, because there are so many variations within qualitative methods – it makes it clear to the reader which kind you are using. This is in contrast to quantitative write-ups where you wouldn't be expected to provide a reference for a t-test, for example.

Design

You are now ready to start describing what you did (your methods). Start with a brief description of your research design – a succinct summary of the structure of your study. For example, it could be 'a discursive analysis of blame management rhetoric on mums net posts about baby lead weaning' or 'an in-depth interview study using interpretative phenomenological analysis to explore the experiences of caring for an elderly relative'. If you have collected data in phases, or have more than one group of participants, then here is where you would state this. The design subsection sets the expectations of your reader for what will follow.

Participants

In the participants section you should give information on who your participants were. This information should focus on characteristics that are relevant to your study. For example, if you are interviewing overseas students consider saying what country they came from, as well as their sex and age, perhaps what they studied. But when you give information be careful that, when combined, it does not allow your reader to identify your participants. In such circumstances give a broader description that will protect their identification, such as a general region rather than a country or a description of them studying social sciences rather than geography. If you withhold information for ethical reasons, say so.

Some participant sections take the form of a couple of sentences that describe the number of participants, their sex/gender, age, location or other relevant features (for instance, if your study focuses on caring, you might specify the length of time they had been a carer). Often you can present this information in the form of a table.

Alternatively, if participant numbers are small, qualitative researchers sometimes provide a short paragraph describing each participant. This structure is often used when the study is looking at individual experiences and wants to personalise the accounts they are giving, highlighting how different circumstances or attitudes may affect a person's experience or understanding of the topic of interest. Note that pseudonyms are always used. So, for example, in Chapter 5 we met Suzy, a student from Singapore exploring overseas students' experiences of their first weeks at university. Since each of her six students were very different, it would make sense for Suzy to give a short biography of each participant, giving demographic details (age for example), but also describing other characteristics that may have structured their first experiences of university (such as when they arrived, if they had been to the country before, and what their social network was like). An example of such a biography is given below:

> Robert is an 18-year-old male from Ghana, studying psychology. He has been to England on one previous occasion. He arrived two days before the first day of university, moving straight into a room in a hall of residence on campus. One of his sisters had a friend who lived nearby and who showed him around the local town the weekend he arrived. He did not know anyone in his hall, but quickly made friends with the six people on his floor, who included UK and overseas students. He described his first few weeks as 'fun'.

Dataset

It may be that you did not recruit participants for your study, but collected data in other ways, for example, online forum discussions. In this context you might substitute the subheading 'participants' with a more appropriate term such as 'dataset'; see the example below from a study on weight-related websites:

> During the data collection period there were 105 contributions by 46 different posters on the recovery site and 107 contributions by 24 posters on the pro-ana site. The mean number of posts per person was 2.52 for the recovery site and 4.48 for the pro-ana site. As far as we could ascertain, all posts were by females, living predominantly in the US, UK or Australia. (Riley et al., 2009: 352)

Procedure

A procedure section is normally written in chronological order, outlining step by step what you did in designing your study and collecting your data. It should contain enough information that someone else could copy or evaluate your method. You might include recruitment procedures, how you elicited data (for example, strategies for systematically accessing online data or your interview technique), information on the types of questions participants were asked, how long the interviews took, where they took place, and so on. Refer your reader to your appendices when relevant. For example, you might say that you asked a range of questions about their experience and then say '(see Appendix A for the interview schedule)'. As with the rest of your project, this should be written in the past tense. You may describe the procedure you followed to analyse your data here or in a following separate subsection.

Procedure for data analysis

Given that qualitative research needs to be both systematic and flexible to the needs of the research question, you usually need to give details of your analytical procedure or 'procedure for data analysis'.

Here you describe what you did with your data; that is, your procedure for coding and analysing your data. Name the method of data analysis you used (e.g. IPA, Foucauldian discourse analysis, discursive psychology, phenomenologically informed thematic analysis), and describe how you applied this method to your data. Give a step-by-step description with enough detail that your reader understands what you did well enough to evaluate it and so that, if they chose, they could apply your method themselves. For instance, if you are discussing how you developed codes into categories in a grounded theory study (see Chapter 8) you could give an example, such as how, in a project on meditation codes of 'contentment', 'oneness' and 'peace' were collated into an overarching category of 'finding serenity'. If you are using an established procedure, refer to relevant methodology literature, list the steps described in that literature and explain how they were applied in your project. For example, in a study using the Foucauldian informed discourse analysis on how people talked about with healthy lifestyle advice, we wrote the following:

> Our discourse analysis combined Willig's (2013) and (Riley et al., 2021) guidelines for a Foucauldian-informed discourse analysis. Each transcript was read multiple times, coding direct and indirect references to health and healthy lifestyle. Each 'health talk' extract was then analysed in terms of 1) what issues, objects, or people were described; 2) what reality was constructed in these descriptions; 3) the wider discourses informing this sense making; 4) rhetoric strategies, which offers important insights into the action orientation of talk (for example, extreme case formulations and active voicing can strengthen an argument, while careful

discursive work highlights an issue of social sensitivity; and 5) the consequences in these accounts for healthy lifestyle practices.

(Robson et al., 2022)

Make sure your description of what you did with your data is consistent with your earlier description of the principles of the approach you are using. For example, if you argued in your methodological approach section that phenomenology is idiographic, then here, in your data analysis section, you might say that you analysed each interview separately before looking at them together. If you did something different to standard procedures, then now is the place to say what you did and why.

If you are going to present transcriptions of talk in your analysis section, you will need to let your reader know what your transcription notation means. Transcription notation is the name for the symbols you use to describe the talk in more detail; for example, the use of an upward arrow to show rising intonation. If you're using a fairly simple form of notation, you can incorporate it in your this section, but if it's a detailed one you may want to give your 'transcription notation' its own subsection below, or save on your word count and put your notation conventions as an appendix. (For more on transcription, see Chapters 7 and 8.)

Ethics

Here you describe the main ethical issues that are relevant to your study and how you addressed them (see Chapter 4 for a detailed discussion on ethics). Look up your ethics document to remind yourself. Remember to include your careful handling and storage of the data. Refer to relevant institutional guidelines, such as the British Psychology Society ethics guidelines, and to your appendix if you put your ethics application there. Try to avoid repetition, for many students this means thinking carefully about when information goes in your procedure and when it goes in your ethics subsection, in your procedure you can always refer your reader to your ethics section for more details.

Reflexivity

Reflexivity involves deep thinking about your role in your study. As a qualitative researcher you need to reflect on the decisions you made and why. Including how your values shaped the research, what worked, or didn't work, and how your participants responded to you – and how you responded back. You might also want to consider how your design shaped the findings (e.g. interviews are likely to give individual stories), or even your disciplinary location (e.g. in psychology we tend to focus on the individual; if you were a geographer would you have focused more on the environment your participants were in?). See Chapter 9 for more on this.

This is not an issue about bias. Many qualitative researchers take the position that all research is subjective because it is made by people, and we bring our socio-historic, cultural and personal experiences to our research, including experimental research – see Haraway (1989) for a convincing case. From this perspective, a reflexivity section helps us understand the context in which the knowledge we produce has occurred, and from that, help us evaluate how useful that knowledge is, and where it might be more or less useful.

There are many ways to 'do' reflexivity; not all qualitative research has a distinct reflexivity section, preferring instead to include reflexivity in multiple parts of the write-up. To do this you might include in your method some reflection on the decisions and practices that led to and produced your data, including how your own perspective or position in relation to the topic might have shaped the project. Then, in the analysis you might include the interviewer's questions in the data extracts. To bring reflexivity in your discussion/conclusion sections you might reflect on the limitations of the study, or how the dynamics between you and your participants co-produced certain understandings. For example, Suzy (who we met in Chapter 5) might reflect upon her own experience of being an overseas student who is researching other overseas students. In doing so she might have reflected on how her similarities to, and differences from, her participants may have affected the way her participants responded to her and how this in turn affected the data she got. (See Chapter 9 for a detailed discussion of reflexivity and how it might apply to your own work.)

The above sections are fairly standard for qualitative research projects. Depending on your project, you may need other subsections, such as apparatus or quality criteria. Include these if you feel they are relevant to your study and the theoretical and methodological approach you've taken. Check with your supervisor if you're not sure.

Apparatus/materials

Here you describe any technical or specialist equipment you used. This section is less common for qualitative projects than quantitative projects but may be relevant if you used specific apparatus or materials. For example, a description of magazine advertisements that you used to stimulate focus group discussion (and in cases like these the section heading would probably be changed to 'materials'). Similarly, if you have used an open-ended questionnaire, you could describe it (and refer your reader to an appendix section where you would have put copies of these documents or images). Documents such as interview schedules are usually described in the procedure section, while those developed for ethics are usually discussed in that section.

Quality criteria

Sometimes write-ups have a quality criteria section, describing the key components of a good project within the approach you are using, and how your project meets them.

If you don't have an explicit quality criteria section, make sure that you embed this information elsewhere in your write-up. Stating your quality criteria explicitly allows you to set the goalposts or targets for your study and then show how you have met them. It's a great way to show methodological understanding, helps you get clear on the criteria you are working towards, and helps your examiner understand why they should give you a good mark! See Chapter 9 for further discussion of research quality.

Analysis

Your analysis section contains both a description of your findings and analysis of those findings, where you interpret the findings in a way that helps you address your research question(s). It is supported with extracts from the data (such as quotes from participants). Many qualitative write-ups therefore have a relatively long analysis section. The fact that results are interpreted in this section means that you may also usually include links to relevant literature and theories, if it helps you to develop the analysis. For this reason, your analysis section might be anything between 20 per cent and 40 per cent of your write-up. The analysis section is therefore not a 'results' section that describes findings without commentary, as you might find in the write-up of an experimental study. Rather, it combines aspects of results and discussion sections of more traditional reporting styles. A minority of qualitative write-ups do still use the more traditional separate sections for results and discussion, so if you are not sure, speak to your supervisor.

Top tips

Presenting data

When you present a data extract (e.g. a quote from a participant), follow this procedure:
   Put quotes of fewer than 40 words in the main text. For example, you might write:

Deborah (25-year-old psychology student) drew on the idea of personality to distinguish between friends and the other people in her class she talked to, saying: 'I'd say because I am chatty I meet so many different people and I wouldn't class them as my friend.' Several other participants also employed friendship categories, variously making distinctions, such as between 'close and random friends' (Paula, 18, geography student) and 'friends and acquaintances' (Laura, 22-year-old psychology student). Combined, the students described experiencing a range of friendly relationships that they had with other people who they did not necessarily consider their friends.

The advantages of the above include demonstrating that several participants described the issue you're talking about and giving a feel for the different ways they talked about it.

The disadvantage is that short quotes don't give you the opportunity to engage deeply with the talk. For that you might need quotes of over 40 words.

Quotes of over 40 words should appear in an indented block paragraph (note, you don't need to use italics, double space or quotation marks in block quotes). So, you would write an introduction to your extract in your main paragraph, present the extract in a block and then continue with your analysis in the following paragraph. Give these more lengthy extracts a title, chronologically numbering your extracts (making it easier to refer to them in your analysis); you might also give other relevant information, such as the participant's pseudonym. For example, you might write:

Deborah draws on the idea of personality to distinguish between friends and the other people in her class she talks to.

Extract 3: Deborah (25-year-old psychology student)

because I am chatty I meet so many different people and I wouldn't class them as my friend, friend [INT: yeah], but like, you know like uni friends and I know loads of people, but I don't know what it was, just, we just clicked

Above, Deborah explained how being a 'chatty' person meant that she socialised with a range of people, and these she categorised as 'uni friends'. But for a person to become understood as a true friend there needed to be connection between personalities, as Deborah states about such a friend, 'we just clicked'.

When making decisions about your analysis section consider the kind of method you're using, and the usual practices associated with writing up studies that use this method. Grounded theory, IPA and the various forms of discourse analysis for example each tend to have their ways of presenting analysis sections that may differ slightly from each other. There is also variation within methods based on researchers' preferences or the kind of question being addressed. This variation is an advantage for qualitative researchers; it means that we can present our work in a way that best suits the specifics of our study. But this can make new qualitative researchers anxious about how to do it 'right'. Therefore below, I've outlined a generic structure for analysis sections, which may be a good starting point for structuring your own specific analysis.

Before I outline a generic structure for analysis sections in qualitative projects, it's useful to note that more unconventional or creative write-ups may employ a different style; for example, imaginary conversations composed from 'real' talk (Ashmore, 1989). If you are using unconventional methods remember to clearly state what you're doing, why, and the quality criteria from which your work should be judged. In general, though, analysis sections often use the following structure:

Top tips

Analysis outline

- A paragraph introducing the overall patterns of your findings (e.g. naming your themes and saying how they collectively offer directions for answering your research question or giving insight into your study).
- Subheading with the title of your first analytic unit, such as a theme, discourse or conversational device. Depending on your method, introduce this section with a general explanation of what this theme/discourse involves.
- Give an extract as an example, label it, give relevant demographic information (e.g. 'Extract 1, Sonia and James, social science students from Eastern Europe').
- Analyse that extract according to the principles of your method of analysis.
- Give a second extract as a further example. This should not simply repeat the point exemplified by your first extract, but develop the nuance of your main argument, show how another participant reproduced this pattern, or show a different way in which the pattern you've identified can occur.
- You can continue this pattern of extract-analysis until you feel you have explored and communicated this first pattern appropriately. How many extracts you need to do this will depend on your analysis (e.g. if you have one major superordinate theme with many sub-themes, or several superordinate themes, with several sub-themes, the latter means that you will have fewer extracts per sub-theme to still be in the word count).
- When you finish this first theme/category/discourse, summarise your take-home point for how it helps you understand your topic (and thus address your research question). Here you might draw on previous research if it helps with the analysis. For example, if your take-home point is that students categorise friendships differently, and previous research has shown that friendship categorisations allow people to make sense of complex social situations, then you could suggest that perhaps one of the reasons why the students in your study used multiple ways of categorising friendships was to manage the complex social situations in university created by expectations to interact with many people in different contexts. When deciding on whether and when to include previous literature in your analysis, base your decision on what works best for your write-up. For example, if several parts of your analysis can be linked to a particular study or theory, avoid repeating yourself and make that point only once, probably in your discussion. In contrast, if there is some literature that is only really relevant to one part of your analysis you may wish to mention that within the analysis section. It's often good to follow the same pattern of writing across your analysis, so usually I recommend either including previous research at the end of each theme/category/discourse, or not including previous research, and saving all discussion of previous research to your discussion section.
- Repeat this pattern for your other themes/discourses/categories.
- Sometimes researchers finish the whole analysis section with a brief overall summary of main arguments and findings, although this can work better in the discussion section.

The structure outlined above allows you to develop an argument and provide evidence for that argument. This makes for a logical approach to presenting your findings and enhancing the trustworthiness of your analysis. The screen capture in Figure 10.1 gives you an example of how I've applied this structure to my own work.

Economic citizens ←————————————— A subheading that is the title of a new theme

In the 'economic citizen' repertoire participants linked controlled drug use with economic participation, constructing magic mushroom use as an occasional leisure activity, in a context in which paid work was normalised and took priority ← A paragraph that introduces this theme
over hallucinogenic drug use.

(Extract 6, focus group 3, Joanne 38):
but I think it's got such (.) if you take them [mushrooms] (.) you've probably got about 8, 10 hours (.) depending on the quantity (.) I think that's why it's a celebration ← An extract that acts as an example of the theme. Indented and titled with a number and description of where and who in the data it came from (in this case the focus group, participant's name and age)
thing (.) you need to take some time out (.) if you've got anything to do the next day (..) like for example if it's mid-week (.) you had to go to work the next day (.) you would not take mushrooms

Joanne associates the longevity of the effects of mushrooms (*you've probably got about 8, 10 hours*) with the need to limit their use to occasions that provide time out from everyday responsibilities (*a celebration thing ... you* ← New paragraph analysing the extract in detail
need to take time out). Arguing that you need to take 'time out' implies that there is something people are typically 'in', this subtly constructs economic participation as normal, an understanding then made explicit with a direct link between drug use and economic participation (*if ... you had to go to work the next day*).

Economic activity is thus constructed as normative and as taking priority over hallucinogenic drug use that may ← New paragraph that links the above in-depth analysis to wider patterns in the data, it also introduces the next extract.
negatively impact on work. An alternative account was raised by some participants, but as in extract five, such apparently deviant cases were mobilised in ways that served to reinforce rather than challenge neo-liberal sense making.

(Extract 7, focus group 1, *Rebrov, age 25*): the majority of people who take mushrooms in their lifetime (..) won't do it for any great length of time (.) for a short ← The next extract, presented in the same way as previous extracts. This would be followed by in-depth analysis, as before, and if it was at the end of the subsection, perhaps discussed in relation to previous literature if that helped develop the analysis.
period (.) maybe their teenage years or (.) early adult hood and then (..) you know (.) go and get a job and (.) calm down (.) and drink beer for the rest of their lives (.) the majority (.) certainly most of my <u>friends</u> (.) erm have gone back to that way (.) of (.) living

Figure 10.1 Screen capture of a page of analysis (from Riley, Thompson and Griffin, 2010).

┌─ Top tips ─────────────────────────────────

Write your analysis like a pro

The analysis section is a very important part of your write-up and often the one that students find hardest. Following these tips will help you develop a strong analysis section:

- Too many cooks themes spoil the broth. A strong analysis tends to have a few core ways of describing the data (whether it's superordinate themes, discourses, or another kind of pattern). Avoid the temptation to include everything, because this can overwhelm or confuse your reader. Research questions are better answered with clear, conceptual and focused analysis. If you're not sure what to include, speak to your supervisor.
- Make sure your quotes support what you want to say. Sometimes students use quotes that do not match the argument being presented.
- Do not present your analysis transcript by transcript; rather, draw from your whole dataset and don't rely on one participant to quote from.
- Make sure there is enough information in data extracts so they makes sense in their own right and so that the context isn't lost.
- Focus on your data. Sometimes students jump straight from presenting an extract to discussing previous literature on the topic – stay with your data for longer by explaining how that data (and not a previous researcher) informs your understanding of an aspect of your study.
- The opposite of students who ignore their own data are those who describe it in detail, but in a way that just repeats that data. Instead, offer a deeper level of interpretation using the techniques of your chosen method of analysis. Phenomenological work will require you to focus on the nature of the experience (that might be embodied, temporal or related to identity). In contrast, discursive work requires a focus on how the language used constructs reality or enables a particular social interaction.
- When in doubt, keep in mind your research question(s) – how is your analysis helping you answer your research question?
- Know the quality criteria for your chosen method of analysis and for qualitative methods in general (see Chapter 9 for how to find these).
- Make sure you know what marking criteria will be used and refer to them as you write.
- For a coherent project, your literature review (see Chapter 6) should reflect the themes in your analysis. Do a preliminary literature review to help write your research question(s). Further literature reviewing, done after or alongside the analysis, allows you to link what you've found to the literature and write a clear rationale for your project.
- While a write-up is presented in a linear way, literature review, method, analysis, etc., it is not carried out that way. Rather, qualitative researchers go back and forth between data analysis and literature as they develop their thinking.

─Success story─

Writing as an iterative process

Tina interviewed female drug users about their drug use during Covid-19 lockdowns. Originally, she thought that the framing of 'drug, set and setting' would provide the structure for her analysis, because it is important in a lot of drug research. But her participants talked much more about gender issues (e.g. how being high involved more risks from sleazy men, but feelings of escaping body image concerns). This meant that in her final write-up, her literature review included a lot less on drug set and setting than she had anticipated, and instead she engaged more with research on contemporary gender concerns for women, using her analysis to show how these concerns took on particular flavour for these female drug users.

One final, but possibly most important, comment about writing an analysis: your analysis develops as you write it. Good data analysis is iterative, you work on some data, develop ideas, these ideas might be relevant for previous data, you go back to that, and so forth. But it is also likely that as you write up your analysis your ideas on how to analyse your data develop again. This is because of the cyclical nature of qualitative research and the associations between writing and thinking. So, it is an excellent sign if, when you're writing your analysis, you can see better, more conceptual or clearer ways of articulating your findings, or even if you begin to notice new things that you hadn't picked up on previously! If this happens, don't think of your previous work as a waste of time, you needed to do it to get to this stage. But it does mean that to do an excellent write-up you need to give yourself enough time for you to use these new ideas to develop your analysis. As a rule of thumb, consider leaving about one-third of the time you have to do your study on your analysis and write up. Leaving more time to do this section than you expect you will need is a good way of allowing you to write the best analysis section you can. (For more discussion on analysis see Chapter 8, and for discussion of planning and management of the project see Chapters 3, 4 and 5.)

Discussion

This section rounds off your write-up. Below, I outline what you need to do within this sub-section and offer advice for doing this well so you can finish on a high note.

Summarise and discuss your key findings

You should begin by telling the reader what the key findings are from your analysis, drawing out how these address your research question(s). Also, discuss how your findings develop previous literature – for example, do you add to, support or challenge previous findings? This section is not much different from a traditional 'discussion' section although it is likely to be shorter if you have discussed your data to some degree in the analysis section (e.g. drawing out links to the literature). But it will be more substantial if you have saved your discussion of the literature until here. When discussing your findings, you should also consider the implications of your study. For example, could the knowledge you have generated be applied by people working with people similar to your participants, or in related institutions like schools, universities or workplaces?

You may also include some reflexive discussion (see Chapter 9) in this section, where you consider your role in producing your findings and experience of doing the study. You could also link this reflection to the interpretation of your finding and their implications or limitations (see below).

Consider limitations

You also need to discuss the limitations of your study. You might do this alongside your reflective section or in a separate sub-section. Here you evaluate the parameters of your study. Avoid using quality criteria that are related to quantitative research to evaluate your study (see Chapter 9). For example, if you have not used a method designed to generalise, don't critique your study for failing to generalise. When discussing the parameters of your research you might consider what areas your findings are relevant to. For example, is your study on overseas student experiences most relevant for overseas students in the UK, or could these findings be transferable to other countries? And what would be your justification of that (e.g. that your findings relate to relatively universal psychological developmental stages for that age group rather than specific cultural issues related to life in Britain). For ideas on what to discuss in your limitations section, consider the contexts to which your project is relevant; what you might do differently now you know what you know at the end of your project; or identify issues in the findings that you didn't have capacity to develop further but which might be fruitful to study in their own right.

Sometimes students struggle with the limitations section of the discussion. It's often hard to consider the limitations of a study in a way that is creative and constructive. Students may not be able to think of any limitations or may only think of simple suggestions for improvement, such as increasing the number of participants. Alternatively, some students can reel off so many things that they would do differently if they could start again, that they give the impression their study wasn't worth doing. Finding a balance between these two positions will allow you to show that you have reflected on your work, and that now, having come through the process of the study, you are able to identify a few key factors that affected your ability to address your research question or contribute to knowledge on the topic of your study. This is why some write-ups include a reflexivity section here. All studies have limitations; the key is to identify how they may have had an impact on the data you collected or the way you did your analysis. For example, you may have used focus groups because they allowed you to see how people made sense of an issue together, but in doing so you will only have accessed information that your participants were prepared to share in this semi-public event.

If you are struggling with this section speak to your supervisor or look at published work in your area for examples of how other people have addressed this issue.

Recommend future research

You also need to discuss future research recommendations that are linked to your findings. You can generate ideas for this section from your limitations section (e.g. you might suggest expanding particular parameters), or an aspect of your findings might suggest more research is needed to unpack that topic further (e.g. suggesting that theme one was important enough to be explored further in its own study, or that needs further interpretation), or you can use your implication section to identify what future research is needed to explore how to better apply what you found in real-world situations.

Top tip

Base suggestions for future research on your findings

The limitations you identify can suggest the direction for the next course of study. For example, if you did an IPA study (see Chapter 8) with students who had given up smoking and identified some factors that seemed specific to the university context, you could then suggest other populations who were also institutionally based with whom you could explore the role of institutions further. So, the limiting factor was that using a student population may have affected your findings, but the future suggestion is that this finding suggests a new area for health promotion research, that of exploring the impact of institutional identification.

Conclude

You should conclude with a final sentence or paragraph summing up the study with a clear take-home message. Sometimes this is given its own subheading of 'conclusion'. If it has its own subheading, then develop into a concise paragraph that sums up the aims of the study and how they have been addressed by the key findings

---

Top tip

Write the project you did not the one you planned

In your write-up, demonstrate methodological coherence across your project, so that your research question, methods of data collection and analysis align. It is perfectly acceptable for qualitative projects to change focus as they go along - e.g. to start off

(Continued)

looking at friendships at university but to end up focused on how financial matters affect friendships or changing from IPA to DA. Developing your project is good. But write up the final project, not the one you thought about doing but didn't. In this way you write a coherent write-up that tells a conceptually coherent story throughout. You can use your reflexivity section to talk about changes to the original project plan to stay transparent about your decision making

References

As with all academic work, list all the references for anything you've cited in the main text. This includes journal articles, books, book chapters and webpages. Make sure you follow your institutional guidelines for how to format these. There are several variations and since a sign of an excellent write-up is attention to detail make sure you're consistent and are using the right one. Your course handbook may specify and give you examples. In general, English-speaking psychology projects use the formatting recommended by the American Psychological Association (look up their APA style tutorials: https://apastyle.apa.org/instructional-aids/tutorials-webinars). You may also want to use reference managing software such as EndNote or Zotero.

Appendices

In the last section of your write-up are your appendices. Appendices house all the extra bits of your project that are not essential for your reader to understand your study, but may help your reader if, for example, they wanted to reproduce your study or wanted to critically evaluate aspects of your study, such as seeing if your interview questions closely match the themes of your analysis – a sign that you only found what you were looking for. Appendices tend to include documents such as: blank versions of consent forms, information sent to participants, interview schedules or other relevant materials (for example, the photographs used in a photo-elicitation study, ethics applications). As such, appendices may not take on the same formatting structure as the rest of your write-up. Each document in your appendices should be given its own heading and be labelled accordingly, for example, 'Appendix A: Consent forms used for first phase of data collection'. Note that all appendices should be referred to in the main text, and if you have several appendices make sure that you refer to the right one!

Writing Style

Do I say 'I'?

Researchers used to write in the third person and imperfect past tense (e.g. 'the results showed a reduction in metabolism between the two test periods'). But (often qualitative)

researchers argued that by writing in the third person, researchers made themselves absent, hiding the fact that there was a decision maker behind the research and creating an illusion of objectivity. This critique led to researchers arguing that academics should write in the first person. However, other researchers argued that using the first person was simply another form of presenting the research and is no more or less transparent than any other. Regardless, current APA style now states that researchers should not use the third person to refer to themselves, and instead use the first person; for example, 'I performed discourse analysis on interviews with …'. We therefore recommend you follow APA style unless your institution tells you otherwise (and whatever you choose, make sure you're consistent throughout). Also see, https://apastyle.apa.org/blog/first-person-myth.

Do I write in the past tense?

Generally, you should also write in the past tense. APA guidelines are that write-ups are written in the past tense (e.g. 'I interviewed eight women who regularly used the drug MDMA'). Exceptions are (1) when discussing the implications of the study the present tense is used ('the implication is that gender profoundly shapes experience of female drug users'); and (2) when signposting what is coming in the document (e.g. 'in the second section of my introduction I will describe the research that …').

What makes good academic writing?

Writing that has style usually has clarity, structure and a 'turn of phrase' that keeps the reader interested. Academics are well known for writing dense prose that sounds clever, but is hard to understand (see Billig [2011] for an interesting discussion of this issue). It's tempting to try and emulate this style. But think about how you feel when you read these kinds of texts. Reading dense, turgid, unclear, ambiguous and overly complicated writing is hard work, and often leaves a reader feeling irritated. And this is not what you want your reader – and marker – to feel when reading your write-up.

Top tip

Writing style

If you find yourself enjoying reading an article, try to notice what it is about the author's style that has made it a pleasant read. Then you can emulate it in your own work.

When someone writes clearly the reader stops noticing that they are reading and instead they become focused on taking in the content of the document. Clear writing therefore allows reading to be enjoyable because the reader can immerse themselves in the ideas. Writing clearly is a skill that develops with time, practice and a bit of know-how. Here are some writing tips to help you develop good writing skills.

Top tip

Writing clearly

- Use fewer words: Avoid repetition, waffle or labouring a point.
- When editing, look for unnecessary words you can cut. For example, in the sentence 'a very important study' the 'very' is unnecessary because the word 'important' tells the reader that this is an issue that needs consideration.
- Have clarity in your sentences. When in doubt have one point in one sentence. Often when I find my writing isn't clear, it's because I'm making more than one point in a sentence, and the meaning can get lost that way.
- Use the simplest word with the same meaning. For example, for 'utilised' write 'used'.
- Use a mixture of short and long sentences. Short sentences add punch. Very long sentences are hard to follow. As a rule of thumb, break up sentences longer than 25 words. Denman (2007) recommends the process of replacing a comma, semi-colon or connecting word (and, but, because, although, since, however) in a long sentence, with a full stop, and then tidying up the subsequent two sentences.
- 'Signpost' to your reader: say what you're going to say, say it, say what you've told them.
- Explain your thinking. Don't assume your reader knows what you're talking about or understands why one concept should be linked to another or what your results mean if you don't tell them.
- Where possible, write in the active tense following a sentence structure of subject, verb, object/noun. For example, in the sentence 'The researcher applied her coding plan to one transcript' we know who did what to what. The 'researcher' is the subject, the verb is 'applied' and the object is her 'coding plan'. If we write this information in a passive way – 'The coding plan was applied to one transcript' – we don't have information on the subject (that is, who did the applying of the coding plan) and we've used two words for the verb 'was applied' when we could have used one. In this example, we can see that writing in the active tense has a logical order and less ambiguity because you know who's doing the deed, and may make your writing sharper because it uses less words. One way to identify 'passive' writing that needs 'activating' is to look for the verb 'to be' (am, is, was, were, are, be, been, being) alongside another verb, such as in the 'was applied' example above. When you find these two verbs, see if you can find one verb that works instead, as in the above, where 'was applied' was replaced with 'applied'.

Language use

Another important aspect of writing style is the use of inclusive language. This includes the use of non-sexist language. APA guidelines also include some useful tips for writing in an inclusive way, which you can find here: https://apastyle.apa.org/style-grammar-guidelines/bias-free-language

Top tips

Non-sexist language

- Avoid using sex-specific forms generically. For example, don't use 'he' when referring to people who might not be male. Instead use plurals, e.g. 'they', which also helps your writing be inclusive of people who don't identify with the binary male/female.
- Avoid specifying the sex of the referent unless it is relevant – e.g. use counsellor, client or participant. An example of when sex is relevant is if your sample is all of one sex, in this context gender neural terms are not appropriate.
- Delete pronouns – e.g. 'the participant completed his/her task' becomes 'the participant completed the task'.
- Use participants' preferred pronouns.
- Avoid making sex-stereotyped assumptions about people, their abilities, attitudes and relationships.

Conclusion

Many people find writing up their research project a daunting prospect. And considered as a whole it may be. But the process of writing can be an enjoyable experience that can let you feel creative and give you a sense of achievement – both in what you've done and how you've communicated it. The aim of this chapter has been to guide you through the process of writing so that it can be a good experience for you. So, I finish with a final set of top tips for getting the job done and wish you happy writing.

Top tips

Getting the job done

- Read your writing aloud – it will let you 'hear' where the problems are in your writing.
- Think of your write-up as a story with a beginning, a middle and an end that takes your reader on an interesting journey that is regularly signposted on the way.

(Continued)

- Writing is a cyclical process. Get your ideas out in draft form, rather than aim for perfection first time round. Return to draft sections repeatedly to polish them.
- If you cannot remember something, then leave a box where the information should go and look it up later.
- You think as you write. Give yourself enough time to be able to develop your ideas as you write up.
- Leave even more time than that. Things always take longer than you think and it's harder to be creative when you're anxious about deadlines.
- Don't write your write-up in the order that you are going to present it. Write your method first to remind you what you did and because it's usually the most straightforward thing to write. This will give you a sense of achievement, and help you carry on. Write your abstract last, because you can only summarise your project when you've written a full draft of your write-up.
- Keep a research diary (see Chapter 9) throughout the project, writing about what you did and why and what you thought. This will be super-helpful for writing your method section. Believe it or not, it's easy to forget what you have done.
- Keep a clear note of where all the information you're using came from. Otherwise, you may spend unhappy hours looking for lost references or, worse, find yourself accused of plagiarism. You are especially vulnerable to producing plagiarised work if you cut and paste from other documents. When using electronic sources, avoid cutting-and-pasting; type what you want to say in your own words.
- You may be tempted to use AI. There is much debate about new developments, such as whether AI can be used ethically in academic work. For example, when writing an essay, you might use it like Wikipedia to give you an accessible introduction to some of the core issues. But don't use it for your actual writing; you are unlikely to get adequate material for your project, it counts as unfair practice and is likely to be picked up by software designed to catch students using it. This would have very serious penalties.
- If having difficulty writing, find a way to get started. Once you begin it's much easier to carry on. Later, you might need ways to keep motivated or to stay focused. Reflect on the things that have helped or hindered in the past to find what works best for you. But the following may be useful:
  - Keep your energies up by eating healthily, avoiding the highs and lows of sugar and caffeine if you can.
  - Go for a short walk. Movement and fresh air can help.
  - Get rid of distractions (turn off your email and phone).
  - Start the day with writing.
  - Set yourself small achievable sub-goals (see Chapter 5).
  - Look up and try the 'pomodoro technique'.
  - Reward yourself.
  - Read this chapter for inspiration – remember you can do it!
  - Do not use reading this chapter as a way of avoiding writing up.

Want to know more about writing up?

Denman, T. (2007) *How Not to Write*. London: Piatkus Books.
Lyons, E. and Coyle, A. (2007) *Analysing Qualitative Data in Psychology*. London: Sage. (This book has examples of project write-ups with author commentaries on them.)

References

Ashmore, M. (1989) *The Reflexive Thesis*. Chicago: University of Chicago Press.

Billig, M. (2011) Writing social psychology: Fictional things and unpopulated texts. *British Journal of Social Psychology*, 50, 4–20.

Denman, T. (2007) *How Not to Write*. London: Piatkus Books.

Haraway, D. (1989) *Primate visions: Gender, Race, and Nature in the World of Modern Science*. London: Routledge.

Parkin, S. and Kimergård, A. (2022) A critical analysis of respondent quotes used as titles of qualitative research papers that are published in peer-reviewed journals. *Accountability in Research*, 29(2), 109–32.

Riley, S. and Paskova, K. (2022) A post-phenomenological analysis of using menstruation tracking apps for the management of premenstrual syndrome. *Digital Health*, 8. https://doi.org/10.1177/20552076221144199

Riley, S., Rodham, K. and Gavin, J. (2009) Doing weight: pro-ana and recovery identities in cyberspace. *Journal of Community and Applied Social Psychology*, 19, 348–59.

Riley, S.C.E., Thompson, J. and Griffin, C. (2010) Turn on, tune in, but don't drop out: The impact of neo-liberalism on magic mushroom users (in)ability to imagine collectivist social worlds. *International Journal of Drug Policy*, 21(6): 445–51.

Robson, M., Riley, S., Gagen, E. and McKeogh, D. (2022) Love and lifestyle: How 'relational healthism' structures couples' talk of engagement with lifestyle advice associated with a new diagnosis of coronary heart disease. *Psychology & Health*. Online first: 10.1080/08870446.2022.2033240

11
CONCLUSIONS: MOVING ON AND WRAPPING UP

Stephen Gibson, Cath Sullivan
and Sarah Riley

The previous chapter focused on producing an excellent write-up and you might think that once you have done that your dissertation is finished. Getting to that stage is a big achievement, but in this chapter we will show you that it isn't necessarily the end of things. There are several ways in which you can build on the work that you have done for your project, and we will briefly outline these. Then, to round things off, we will provide an overview of the key themes of this book, draw some conclusions about the process of doing a qualitative project, and consider some of the joys and frustrations of doing academic research.

What Next?

You can build on the work you have done for your project by:

- using it as evidence to demonstrate your skills;
- writing it up as a journal article;
- using it as a basis for a proposal for further research.

Demonstrating skills

Doing your project helps you develop skills that will be useful in employment, further study and everyday situations. When applying for courses or jobs you can use the work you did to plan, conduct and write up your project to illustrate many skills. It's also useful to reflect on the skills you've practised and how they might help you in other parts of your life.

····In a nutshell··· ···

Your project is evidence of ...

- **Critical evaluation:** For example, you examined a body of literature, critically evaluating it to construct a rationale for your study. Considering links between your findings and other literature, and reflecting on your project's limitations, involved you thinking critically about your findings and those of others.
- **Time management:** To complete your project you had to manage your time properly. You can demonstrate this by, for example, referring to the timetable that you will have created to help manage your project. You might also want to think of examples of where you adjusted this timetable as the process went along.
- **Research skills:** Your project provides many examples of research skills. You could point to generic skills, such as successfully applying for ethical approval, or more specific skills associated with data collection, management and analysis.
- **Working independently:** You could talk here about how you set your own deadlines to help progress towards your goals, how you shaped the project so that it reflected your interests or how you identified what makes a good project and took steps (like reading this book!) to make your project a good one. Obviously, you didn't work entirely unsupervised, but you could also use this as a strength here, by giving examples of how you made decisions that allowed you to put into practice your supervisor's advice.
- **Interpersonal skills:** You will have used various skills in dealing with other people in your project. You might want to draw upon examples of how you have answered queries from prospective participants or had to deal with the communication of technical ideas in everyday language in participant materials.
- **Communication and presentation skills:** Examples in this area could include clear writing for a variety of audiences and possibly also verbal skills if you conducted interviews or did an oral exam as part of your assessment. Good listening and learning to ask the right question are also some of the transferable skills you can get from doing qualitative research.

Being able to use your student research experience to give tangible evidence of your skills is important. Many of the skills above are valued by employers (e.g. Sarkar et al., 2020). Research also shows that employers want graduates to draw on specific experiences that show their skills and highlight the value of those skills (Tomlinson and Anderson, 2021). So, providing concrete examples from your project (and other areas) will take you much further than just saying you've got the skills and hoping that people will take your word for it.

The project as evidence of skills

For her undergraduate project Baljit did an interview study with British Asian students about their attitudes to marriage, using thematic analysis to analyse the data. After university, she applied for a research assistant job with a national charity, who wanted somebody with qualitative research skills for a project interviewing people about domestic violence. Baljit wrote in her application that she had the ability to work independently and that she had skills and experience in qualitative research (as these were highlighted on the job description). She was pleased to be offered an interview for the job. In the interview, she was asked to provide an example of her qualitative research skills and she was also asked to talk about her ability to work independently. Baljit drew on two practical examples from her project to show evidence in these areas.

First, she described writing a semi-structured interview schedule in line with principles of good practice, such as using open questions to elicit a fuller account and preparing prompts to help with this. She then talked briefly about how she had managed her project partly by identifying small achievable sub-goals (e.g. 'transcribe two interviews this week') as she went along. Baljit was told later that she had interviewed very well and was offered the job.

Doing your project is a great achievement, but sometimes the write-up can be developed further and published or disseminated in other ways. For example, could you find a local group of practitioners who might be interested to hear a presentation, or read a newsletter article, about your project? Another option that is sometimes available is to try and develop your write-up into a journal article.

Writing a journal article

Most dissertation work doesn't get published, and it would be a mistake to think that your work isn't good if it's not published. The most important criterion for deciding if a dissertation is publishable is the quality of the data, and not the quality of your write-up or even analysis (Wood et al., 2012). It is possible to do an excellent dissertation that is well planned, executed and written up, but does not have data that is publishable. For example, your sample size may be acceptable for a project but considered too small for publication in many journals.

Your project is all about your development and learning. An excellent project is feasible in the time available, applies and extends your research skills and meets the associated learning outcomes. Poor dissertations can result from over-extending yourself, or getting too fixated on the idea of doing something publishable or that makes a unique contribution to knowledge (this is expected, to some extent, of postgraduate students but seldom required of undergraduates). Those students who have aspects of their dissertation work published have not necessarily done a better dissertation. However, some of you may be approached by your supervisor about the possibility of publication and it may be something you are keen to try. Below we present our top tips for students in such a situation.

Top tips

Developing your write-up into a journal article

- Talk to your supervisor and as many people as possible about how journal articles are written and published so that you know what you are letting yourself in for (see Silvia, 2015).
- Discuss with your supervisor how you will share the work of writing the article and what order your names will be presented in (see Game and West, 2002).
- Decide on a journal before you start writing and tailor your article to match the aims and scope.
- Make sure you find and follow the instructions for authors for the journal you aim to submit to (for example, about word length, format).
- Be aware that your article, like many other pieces of writing, will probably go through many stages before being ready – get feedback from as many people as you can on the drafts and try your best to use it when revising.
- Use similar published work in that journal as a guide to the length, format and style that you are trying to aim for (note that journal articles are different from project write-ups).
- Remember that writing a journal article will be a useful experience, whatever the outcome. Many articles are rejected, and competition is fierce even for experienced researchers. The goal is to write and submit, rather than to get published (as the latter is usually out of the author's hands).

A third way that your project can provide a useful springboard for the future is as the basis for developing a proposal for future research. This is considered in the next section.

Developing a proposal

Some of you will want to go on to further study – at masters (for example, MSc, MA, MRes, MPhil) or doctoral level (for example, PhD, DClinPsy). Study at this level varies, but generally has at least some element that involves conducting a significant independent research project. In many cases, this will involve you having to develop, in conjunction with a supervisor, a proposal for a research project. It isn't necessary, when doing this, to build on previous project work, and it may not be appropriate. But there can be advantages; for example, you will already be familiar with the literature and the process of doing the dissertation will have probably left you with good awareness of the gaps in knowledge on that topic.

The earlier chapters of this book describe many processes that will be the same for developing research ideas and proposals at any level. So, you can use these to help you with proposals that you might do after your undergraduate work. If you find yourself trying to build on your previous project to develop a proposal, here is our advice.

Top tips

Developing a proposal from your project

- Talk to your ex-supervisor to identify possibilities for developing your research and advice about how to do this.
- Go over your write-up carefully and reflect on areas you identified for future research. These may be things that you can turn into a proposal, as part of your rationale will already be there.
- Think about what you learned about the methodology you used – how can you improve on this in the future? What methodological choices would you make differently in the future? Again, some of this will be there in your write-up.
- As you develop your ideas, incorporate any feedback that you obtained on your project (either at the draft stage, at the final stage or in relation to a viva or presentation if you did one).

We have considered three main ways in which your project work can be useful for future activities. Next, we want to encourage you to reflect on the key themes of this book, as outlined in Chapter 1.

Drawing it All Together

In Chapter 1, we used the metaphor of the methodological kite to try and show how methodology is about the connections between different elements of the research process (see Figure 11.1).

Flying a kite isn't as easy as it looks. Sometimes you can't get it airborne, sometimes you think it's flying brilliantly and then it nosedives, sometimes the person next to you has a better kite. We wrote this book so that you can be the person who *can* get their kite airborne, successfully ride out difficult conditions and perhaps even be the envy of other kite flyers. To be that person, you need to make good decisions, think critically and appreciate the different aspects of methodology.

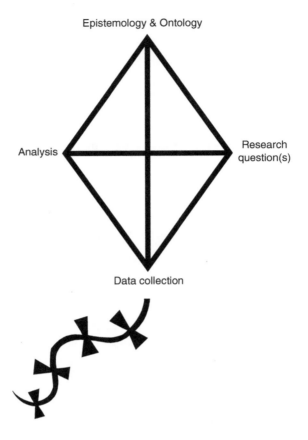

Figure 11.1 The methodological kite flies again

Key themes of the book

Methodology: Appreciating the links between epistemology, ontology, your research question(s), data collection and analysis will ensure that your project 'gets off the ground' and remains airborne.

Decision making: Making timely and informed decisions will help you steer your project in the right direction and prepare for the unexpected.

Critical thinking: Evaluating your own and others' work according to appropriate criteria will demonstrate your grasp of the core principles of good scholarship.

We emphasised decision making at the start of this book because, as you will appreciate by now, doing a research project requires you to make many decisions. There are lots of options available, and deciding which ones to go for can be daunting. A good grasp of methodology and sharpening your critical thinking skills will help you do this. As we noted back in Chapter 1, you might underestimate how good you are at thinking critically, and it's a skill that develops as you progress through your project.

In our experience, students can struggle with the idea that they are allowed (indeed, expected) to take a position on a debate. Often, there is a vaguely misguided attempt to sit on the fence in the name of 'fairness', something which can lead to banal conclusions along the lines of 'every approach has something to offer'. What your markers are looking for is a scholarly, well-argued position – so tell them why you used the approach you did, why you interpreted your findings in the way that you did and why your work is important. Use your reading to develop your position and learn how to make an argument. Enjoy the chance you have to be an apprentice academic.

··· ··In a nutshell· ·· ···

Be a scholar

While doing your project you are an academic-in-training, starting to make a contribution as a member of a scholarly community. Scholarly communities, which exist in universities and beyond, are important. Such communities produce academic research that, at its best, has the power to show us new ways of thinking about the world and new ways of being in the world. Don't lose sight of that even if this is your first or only foray into the world of academic research.

···

While decision making, critical thinking and methodology are key themes in this book, you may notice other themes around good practice in qualitative projects that run through the chapters. In the following section we draw these themes together as our final list of tips, highlighting how they relate to the various stages of the research process.

- **Be systematic:** Whether you're planning your project, conducting your literature review, collecting or analysing your data, being systematic is crucial. If you're not sure what this means think back to previous chapters. In Chapter 3 on planning, we talk about producing a plan early on that spells out what you will do and when. This is being systematic. Chapter 6, on literature reviewing, describes making rigorous notes on the articles you read using key questions to identify relevance. This is being systematic. Chapter 7, on data collection, encourages you to be aware of the possibilities available to you for data collection, and develop a rationale for your choice. This is being systematic. And Chapter 8, on analysis, recommended keeping a record of the analysis process (e.g. a research diary). This is being systematic. There will be examples in the other chapters too.

- **Consider quality:** If you're new to qualitative research, you'll need to get familiar with ways of assessing its quality. This is because there is no single unified entity called 'qualitative research'. Instead, as you will have gleaned, there are a multitude of perspectives on methodology (see Chapter 1), data collection (see Chapter 7) and analysis (see Chapter 8). These perspectives sometimes contrast with one another as sharply as they do with quantitative research. As noted in Chapter 9, there are some common indicators of quality (for example, good evidence use), but quality criteria also vary across different approaches. So, for example, if you're doing interpretative phenomenological analysis (IPA), evaluate it according to the criteria for evaluating IPA, but if you do discourse analysis (DA), evaluate it according to the criteria for evaluating DA.

- **Know your approach:** Don't rely only on textbooks! We hope you find this book useful in thinking about the project process, but you need to build on what you read in textbooks like this one. In particular, don't neglect reading about your research methods. Students sometimes get so focused on reading the literature on their topic that they forget to read about methods. Once you've settled on an approach (e.g. IPA or discourse analysis), you must immerse yourself in it. See Chapters 7 and 8 for further reading suggestions, and Chapter 6 for literature searching tips. Immersing yourself in your methodology matters increasingly as you progress through academia; it is essential for all postgraduate projects and for excellent undergraduate projects.

- **Be ethical:** All research must be designed, carried out and written up ethically. And your project is no exception. There is a temptation to think of ethics as a box-ticking exercise that you go through before getting on with the business of doing the research, but being ethical is integral to being a researcher at all stages of the process. Ethics is dynamic, as we saw in Chapter 4, and it is integral to the relationships you have with others during your project (see Chapter 5).

- **Make it your own:** It's your project! Take control, relish the opportunity you have to find out about something that interests you, and don't sit back and wait for your supervisor to start pushing you. You'll get much more out of it if you can feel like it really is *your* project.

- **Ask for help:** Yes, it's yours, but you're not on your own. A student project is an independent piece of work with supervision. Those last two words are crucial – your supervisor is the best resource you have for your project, so make the most of them! If you feel you are struggling, don't shy away from them – tell them, and ask for their suggestions on how to get over your difficulties. Similarly, make sure you draw on the expertise of other people who you may have access to for assistance in your research (for example, technical staff, librarians).

- **Stay flexibile:** One of the most important things as you plan and conduct your project is remaining flexible. Without doubt, good planning at the outset – as discussed in Chapter 3 – greatly enhances your chances of doing an excellent project, but your plan must allow room for manoeuvre so that you can respond flexibly to changing circumstances. It's okay for your project to evolve in unanticipated directions as you go along. The capacity to be led where the project takes you is one of the hallmarks of excellence. If your project surprises you, this indicates that you have an open and curious approach and haven't forced the research to conform to your own views. This is a good thing, but it can lead to some anxiety, and highlights two differing types of uncertainty, which we will (imaginatively) call bad uncertainty and good uncertainty.

··· ···In a nutshell··· ·······································

Good and bad uncertainty

Good uncertainty: Your research throws up something (such as a finding or a possible avenue for further data collection) that you simply hadn't (and couldn't) have anticipated.

Bad uncertainty: Something crops up unexpectedly that you really could (and should) have planned for!

· ·

Getting to grips with bad uncertainty and learning to embrace good uncertainty is central to the success of your project, so let's say a bit more about them.

Managing uncertainty

There are some unexpected events that you really should expect – for example, you should expect that not all the people you invite to participate in your research will agree to do so. If you haven't prepared adequately for this kind of thing, then your project may suffer. However, there are other unexpected events that might well indicate that your project is a well-designed and interesting piece of work. Think about it like this: if we could plan every detail of a study to the point where there was nothing that could surprise us, then would there be any point in conducting the research in the first place? A good project will strike a balance between those aspects of the research process that you can – and should – prepare for, and those that you simply can't. Indeed, it is one of the most satisfying and exciting aspects of qualitative research when your findings open possibilities that you hadn't previously considered. This is not to suggest that every student will have this experience with every project – even seasoned academic researchers don't feel this way about every project they're involved in – but you can at least feel relaxed about the possibility of being surprised.

So, what sorts of things can we anticipate – or, what things shouldn't be unexpected? Well, you will have gleaned from many of the chapters that the links between the assumptions you make about the nature of knowledge (epistemology) and reality (ontology), the research question(s) you ask, and the way in which you collect and analyse your data are inextricably connected.

So, if you realise that your findings are inconsistent with the epistemological position that you had in mind, or that your analysis isn't addressing your research question(s), then you are most likely coming across something unexpected that you really should have expected. As you will appreciate by now, good planning from an early stage will help you to avoid this.

However, if you begin to analyse your data and find that a new research question springs to mind, which potentially takes you down a different path, then this is an encouraging sign because it shows a development in your thinking that could only have come about by engaging in the processes of qualitative research. This is an example of how qualitative research is cyclical.

Qualitative research: Going round in circles

Qualitative research can be thought of as being cyclical in two ways. Firstly, each stage, such as developing your research question, reviewing literature or doing analysis, is in itself an iterative process. For example, when analysing data qualitative (see Chapter 8), researchers usually engage in several rounds of analysis before moving on to the next stage. These cyclical processes allow researchers to develop deeper and more conceptual ways of thinking about their project.

The second way that qualitative research is cyclical is that the conceptual thinking produced by approaching each research stage iteratively may lead you to ultimately take a different path from that which you originally planned. This will often require you to go back to earlier stages in your project with a new perspective or a more knowledgeable standpoint (see Chapter 2).

Re-visiting early stages in your project with a new perspective can be a very exciting aspect of qualitative research, but it can also be daunting, leaving you faced with some important decisions about the ways in which you develop your project. Discuss things like this with your supervisor as they can support you and help you to be confident about your decisions (see Chapter 5).

New ideas can lead to you wanting to collect more data, or to re-assess some of your assumptions. They might even lead you to wish you'd done a completely different project altogether! This is where the first part of this chapter is useful in reminding you that your project needn't be just an end-point but can be the starting point for so much more. Nevertheless, you may have to deal with the potentially tricky issue of managing the cyclical nature of qualitative research – with its associated heavy toll on your time – and the necessity of having to produce a piece of work by a specified deadline.

One way to manage the cyclical nature of doing qualitative research with a limited time frame is to remember that while qualitative research can be thought of as cyclical, these cycles take place over a set period and reach an endpoint. You might therefore think of your project as both cyclical and linear at the same time (see Figure 11.2), with several cycles of, for example, data collection and analysis taking place along a broadly linear trajectory.

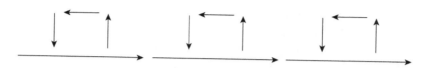

Figure 11.2 The process of a qualitative research project

It can be useful to build these cycles into your project timetable by, for example, doubling the amount of time you think it will take you to do an activity (see Chapter 3). But, since it can be difficult – if not impossible – to identify in advance precisely where your project is going to take you, you also need to draw on your critical thinking and decision-making skills. In consultation with your supervisor, you should have the confidence to say 'this is good enough' and move on at appropriate points.

You may feel that you have yet to fully mine your project for all its varied and rich possibilities, but at some point you will need to switch from exploratory-researcher mode to deadline-chasing-student mode. If you are so wrapped up in your project that you feel as though there's still much more to be done, then it sounds like you've caught the research bug – maybe you should stick around academia a while longer?

Success story

Catching the bug

Not all students who undertake a research project as part of a degree course will go on to further study, let alone a career in academia, but the authors of the chapters in this book have tried to convey the excitement of research, and particularly qualitative research. We all caught the bug at some stage - some of us as undergraduates, some much later, but we're infected beyond all hope now regardless. We've tried to leave traces of the bug all over this book in the hope that some of you might catch it too.

It's worth emphasising again that high-quality projects tend to involve, amongst other things, wide reading and thorough knowledge. So, our final tip concerns something which we've found to mark out the most impressive projects from all the rest – the importance of reading.

─Top tip─

Read, read and read some more!

The very best student projects will demonstrate engagement with a broad array of sources, so make sure that you keep your reading going throughout your project. It sounds so simple, doesn't it? The more you read, the more you will grow in confidence as you begin to consider the options available to you from a position of expertise. So, try to build in time for regular reading throughout your project.

We conclude this book by pointing out that if you've gone to the trouble of reading this book, you're most likely doing things the right way already. We wish you the very best in your journey through the world of qualitative research and hope that this book has given you an idea of the routes available to you, what the terrain might be like and where you can catch a lift along the way.

References

Game, A. and West, M.A. (2002) Principles of publishing. *The Psychologist*, 15, 126–9.

Silvia, P.J. (2015) *Write It Up: Practical Strategies for Writing and Publishing Journal Articles*. Washington, DC: American Psychological Association.

Tomlinson, M. and Anderson, V. (2021) Employers and graduates: The mediating role of signals and capitals. *Journal of Higher Education Policy and Management*, 43(4), 384–99.

Sarkar, M., Overton, T., Thompson, C.D. and Rayner, G. (2020) Academics' perspectives of the teaching and development of generic employability skills in science curricula, *Higher Education Research and Development*, 39(2), 346–61.

Wood, C., Giles, D. and Percy, C. (2012) *Your Psychology Project Handbook: Becoming a Researcher* (2nd edn). Harlow: Pearson Education.

Index